TOUCHDOWN
AUBURN!

*Carrying on the Tradition
of the Auburn Tigers*

Rod Bramblett

TRIUMPH
BOOKS

I dedicate this book to Paula, Shelby, and Joshua.
Thanks for your understanding, support, and love.

I also dedicate this to my mother and grandfather, who gave
me the values and work ethic to believe in myself.

Finally, to our entire broadcast crew, past and present; you are the best
in the business, and I love each and every one of you. War Eagle!

This book is available in quantity at special discounts for your group or organization. For further information, contact:

Triumph Books LLC
814 North Franklin Street
Chicago, Illinois 60610
(312) 337-0747
www.triumphbooks.com

Printed in U.S.A.
ISBN: 978-1-62937-108-5
Design by Patricia Frey
Photos courtesy of Rod Bramblett, Auburn Athletics, Auburn IMG Sports Network, Auburn ISP Sports Network, Todd Van Emst, and John Reed

Contents

Introduction:
How Did I Get Here?

The date was Friday, September 7, 1990. I arrived at Chambers Academy in LaFayette, Alabama, with a Marantz recorder, a Shure mixer, two headsets, and a crowd mic in hand. Alongside me was my first color analyst, Phil Dunlap. This was it, my first game as a play-by-play announcer. I was the voice of the Lee-Scott Academy Warriors, a small private school in Auburn, Alabama. The games weren't aired live; I brought the tape recorder so my call could be played back Saturday morning on WAUD-AM 1230.

I walked up to the press box at Chambers Academy and asked someone where I needed to go. That person simply pointed straight up. There was a ladder that led to the top of the press box, where there were two chairs and a stack of plastic two-liter soda crates (aka, my table). I don't remember much about the 19–12 Lee-Scott win, but I do remember thinking, *"My gosh, my dream has come true. I'm a play-by-play announcer."*

At that point, I was on top of the world. I could not see past that hot, humid night in September on top of that old press box at a private school in east central Alabama. That moment was all that mattered. I had no idea—how could I?— that this was the start of a career that would consume half of my life. A career that a little over 23 years later led to this...

"Well, if this thing comes up short I guess he can run it out. Here we go...the kick has...no does not have the leg and Davis takes it in the back of the end zone. He'll run it out to the 10, 15, 20, 25, 30, 35, 40, 45, 50, 45...Oh my god!...Davis is gonna run it all the way back. Auburn is gonna win the football game! Auburn is gonna win the football game! He ran the missed field goal back! He ran it back 109 yards!

They're not gonna keep 'em off the field tonight! Holy Cow! Oh my god! Auburn wins! Auburn has won the Iron Bowl in the most unbelievable fashion you will ever see! I cannot believe it! 34–28!"

With those words my professional broadcasting career had reached its peak. How could it get better than that? History had been made, and for some inexplicable reason the good Lord above put me right in the middle of it. There I was alongside my color analyst, Stan White, and the best radio crew in the country, watching it all unfold. The next day after the dust had settled, I truly thought, *"I've been doing this for almost 25 years. I really should think about calling it quits because there's no way you'll ever top that."*

On Saturday, November 30, 2013, there I was…sitting in the home radio booth of Jordan-Hare Stadium, my face in my hands, not quite realizing what I had just witnessed. I knew it was special, but so was two weeks ago when my eyes had seen something that I thought at the time was the most unbelievable finish to a football game I had ever seen. I didn't think it could be duplicated. The Auburn Tigers football team had blown a 20-point fourth-quarter lead in the span of 10 minutes at home versus Georgia. The Tigers facing fourth-and-18 from their own 27 found lightning in a bottle. Quarterback Nick Marshall heaved one to Ricardo Louis, who reeled it in after two Georgia defenders graciously tipped the ball in the air. Seventy-three yards later with 25 seconds to go it was Auburn 43–38, and that was your final. Remarkable, there was no way it could be topped—one of the best ever in the Deep South's oldest rivalry. However, I guess lightning does strike twice. It just took place before my very eyes.

On the field below me was a tapestry of Orange and Blue made up of thousands of Auburn fans all sharing in the joy of beating their archrival in the most amazing fashion you could ever imagine. "The greatest college football game ever played" is what some called that night. Auburn fans preferred "Kick Six." Alabama fans, well they don't prefer to talk about it at all. At the time, I didn't know what to call Chris Davis' 109-yard missed field goal return for a touchdown to give Auburn a 34–28 win. Heck, I didn't even know what I had said until I heard it played back on the radio on my drive back home. I only knew that my broadcast career would never be the same. I knew Auburn would never be the same. I knew the college football world would never be the same.

Auburn athletics has been my life for the past 25 years. It has been my profession and my passion. I care deeply about what happens on that football field on Saturdays in the fall. The same can be said for basketball, baseball, and any other sport at my alma mater. That's why I consider myself to be so lucky. Over the last quarter century I've either covered the games as a member of the media or as my school's "Voice." This job has allowed my family and me to visit places around this country that wouldn't have been possible otherwise. The people I've met, the relationships developed transcend the wins and losses. Those are the things that stand out the most.

I don't want this to be an autobiography, but I feel it's important to talk about where I came from. The influences I had when I was younger and the choices made were integral in setting me on this less than straight career path. There are hundreds of great stories to be told. Every broadcaster has them. The tales are funny, sad, and dramatic. They cover the spectrum of emotions, much like the games we broadcast.

However, at the end of the day, it's all about the fans. Without the fans none of us play-by-play guys would have a job. Their passion is our passion. We are there for them. Auburn fans listen to our broadcasts because they want the Auburn perspective. An Alabama fan living in Centreville should despise listening to my voice...that is unless Auburn is losing, then there's a sadistic joy involved. The majority of our audience wants to know that you are living and dying with every play that takes place...and we are.

It's because of that fact that I hope I don't have to give this up anytime soon. Good Lord willing and Auburn still wants me around, I want to continue being the "Voice" for a very long time. Those moments like we saw at the end of the 2013 Auburn football season, that's what keeps me coming back for more. While there haven't been any quite like those two over the course of the last 25 years, there have been plenty that will make the hairs on the back of your neck stand up. There are plenty more of them to come. So sit back and I hope you enjoy this tale of an ordinary guy and some of the extraordinary things he has witnessed. Auburn is a special place with special people. I'm proud to say I belong to that very special group as an alum, a fan, and as their "Voice."

Chapter 1

Family and Influences

There are certain people I want to mention who shaped my life—personally and professionally—in many ways. Whether it was something that pushed me in one direction, or gave me an opportunity that led to something unexpected, or just simply inspired me in one fashion or another. I also realize I will probably leave out someone, so my apologies to anyone I forgot. These are the people who influenced my personal and professional life. Without them I certainly wouldn't be writing a book about the 25 years I've spent as a play-by-play man.

My Wife and Kids

I would not be where I am today without my wonderful wife's support and the support of my two kids. They make the biggest sacrifices having to deal with things that should normally fall on my shoulders but fall on theirs just because I am on the road so much.

My daughter, Shelby, has turned into a beautiful young woman. She is incredibly intelligent. I know whatever she chooses in life she will have great success. My wife and I call her our "angel baby." After years of unsuccessfully trying to have a child we were just about ready to give up; that's when the good Lord above delivered us a miracle in 1998. I will never forget November 5 of that year. It's when Shelby Grace came into our world and when I no longer celebrated my birthday—that's right, she and I were born on the same day. Best gift ever!

Five years later we were blessed with our first son, Joshua Baird Bramblett. He came to us in a much easier fashion. His personality matches the ease with which he arrived into this world. He shares his father's affection for superheroes and comic books. He is creative, imaginative, and funny. He makes us laugh every day. He is a mama's boy, but that's okay. He is going to make a very good husband one day because of his loving heart and sense of humor.

And then there's my wife, Paula. I'm still trying to figure out why she has stuck with me all these years. I'm grateful she has. She provides great balance in my life. The former Paula East doesn't really care about sports. Unlike my world, hers doesn't revolve around what a bunch of 18- to 22-year-old kids do on the field, court, or diamond.

Throughout this book, I am going to share with you columns I've written over the years. Most are related to games I've described, but some are personal like this one I wrote the week that my son, Joshua, was born. I was in my first season as Auburn's lead announcer. Auburn was preparing to play Tennessee on October 4, 2003. I was, on the other hand, preparing for something much more important. It was a special week for multiple reasons.

This week I want to talk about something a little different. I know...the Auburn-Tennessee game is on the forefront of everybody's mind, as well it should be, but my mind is wandering a little bit this week. I've got other things floating in this feeble brain of mine. They say this is my column and I can write whatever I want...so forgive me while I ramble.

This week I feel the need to tell you about a girl I know and someone I dated a long time ago...or was it so long ago? I guess it depends on how you look at it. The date (on the calendar) was September 30, 1983. Twenty years ago this week. It was the night of the Homecoming football game at Valley High...my alma mater. It was a great football game with a miracle finish. I think we played Smiths Station, and Willie Atkinson caught a touchdown pass in the fourth quarter to give my Rams a come from behind victory. Hey...I even got to escort the Homecoming Queen! It was a pretty big night, but not because of any reasons I've already mentioned...it was a big night for one reason and one reason alone...that girl.

This particular girl was meeting me at the homecoming dance after the football game. She actually attended Lanett High School. For those of you who don't know, they are Valley's biggest rival. Back then it was a lot like Auburn-Alabama but on a smaller scale. She was in the band at Lanett so I had to wait until she got done with their football game before she could make the 10-minute drive to the National Guard Armory where the dance was being held. We had a great time. We laughed and danced to some really bad '80s music. We enjoyed each other's company enough to set up our first "real" date the next night.

The first "real" date consisted of dinner at a local pizza establishment. Not real glamorous by most standards, but I remember it like it was yesterday. She was wearing a simple flannel shirt and blue jeans. I was wearing a big grin on my face the whole night. This girl was special.

As the years went by this particular girl worked her way through college. Sometimes she would take whole quarters off while she worked to earn enough money to get by living on her own and going to school. It took her six years, but she obtained her degree from Auburn University in 1991. She became the first member of her family to earn a four-year degree. This girl was special.

It's 20 years later and I'm still amazed by this girl. It's 20 years later and I still think about this girl every day. It's 20 years later and I count my blessings every second that this girl is my wife. Life is amazing...20 years to the day (October 1, 2003, if the doctors are right) after our first date this girl is giving us our second child...our first son.

Joshua Baird Bramblett, let me introduce you to your mother. Always do what she says and never forget...she is a very special girl.

Special indeed...she truly is my soul mate.

Looking back now, we were just children. I was not quite 18, she was not quite 17. There have been ups and downs (mostly my fault), but we are still together. Sure Chris Davis' "Kick Six" was amazing, but nothing is more amazing than my marriage to my best friend and through the years how we have persevered and never given up on one another. There is such a thing as "love at first sight," and September 30, 1983, proves it.

My Mother

I know this seems like an obvious one because without her I would not be here, but there are other reasons she has been important to me and my career.

She'll probably shoot me for saying this, but she did not have a great relationship with her mother. Now I'm not talking anything too terribly unusual for a teenage daughter and her mother, but still, being the youngest of four and the only girl came with benefits and disadvantages. Thankfully, that rebellious side allowed me to come into this world…if you know what I mean.

My mom had me when she was just 19. In 1965, I guess having a child without being married yet was still a rather scandalous thing…particularly in South Georgia. However, she never let it slow her down. She had to put off college plans, but that was okay. Even with the relationship with her mother (my grandmother), the whole family rallied to help raise me. I'm sure it wasn't easy at times, but I never knew it.

Mom and I lived with my grandmother and grandfather. In 1971 he got a job in Langdale, Alabama. He was in the textile industry and moved around regularly. In this case, it was West Point-Pepperell who wanted him as an assistant manager. This also gave my mom the chance to get her college education. The nearest school was Auburn University. That little connection will come up again later. She finished her degree. She went on to become a teacher at Valley High School where she later was principal.

She showed her toughness after suffering a stroke several years ago by not letting it slow her down. She lost partial use of her left arm and leg. However, she has fought through it and adjusted her life without making many sacrifices. She's provided me with inspiration fighting and winning her battle with cancer. There's not much that can hold her down. She remains my biggest fan.

My Grandfather

Growing up without a relationship with my real father, my main male role model was my grandfather. Boyd Lee Cates was born in 1918 in western North Carolina. He grew up around the textile industry. He was too skinny to join the military so he went back home to work. He never got his high school diploma, but what he lacked in education he made up for in work ethic.

When I was small he traveled a good bit. I always remember him bringing me home a toy from wherever his travels took him. It's one of those memories you never lose. He'd make it a point to take me down to the local drug store every week to see what new comic books had come in. He introduced me to the game of golf...for which, I'm mostly grateful. Although, when I was acting like a fool throwing my clubs around when learning the game I know he wondered why he ever did it.

When I needed summer work, he made sure I had a part-time job in the textile mills. The mill was the one place he was most comfortable. In fact, even without a high school degree, he ascended to the job of manager at one of the textile mills located in nearby LaGrange, Georgia. Pretty amazing for the level of his "book learning," however, I doubt there were very many people out there with the "textile" smarts that Boyd Cates had accumulated over the years.

He also realized the best way to assure I went on to college was to put me in the mills where the work was incredibly difficult, the conditions were not the best, and heat of the summertime weighed on you when working amongst the cotton. He, like my mother, had great influence on my path...again, more on that later.

In his later years, when I was well into my career as Auburn's baseball play-by-play announcer, he was one of my biggest supporters. Although he didn't think I should get into the radio business, he never once said I couldn't do it. He believed in my ability. In fact, he would come to almost all of the home baseball games with his old-school Sony Walkman with the big headphones so he could listen to our broadcast while he watched the games. To this day, I still glance to the right of our press box at Plainsman Park where his seats were and think about him.

The grandkids called him "PePaw." When he passed several years ago it was tough for the entire family, but at the same time there was a sense of relief. He had battled congestive heart failure for years. His quality of life had declined. It was time for him to move on to a better place. I'm not sure if he ever knew how much I appreciated his role in my life. It's one of my biggest regrets; hopefully, he knew how much he meant to me.

In a column I wrote just prior to the start of the 2006 football season, I tried to put into words what he meant to me...it would be my first broadcast season without my grandfather:

Remembering PePaw

Well here we are again, on the cusp of another football and broadcast season. Unfortunately, the Auburn family and Auburn Network will be minus one of their most ardent followers. Boyd Lee Cates passed away Thursday, July 20. He was just a few weeks shy of his 88th birthday.

"PePaw" is how everyone knew him in Valley, Alabama, a name he picked up when his youngest grandson started calling grandma "MeMaw" when he was a little boy. Quickly, he became known as PePaw. At first I don't think he cared for it, but he grew to appreciate and love the fact that everyone else started calling him the same thing.

PePaw was born in Burlington, North Carolina, in 1918. He was one of four children. He did not finish high school, but instead went into textiles. It would be the business in which he stayed until he retired about 15 years ago. PePaw traveled quite a bit in his career. His final stop would be Langdale (now part of Valley), Alabama.

He married early in life and had four children of his own, three sons and one daughter. The daughter was the youngest and the one that was taking care of him in his final days. PePaw had four grandchildren, two boys and two girls, and four great-grandchildren, three girls and a boy.

PePaw loved the Auburn Tigers. However, like one of his grandsons, he was a Georgia fan for many years. It wasn't until the mid- to late-'80s that his allegiances switched totally to the Tigers. He listened to every radio broadcast if at all possible. And when I say every radio broadcast, I'm not talking about just football. He also listened to basketball, baseball, and Tiger Talk. He was a devoted listener.

Now you may ask why I chose to write about this particular person in this my first column of the new season. Well you see, that youngest daughter who was taking care of this man in his final days is my mom, and PePaw was my granddaddy. One thing is for sure, without him I would not be where I am today.

He introduced me to sports. He took me to my first college football game, my first Braves game, my first Falcons game, my first Atlanta Hawks game, and my first PGA Tour event. From the time I was a small child up into my college days he was the one I wanted to sit down and watch a big game with. Since becoming a so-called "responsible adult," we hadn't been able to do that very often. I missed it.

He introduced me to the infernal game of golf. He gave me my first set of golf clubs Christmas of 1978. We were out on the links the very next day, and I haven't stopped playing since.

He made sure I got into Auburn University. It was the summer of 1984 and a scholarship to Samford University had unexpectedly fallen through. At that time Auburn was my second choice, so it was next in line. Unfortunately, the admissions date had passed. PePaw made a few calls to the Textile Engineering School. They still had some openings for students majoring in Textile Engineering. He pulled some strings, and I was in. Sometimes I wonder where I would be right now if he hadn't used his influence to get me on the Plains. I certainly wouldn't have what I consider to be the greatest job in the world right now.

The words in this column can never adequately sum up what PePaw meant to me. I never got a chance to tell him, either; however, I'm sure he knew. Since his death I've had several people tell me how proud PePaw was of me. At the funeral I was told by a second cousin that the first time CBS used my play-by-play on one of their television broadcasts he apparently immediately called to tell him. I never knew that…I'm glad I do now.

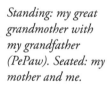

Standing: my great grandmother with my grandfather (PePaw). Seated: my mother and me.

My Grandmother

I can't mention my grandfather without mentioning my grandmother. She helped raise me when my mom was either working or finishing her college degree. She was "MeMaw." My grandparents were married well over 50 years before she passed away in 1996. She was…as they say in the South…a mess. She was extremely protective of her family…particularly the grandchildren. My mom and her mother didn't always see eye to eye, but they both always had our best interest at heart.

My favorite MeMaw story occurred when I was around 10 years old. It was the summertime and I was playing downstairs in the basement of the house. She always made me read for an hour and "rest." This typically took place around 2:00 in the afternoon. Well on this particular day I wasn't ready to go "read and rest." She came down the steps and said, "Roddy, it's time to go read." I argued a little bit as I was right in the middle of a thrilling adventure involving my superhero action figures, but she finally got a little agitated and told me to "get up the stairs right now!" I huffed and grunted. I also thought she had gone back up the stairs to wait on me when I said, "You make me sick!" Mistake! She was still standing there. MeMaw wasn't a big woman. She only stood about 5'1", but as I found out, she was a strong woman. She jerked me up by the arm and proceeded to drag me up the stairs. There were 12 steps to that staircase. I know that's because my butt hit each one on the way up. Needless to say, I never talked back to her again.

Andy Burcham

I could easily put Andy in the category of professional influences, because he is. But more important to me, he is a dear friend. Andy and I have now been doing Auburn University baseball together since 1995. We have been to two College World Series, two BCS National Championship Games, multiple NCAA Regionals and SEC Championships. We are roommates on the road for football and basketball. We have become so close that our spouses joke that we each are the other's "second wife."

I can't begin to describe the respect I have for Andy. He is the longtime "Voice" of the Auburn women's basketball team. For a quarter century, he's held that position. In fact, he is the "dean" of women's basketball play-by-play announcers in the SEC.

Andy and I first met back in the early 1990s when we each covered Auburn football for competing radio stations. He offered me great advice along the way. In 1995, we started doing Auburn baseball. Since that time, we have seen great ups and downs in the baseball program.

Along the way, our families have become close. Personally, we've been each other's sounding board when we've needed to vent. Professionally, Andy has set an example for me on how broadcasters should act, present themselves, and do their jobs.

But it's the relationship that I cherish most. In a business where egos run high, it's nice to have a peer and friend in the business that you can trust. It's nice to work with someone that you truly like and respect.

Andy Burcham and myself at Rosenblatt Stadium prior to the 1997 College World Series.

Professionally, there have been almost too many people to mention that have had an influence on my career. There were a few that had a direct impact. These are the ones who helped pave my path to the greatest job in broadcasting, and they include broadcasters and coaches I've worked with in some capacity.

Barry McKnight

Barry McKnight is one of the most talented broadcasters in the business. He is currently the longtime play-by-play voice of the Troy University Trojans. He also just happens to be a good friend and quite possibly the one person that set me on my ultimate path. I first met Barry when I was a part-time employee at WAUD Radio Station in Auburn, Alabama. I was hired in late 1988 but didn't start my part-time work until right after New Year's Day 1989. Barry was the sports director, and I was but a lowly weekend DJ. At the time Barry was the play-by-play voice of the Auburn University baseball team. Barry was born to do baseball on the radio. His idol is Vin Scully, and you could tell it on the airwaves.

Here I am at the WAUD radio station in 1993. Barry McKnight had just hired me as news/sports director and play-by-play man for Auburn University baseball.

Barry gave me my first shot as a sportscaster when he allowed me to do sidelines for Auburn High School football. I thought I had hit the big time. All bets were off from that point on. I knew this is what I was meant to do.

The following fall I became the play-by-play man for Lee-Scott Academy, a small private school in Auburn. I did that for two seasons. The first year, the Warriors won a state championship. Being the naïve broadcaster that I was, I thought, *"Wow, this is easy."* It always is when you're winning.

After spending 1992 working in Morristown, Tennessee, Barry called me in the late fall. He had been promoted to station manager at WAUD, and he needed someone to come back and be his sports director and do the play-by-play for Auburn University baseball along with Auburn High School football and basketball. The offer was too good to pass up. I am forever grateful to Barry for giving me the opportunity. Without it I'm not sure I would even be in this business today.

Bill Gardner

I knew Bill Gardner all of five months, but I will never forget his generosity and how it ultimately affected my career. Bill worked at a radio station in Morristown, Tennessee. I met him when I started working at the station shortly after moving there with my wife in late 1991. Bill was a retired broadcaster who did the Baltimore Bullets of the NBA. He was there simply because his daughter was on the volleyball team at nearby Carson Newman University.

Bill was set to do play-by-play in the fall of 1992 for the Morristown-Hamblen West Trojans football team. I begged to be on the broadcast. I didn't care if I got paid or not, I just wanted to be on the air in some capacity. Station manager Robin Keith agreed to let me do color. About a month before the season started Bill Gardner came to me with an offer I couldn't refuse. He knew what my long-term goals were, so he relinquished his duties as the play-by-play man to me. He became the analyst and offered me guidance I couldn't get anywhere else. That one football season molded me as much as any because of the mentoring that Bill gave me. His lifetime experiences were more than I could ask for.

It's a shame. When leaving Morristown to come back to Auburn I lost touch with Bill. I have no idea where he went or if he is even still alive. I'd love to tell him face to face how much he helped me with career. He was truly a great man.

Mike Hubbard

In any successful career there is that time where all your preparation, all the relationships you've developed, all the "putting" yourself in the right position builds toward that moment when your career needs or gets that final push. In most cases, you need to have someone trust and believe in you to give you the shove. That person for me is Mike Hubbard. Like me, Mike was a Georgia fan growing up (he actually attended the University of Georgia) but found a new home and loyalty when he came to work at Auburn in the athletics department.

Around 1990, Mike took over the multimedia rights for Auburn athletics. What that basically means is that Mike ran the radio network. His attention to detail and demand for excellence made the (as it was known then) Auburn Network one of, if not the best, radio network broadcasting a single school's football, basketball, and later baseball games.

Mike and I first got together professionally when he asked me do sidelines for some of the Auburn football pay-per-view broadcasts in 1994 and 1995. In 1996, he hired me full-time at the Auburn Network as director of broadcast services. It also allowed me to continue as Auburn baseball's play-by-play announcer.

Two years later in 1998, Mike made me Tiger Talk host and then in 2003 when Jim Fyffe passed away it was Mike who gave me that shove. He had many options to replace Jim—most of them had much more experience than I did. However, Mike had my back and eventually I was named the next "Voice of the Tigers."

Ben Sutton Jr.

When Mike Hubbard sold the Network to ISP, I went to work for a different boss. Ben Sutton Jr. founded ISP in April 1992. He started with just Wake Forest, but quickly grew the business to include more than 60 schools. He took over the same year Jim Fyffe passed away. Ben could have easily come in and said he didn't want me, but he trusted Mike's choice and stuck with it. I am forever grateful for that trust and the fact he continues to trust in the work I do. Ben Sutton Jr. continues to be an innovator in the collegiate sports marketing world. In the early days of ISP, Ben would gather all his play-by-play guys together every summer for a two-day retreat. He once told a group of 12 (jokingly I hope), "You guys are a dime a dozen!" From that point on every summer the group would present Ben Sutton a dime for every "new" dozen of play-by-play guys that gathered as the company continued to grow.

Jay Jacobs

Most know Jay Jacobs as Auburn's athletic director for the past decade—a decade that has included some of Auburn's greatest athletic success both on the field and in the classroom. But I know Jay Jacobs as someone who also spent some of his younger days in Chambers County where I grew up, and who, like me, is living out his dream at his alma mater. Back in the mid-'90s when Jay was director of operations in the department, he would occasionally travel with us on baseball trips. I believe it was 1995 when we all traveled to Starkville, Mississippi. A round of golf was in order. Andy Burcham and I were paired up with Jay and Auburn media relations associate Scott Stricklin. We were winning going into the final

From L to R: future Auburn athletic director Jay Jacobs, me, and future Miss. St. AD Scott Stricklin in 1995. Jay was a sports administrator at Auburn and Scott was the sports information director for Auburn baseball. We had just played a round of golf in Starkville, Mississippi, prior to the Auburn–Miss. State baseball series. Not shown: my broadcast partner Andy Burcham (he was taking the picture).

hole when Scott chirps in, "Double or nothing?" Those were big words coming from someone who had contributed very little on that day. The look on Jay's face was priceless. Andy and I won the hole, but I don't think we ever collected. By the way, little did we know at that time we were playing with two future athletic directors. Scott is now, of course, athletic director at Mississippi State. Meanwhile, 20-plus years later Andy and I are still doing Auburn baseball.

I appreciate Jay's continued support in what I do. He constantly pushes the department to be better and the people (like me) who are out there speaking on behalf of Auburn athletics to do the same.

Larry Wilkins

I have to mention Larry Wilkins. Larry was the chief engineer for the Auburn football (and sometimes basketball) broadcast for the majority of the years dating back to the early 1980s. Don't let appearances fool you. When you meet Larry for the first time, odds are he will be wearing a plaid shirt with suspenders holding up his blue work pants. You probably would be left thinking that this guy works down at the general store, but he is truly one of the most brilliant guys I know. He can solve any problem that arises during a broadcast. I've learned just enough through Larry to make me think at least that I know what I'm doing when setting up my own equipment—and, most important, when rolling up cable, believe me there is a secret to getting that right. His induction into the Alabama Broadcasters Association in 2012 was well deserved.

Larry retired three or four years back, but you still see him at Auburn football games. He coordinates the hundreds of radio frequencies different folks use on a gameday. The biggest compliment you can get from Larry is when he calls you an "ignorant." Trust me…it's a good thing. He and his wife have lived in Prattville, Alabama, for many years. He is one of the true gentlemen in the business and one of most respected engineers around. Our current engineer, Patrick Tisdale, will tell you, Larry Wilkins is the gold standard.

The Media Relations Gang

There are so many others I'd like to mention. In our business, you work closely with the school's media relations directors for each of the sports you cover. I consider all of these people friends more than co-workers—Kent Partridge, Scott

Stricklin, Kirk Sampson, Meredith Jenkins, Dan Froehlich, Chuck Gallina, Shelly Poe, and Taylor Bryan all have made my job so much easier. I have some great stories I could tell about our time together but that would be another book altogether. From the bathroom stalls at Middle Tennessee State University (don't ask), to hoping we don't get caught for speeding leaving the Grand Canyon, to taking your shirt off in a parking lot in Knoxville, to an unexpected stop in the lawn of the old Carolina Arena, to the 3-finger combo at Raising Cane's. Here's to all the fun times we've had. I love each and every one of you.

In this profession you meet so many interesting characters, whether they are coaches, athletes, administrators, or fans. It's one of the most rewarding parts of the job. I've had the good fortune to get to know some of the great legends in coaching and broadcasting...and some of them have left an indelible mark on my life.

Hal Baird

Harry Bailey Baird Jr. was born on August 23, 1949, in Petersburg, Virginia, and there is not a man I respect more. "Hal," as he is known, married his high school sweetheart, Janie Magee, from Corpus Christi, Texas. He earned a B.S. and an M.A. from East Carolina University, where he also pitched for two years. Most of his seven-year professional career was spent with the Kansas City Royals. After his time in pro ball was over, he coached at his alma mater, where he became the head coach and led East Carolina to three consecutive NCAA Tournaments.

Baird was hired at Auburn in 1985 by athletic director and head football coach Pat Dye. Dye knew Baird from his time as head coach in Greenville, North Carolina. Hal Baird immediately had an impact. Playing in an antiquated stadium until 1996, he never used that as an excuse while turning the program around. He took the Tigers to two College World Series and nine NCAA Regionals during his tenure. He coached the likes of Bo Jackson, Frank Thomas, Gregg Olson, and Tim Hudson. Those players still recognize Coach Baird as their biggest influence.

I can say the same thing. My first interaction with Coach Baird came prior to the 1993 baseball season, my first as play-by-play man for the Tigers. At that time, the baseball games only aired locally on a 1,000-watt AM station, WAUD.

One of my most cherished possessions: a signed picture from Hal Baird, with former Auburn head football coach Pat Dye. Coach Baird gave me this shortly after I was named lead announcer in 2003.

As sports director I was responsible for sitting down with the head coach for 30 minutes.

So there I was, sitting in the old dugout at Plainsman Park. Surrounded by metal bleachers that would embarrass some high schools, we proceeded to talk about the 1993 team. I was scared to death. Coach Baird could probably tell I was nervous, and being the gracious man that he is, after the interview was over he told me, "I'm looking forward to working with you…and by the way…you have a great voice." I'm sure he was just trying to make me feel better, but I didn't care. He put me at ease, which is what I needed.

We would go on to develop a professional/personal relationship that is rare in this business. To be honest, we probably got too close. When he announced the 2000 baseball season would be his last, it hit me hard. I wasn't ready for the ride to end, but it was time. He was ready to move on due to some health concerns. Thankfully, he continued to work at Auburn, serving as associate athletic director and eventually interim athletic director when David Housel retired.

Our families became close—so close, that my youngest son Joshua's middle name is Baird. I remember the day he came to my office so I could ask his permission. Janie and he never had children, and I wanted to do something to honor what he meant to me. It seemed like the perfect fit. To this day, he regularly checks in on his "namesake." A few years ago he brought one of his jerseys he wore at Auburn when he was head coach. He could have given me a million dollars and I would not have been more honored.

Hal Baird is Auburn's winningest coach with 634 victories. Yes, that is a great achievement, but his greatest achievement was the way he ran the Auburn baseball program, and for a shorter time, the Auburn athletic department, with the highest level of integrity. Till the day I die, I doubt I will ever meet a greater leader and person than Harry Bailey Baird Jr.

Larry Munson

I'm asked at almost every speaking engagement I attend, "Who did you listen to growing up?" Or "What broadcaster influenced you the most?" That's really a hard question to answer. I could go back to the great Atlanta Braves broadcast team or Ernie Johnson Sr., Pete Van Wieren, and Skip Caray. My grandfather and I listened to them almost every day during the summer. They were three very different personalities that made a perfect combination of professionalism and wit. They just seemed to be having so much darn fun. I could put them at the top of the list, but I think the broadcaster that made me realize this was the business I wanted to get into was Larry Munson. He had a long and diverse career, but it was his work as the University of Georgia play-by-play man that had the most influence on me.

Until I started at Auburn University in the fall of 1984, I was an avid Georgia fan. I was close to an uncle and aunt that attended/worked at the University of Georgia. My first football game I ever attended was an Auburn-Georgia game in 1976. But I really would have rather listened to Larry Munson. My favorite Munson call came in 1980 and the famous "Run, Lindsay, Run" call in the Florida game. Lindsey Scott making the catch on a pass from Buck Belue for 93 yards and the score that would win the game for the Bulldogs and keep them on track for a national championship that season was the moment I thought, *"I want to make a call like that one day."* In fact, I referenced Larry's famous line, "I broke my chair, I came right through a chair, a metal steel chair with about a five-inch cushion, I broke it!" after Ricardo Louis made his miraculous catch against Georgia in 2013. It was the first of two incredible finishes at the end of that regular season.

In 2005, we played at Georgia, and little did we know going in that it would be another classic finish in the rivalry. Brandon Cox hit Devin Aromashodu on fourth-and-10 with 2:05 to go in the game trailing 30–28. It appeared to be a touchdown but was ruled the ball came out on the fumble before he crossed the goal line. Auburn recovered and it set up a game-winning field goal by John Vaughn, but we'll talk about that game later.

Larry Munson's 40th anniversary as the "Voice of the Dawgs" occurred in 2006. We'd always tried to have Larry on our pregame radio show whenever we went to Athens. Football was almost always the secondary topic of conversation. On this particular occasion, we talked more about the group of co-eds Larry would attend movies with on a regular basis. After the movie, they would always critique what they had seen…classic Larry. That week I wrote this about getting to visit with one of my longtime idols:

Larry Legend

This week is one of my favorites of the year…actually one of my favorites out of every two years. The Auburn Network's trip to Athens always means we get to have Georgia play-by-play announcer Larry Munson on our Tiger Tailgate Show. For me personally, it's one of those times where I can't help but feel like a little kid. You see, Larry Munson is probably the first radio play-by-play voice that I really noticed growing up. Looking back, it was listening to him call Georgia games in the late '70s and early '80s that piqued my interest in this profession.

I'm sure you're wondering why in the world Rod Bramblett was listening to the Georgia games growing up. Confession time…from the time I was, oh, probably 9 or 10 years old all the way up to my senior year in high school, I was a Georgia Bulldog fan. That's right, Red and Black were my colors. To make a long story short, I was very close to an uncle who earned two degrees from Georgia. He got me interested in football in particular and thus I became a follower of the Dawgs! Of course, that all changed the first day I stepped on Auburn's campus as a freshman in college. I was immediately weaned off the Red and Black.

Back to the original story...I listened to Larry Munson call game after game with a style that no one else can copy. He's probably the only play-by-play announcer in the country that can get away with it. Munson abandons all sense of professionalism in the way he calls a game. "We" this and "us" that. The opponent is always "they." Sometimes you don't know what's happening but there's never any doubt whether it's good or bad for the Bulldogs.

Where Munson comes up with some of his calls I'll never know. I honestly think they are spur of the moment. Who can forget, "run Lindsay, run Lindsay"—he never called it a touchdown, but you knew. What he did describe was how he broke his chair in the booth: "I came right through a chair. A metal steel chair with about a five-inch cushion, I broke it!" Another one of my favorites, versus Tennessee in 2001: "We just stepped on their face with a hobnailed boot and broke their nose. We just crushed their faces!"

Larry Munson is calling his 40th season of Georgia football this year. Meanwhile, I'm calling my third for Auburn. I certainly hope that one day I'll be calling my 40th season of Auburn football. I don't know if that day will ever come, but if it does I hope I'm as beloved as Larry Munson.

Also, forgive me this Saturday as you're listening to us talk to Larry about anything from football to movies, if you hear me giggle like a little kid. After all, wouldn't you, if you were standing side-by-side one of your idols?

This is one special series...the connections are too numerous to count between Auburn and Georgia. Throw one more in the mix. A young man who grew up a Georgia fan getting to interview the legendary Georgia announcer Larry, the two now peers in the business. A young man who now bleeds Orange and Blue...a young man living out a dream as the play-by-play announcer for his alma mater.

Sonny Smith/Joe Ciampi

I have had the honor over the last four years of my broadcasting career to have two of Auburn's all-time greatest basketball coaches as my color partners. Both are Hall of Famers. I attended Auburn when these two men had their respective basketball programs at the top of their game. Two decades later, I have the privilege of working with both gentlemen.

Coach Smith was Auburn's head coach from 1978–89. It wasn't until his sixth year that he took the Tigers to the NCAA Tournament. Once he did, they were there for five straight years. No one has done that since at Auburn. He was incredibly popular with the student body. A lot like Auburn's current head basketball coach Bruce Pearl, Sonny was a promoter as much as a head coach.

In his career, he won 339 games and lost 304. Granted, not the best winning percentage, but because of his personality and the way he treated the people around him, Sonny Smith is still considered one of the best basketball coaches of his time.

My most vivid memory of Coach Smith when I was a student came on February 1, 1987, when the second-ranked Runnin' Rebels of UNLV came to town. Old Beard-Eaves-Memorial Coliseum was sold out. The Tigers had beaten UNLV the previous season in the Sweet 16 of the NCAA Tournament in

Hall of Fame head coach Sonny Smith has been my full-time broadcast partner on basketball since the 2012–13 basketball season. It's amazing that I get to work with one of my sports idols. He was head coach at Auburn while I was in school on the plains.

Houston, Texas. The odds were stacked against an Auburn basketball team that had played and beaten Florida the day before at home...now they were asked to play a UNLV team that would go on to play in the Final Four that season.

The building was electric and even though the Tigers ended up getting blown out 104–85, Coach Smith and his team made a statement...basketball mattered at Auburn. He had convinced one of the nation's perennial powers to travel from Las Vegas to Auburn, Alabama, to play a basketball game.

At almost 80 years old, Coach Smith is still sharp as ever. He brings his homespun style to the broadcast that you couldn't get anywhere else. His ability to tell a story is unmatched. Coach Smith also wants to get better...he is constantly asking me to critique his performance on the radio. I'm not sure he believes me when I tell him, "Coach, just be yourself and everything will be fine."

I've also had the pleasure of working with former Auburn women's head coach Joe Ciampi. A defensive genius when he was coach, Ciampi mastered the "matchup zone" defense that was a big reason he had so much success. Coach Ciampi and I have done numerous Auburn men's radio broadcasts and a couple of SEC Women's Tournament Championship games. I hope folks realize what Coach Ciampi means to Auburn and college basketball as I pointed out in a column I wrote in 2004...a season that would turn out to be his last at Auburn after 25 years at the helm.

Sunday, January 25, 2004, was a historic day for Auburn athletics as the Auburn women's basketball team defeated Arkansas in easy fashion 71–44. In the second half the Auburn women flexed their muscles and overpowered an overmatched Arkansas team to get a highly coveted road win in the SEC. The reason it was such a historic day was it marked the 600th career win for head coach Joe Ciampi.

I hope Auburn people everywhere realize what an achievement that is. If you don't, let me put it in perspective for you. Ciampi is the fourth fastest women's coach to reach the 600-win plateau and only the 10th coach in the women's game to notch 600 victories. Ciampi is 600–208 in his 27th year. He coached two years at the U.S. Military Academy before arriving at Auburn in 1979. Over the entire history of women's collegiate basketball there have been ONLY 10 coaches to win 600, and Auburn is lucky to have one of them.

Auburn is lucky to have Coach Ciampi not only because of his victories on the court but because of everything he stands for. Discipline, team, academics, and class are terms that are synonymous with the Auburn women's basketball program under Ciampi's leadership. Over 90 percent of Ciampi's players go on to get their degrees. His list of former players is a who's-who of some of the greatest athletes to play the game. Ruthie Bolton-Holifield participated in two Olympic Games. All-American Carolyn Jones-Young and Vickie Orr both participated in one. Other All-Americans include Lauretta Freeman and Becky Jackson.

Now on to his accomplishments on the court. Three Final Four appearances, six Elite Eight, 10 Sweet Sixteen, and a total of 15 NCAA Tournament appearances. On top of that, he has won the SEC Tournament four times and the regular season title on three different occasions. And just this past year the Tigers captured their first WNIT Championship, becoming one of only two teams in the country to finish the year with a win.

Despite all of this I can't help but feel his accomplishments have been underappreciated by a majority of Auburn fans. So let's rally the troops because the most successful coach in Auburn basketball history deserves our support. Make a point to take your family to a game before the end of this season. The Tigers are ranked in the top 25 and are in the thick of a Southeastern Conference race. Now is the time to show your support for one of the best basketball teams in the country and for one of the best coaches in the game's history.

Ciampi finished his career with 607 victories and was inducted into the Women's Basketball Hall of Fame in 2005.

I love both these men. They bring two very different perspectives to the broadcasts. Sonny Smith looks at things from more of an offensive perspective, and Joe Ciampi is the opposite with everything coming from defense. Our listeners are very fortunate to have both still involved with Auburn athletics.

As I said, I know I've left many out, haven't talked enough about others. When you've done this for as long as I have the relationships are the most important thing—not necessarily the wins and losses—I struggle sometimes to remember that.

Chapter 2

Auburn Baseball—Where It Really All Began

Scared to Death but Having the Time of My Life

It was 70 degrees and partly cloudy in Kissimmee, Florida, on February 5, 1993. It was a beautiful day for baseball at Osceola County Stadium. In the press box of the spring training home of the Houston Astros—to be more specific the home radio booth—it might as well have been 100 degrees because I was sweating like a stuck pig and unbelievably nervous as I prepared to broadcast my first Auburn University baseball game. I haven't admitted this to many people but I will here—I had not done very much baseball play-by-play when asked to be the voice of Auburn baseball. So I was terrified over what was about to happen. I really wasn't sure what would come out of my mouth.

I was by myself—back then the Auburn games were only broadcast on WAUD AM 1230. In fact, this would be the first season all games would be on the radio. In the past, some of the road non-conference games were not on the air. So obviously the station was not going to pay to have a two-man crew. I was alone and about to try and fill nine innings of baseball—a scary proposition to say the least.

The season opener that year was part of a four-team round-robin event called the "Olive Garden" Classic. Defending national champion Pepperdine, host school Central Florida, and Georgia Tech were all part of the three-day tournament. On the first day, the Tigers played a doubleheader starting with

Georgia Tech. I look back at my scorebook now and realize how good that Georgia Tech team was. Their leadoff hitter was Nomar Garciaparra. Their No. 3 hitter was Jay Payton. Their cleanup man was Jason Varitek. All of whom went on to have pretty darn good major league careers.

Auburn had their little right-hander on the hill, John Powell—a strikeout machine with his split-finger fastball. The Tigers also had a future major leaguer in their lineup with true freshman Mark Bellhorn at second base. Bellhorn hit a home run in his second at-bat in the fifth inning to give Auburn a 1–0 lead, but in the top of the sixth Garciaparra led off the inning with a triple, Jay Payton singled, Varitek reached on a third-strike wild pitch that got away, and then a walk to the next batter led to a bases-clearing double from a kid by the name of Brandon Hensley. And just like that the game was broken open, and the Yellow Jackets led 4–1. Auburn cut it to 4–3 in the bottom half of the inning, but a two-out solo home run in the seventh by Georgia Tech's David Newhan made it 5–3. Auburn would go on to fall, 5–4.

Speaking of major leaguers, Auburn did have another one who pitched in that game. Scott Sullivan was Auburn's closer that season. He pitched the final two innings. Sullivan is a great story. He came to Auburn as a shortstop but had very little chance of playing. He was a tall kid at 6'3". Head coach Hal Baird loved his makeup, and he had all the characteristics of a great leader. He knew he had to figure out a way to get him involved, so he decided to make him a pitcher. When Sullivan first tried it he went with a standard delivery and could barely throw over 80 mph. So that's when Coach Baird dropped him down to a sidearm delivery, and all of a sudden he was up to 90 mph with a brutal slider to go with his fastball. He was 4–3 with an ERA of 2.55 in his final year at Auburn. He did enough to catch the eyes of major league scouts. The Cincinnati Reds drafted him in the second round of the June draft. Two years later, he was in the bigs with the Reds. He ended up enjoying an 11-year major league career with the Reds, White Sox, and Royals. Scott is back in Auburn now with his family. He is still one of my favorites.

But I digress…back to my first game. I was awful! I was so bad, I refused to go back and listen to the game. I was slow in my description. I lost track of what was happening on the bases. I was scared to death to let my emotions go because I was more concerned about getting the names of the players right. Mike Lude was the athletic director at the time. He actually called the baseball media relations director at the time, Kent Partridge, and asked if I was okay? I think he was genuinely concerned that I would not make it through the broadcast. Kent... being the good, level-headed friend that he was...calmly explained that I would be okay. He told him to please realize that I was doing my first game and to be patient. I wish I could tell you I was as confident as Kent.

It didn't get any better in game two of the day against Pepperdine. Auburn hung in there until the fifth inning when the Wave scored five runs and went on to win, 7–1. So there I was 0–2 as Auburn's baseball play-by-play man and was really bad in the process. Please God...just let me go crawl in a hole somewhere!

The next day was a little better. At least Auburn won a game as they dismantled the host school, Central Florida, 12–1. I finally got into a little bit of a rhythm, but it was still far from satisfactory. The best thing for me was to decompress, force myself to listen to at least one of those games from my first weekend, and get back to Auburn.

As the season went along, things got better with every game I called. My color partner that season was Mark Littleton. He did all the home games with me and actually paid his own way to go on the road. Mark had a bright future in the business but later decided to get out of broadcasting.

I will always cherish that 1993 baseball season. That team that started the season 1–4 actually turned out to be a really good ball club. They won all but one of their Southeastern Conference series—the only series loss coming at South Carolina where they were swept. I remember Coach Baird being particularly terse on the postgame show. It was not a fun bus ride home for the guys. Auburn then proceeded to take it out on UAB in the midweek, 20–1. After that South Carolina sweep, Auburn went 18–5 the remainder of the regular season. Included in that stretch was a series win at eventual national champion LSU.

From 1993 to 1995, the SEC Baseball Tournament was actually split into two separate tournaments with a Western Division tournament and an Eastern Division Tournament. At the time, it seemed like a stupid idea...looking back it was a really stupid idea. You had two different tournament champions, but the overall champion was determined by your conference record (that included the tournament games you played). Crazy stuff but they rectified that problem in 1996 by going with one SEC Tournament.

In 1993 the Western Division tournament was at LSU. Auburn won the first two tournament games with a 13–4 win over Alabama and a 3–1 win over

Arkansas. Personal tragedy struck at this time for me as my stepfather, who had been battling an illness brought on by a golf cart accident, passed away. I missed the next two games of the tournament as I rushed back to my hometown of Valley. The tournament was a double-elimination event. Auburn dropped their next two games to LSU and Mississippi State. Even with the two losses to close out the tournament, Auburn was poised to make the postseason for the first time since 1989.

The NCAA Selection Committee sent the Tigers west to Stillwater, Oklahoma. At that time there were only 48 teams selected to the tournament with eight different NCAA Regional sites. In what was called the Midwest Regional, North Carolina State was the No. 1 seed. The Wolfpack were coached by future South Carolina head man Ray Tanner (who is now athletic director in Columbia). The host school, Oklahoma State, was the No. 2 seed, followed by Arizona as No. 3, Auburn No. 4, UConn No. 5, and Fordham No. 6.

In the NCAA baseball regionals (which are double elimination), it's imperative to stay in the winner's bracket. If you fall into the loser's side you have to play so

Me in the broadcast booth at old Plainsman Park in 1993 or 1994. The broadcast booth was nothing more than a metal building with three separate rooms.

many more games to have a chance to win it all. Most college teams do not have the pitching depth for that to happen. That was very true for this Auburn team where pitching depth had been one weakness. Having said that, Auburn's No. 1, John Powell, was set to pitch against Arizona, a team that brought one of the most prolific offenses in NCAA history to that point into Stillwater.

The Wildcats led the nation in home runs with 115, they were third in team batting average at .343, first in scoring at just over nine runs per game, first in slugging percentage, third in doubles, and the list goes on and on. Powell was magnificent against the Wildcats as Auburn won the game, 9–1. Later that night we were out for dinner at a local restaurant and heard some of the Arizona players talking with their families and making note they had never seen anything like John Powell in any of their games that season.

That was the highlight of the trip to Stillwater. Auburn dropped the next two games to end the season. However, the foundation was laid for what became something of a renaissance for Auburn baseball. The program would go to the NCAA Regionals 10 of the next 11 years and the following season would be very special.

1994—Tigers Make it to Omaha

The 1994 team had many of the same guys back from the 1993 team, particularly on the pitching staff. John Powell returned for his senior season. Ryan Halla was a sophomore and eventually became the closer on that team. Chris Morrison and Kevin Humphreys were two new arms that would have a tremendous impact on the team. Morrison was typically described as a "bulldog" type pitcher. He had good stuff…not great. But he was a tremendous competitor on the mound. Morrison went 9–2 that season. Humphreys was also key on the 1994 squad. All he did was win, going 12–4 with an ERA of 3.66. For the first time in a while, Auburn had a true three-man weekend rotation that could compete week in and week out in the SEC. Throw in Jason LaBoeuf as the setup man, and it was a pretty complete staff.

Offensively, there were a few that had to be replaced but the core was back, including Jay Waggoner, Mark Bellhorn, Brandon Moore, Mike Killimett, and others. New faces included Dallan Ruch, Ken Key, Kevin Chabot, Shawn McNally, Robert Lewis, and a young man by the name of Frank Sanders. Sanders came over from football and was one of Auburn's all-time best receivers. He made some of the biggest catches in Auburn history over the course of his career. The biggest was a game-winner at Florida in 1994 when Auburn defeated the No. 1-ranked Gators. He had played baseball in high school and wanted to give it one more try before leaving school. He was a little slow to come along, but by the end of the season he was a pretty darn good player.

Auburn started the season 16–3 before hitting a rough patch midway, going 8–10. They opened the season inside the Louisiana Superdome in a round-robin tournament similar to the one the previous season in Kissimmee. For the second straight season, Auburn faced the defending national champion on its opening weekend. It was Pepperdine the year before, this time it was LSU. It was considered a non-conference game, and Auburn won it, 3–1. I think the Fighting Tigers remembered that loss as they swept the conference series later that season in Auburn.

Speaking of that LSU series, despite losing all three games history was made at Plainsman Park. Auburn's John Powell was chasing the NCAA strikeout mark. There was little doubt he would shatter the mark, it was just a matter of when. It occurred on a sunny Saturday afternoon. The date was May 7, and LSU's Warren Morris (who I believe was a freshman) was the victim.

LSU went on to win the game 4–3, but I got a chance to broadcast what was probably my first really important radio call. Powell went on to strike out 602 batters in his career…that is still the NCAA record. Meanwhile, don't feel too bad for Warren Morris. He went on to hit the game-winning home run for LSU against Miami at the College World Series to give LSU yet another national title.

The following weekend Auburn took two of three at Alabama. Actually, game one was played in Huntsville and Auburn lost that one, 6–5. The series returned to Tuscaloosa the next night. Auburn held on to win that one 5–4, but out of that game comes one of my favorite stories.

At Sewell-Thomas Stadium in 1994, the home and visitor radio booths are side by side with a glass between the two. The Alabama booth was to our right. Auburn led 5–1 going to the ninth inning. Chris Morrison was his usual spectacular self, going the first eight-plus innings. However, a leadoff walk to start the inning brought Hal Baird out of the dugout to make the change to his closer, Ryan Halla. "Rhino," as we called him, wasn't as sharp as usual. Before you knew it Alabama's Anthony Box had hit a three-run homer, and it was 5–4 with two outs. The next batter was Brett Taft. He doubled, and the tying run was in scoring position. Anthony Hill stepped to the plate and proceeded to hit one to deep left field…and I mean deep left field! With his back to the wall, Kevin Chabot made the catch to preserve the win. When it left the bat I thought it was gone.

I looked to my left and Alabama's guy doing the play-by-play was going nuts, and I really couldn't figure out why. It almost looked like he thought they had won the game. Oh well…maybe I was wrong. The next day we show up at the ballpark to get the full skinny on what happened.

Apparently, Alabama's announcer (who will remain nameless because I consider him a good friend to this day) called it a home run, "Alabama wins, Alabama wins!" He was going crazy. His broadcast partner leaned over and said, "He caught the ball." The response: "Well, damn him." It gets better. Apparently Alabama's athletic director, Hootie Ingram, was listening to the broadcast. He turned off the radio as soon as he heard the Alabama announcer scream the ball was gone and the Crimson Tide had miraculously won the game.

He comes to the Alabama radio booth and says something to their play-by-play man along the lines of, "When I went to bed last night we had won the game. When I woke up this morning and opened up the sports section to the newspaper it says we lost! What the hell happened?" Upon which I'm sure Alabama's guy went white as a sheet. We still tell that story when together.

Six days later, Auburn opened the SEC Western Division Tournament against Arkansas in Oxford, Mississippi, and that opener would turn out to be one of the most amazing games I've ever called.

John Powell started on the mound for Auburn. Barry Lunney Jr. got the call for Arkansas. The game was scoreless until the ninth inning. Auburn was the visiting team and scored a run in the top half of the inning on a wild pitch. Arkansas answered with a run in the bottom of the inning, scoring on an error. Powell had gone the distance for the Tigers, striking out 13 batters in the process, and Lunney was lifted with one out in the ninth. So it was off to extra innings and the game was in the hands of the bullpen. The Razorbacks went to Todd Abbott, while Auburn rolled the dice and went to its closer, Ryan Halla.

Nothing doing for either side in the 10th…or the 11th…or the 12th…or the 13th…or the 14th…or the 15th (by the way both Halla and Abbott were still in there pitching)…or the 16th. Both teams had a few scoring opportunities, but not many. The 17th rolled around and finally Auburn started making some noise. Shawn McNally singled, and Mark Bellhorn sacrificed him over to second. Mike Killimett then singled to right field, scoring McNally and breaking the tie. Later, Frank Sanders drove in Killimett to give the Tigers some insurance going to the bottom of the 17th.

Halla came out and struck out the side (sandwiched around one hit) to finish the game. I had just witnessed a 17-inning marathon where Auburn used only two pitchers. John Powell and Ryan Halla (remember he had been a starter his freshman season) combined to strike out 25 Arkansas hitters. Arkansas only used three pitchers! The game lasted 4 ½ hours and it is still one of the most remarkable ballgames I've ever seen.

Auburn won a couple more games in the tournament, eventually getting ousted by LSU, who they lost twice against (by one run in both games and with the one run coming in the ninth inning). It also marked the fourth-straight one-run loss to LSU. As we were headed back to Auburn, we stopped by the team bus to get some food where then assistant coach Mitch Thompson said, "Well boys, I guess LSU is one run better than us!" So true, so true. It was then back home to find out where the Tigers would be sent for the NCAA Tournament.

Auburn was sent to Clemson for the East Regional at Tiger Stadium. Clemson was the No. 1 team in the country going into the postseason. Auburn was the No. 2 seed with the rest of the field being Old Dominion (No. 3), Notre Dame (No. 4), Virginia Tech (No. 5), and The Citadel (No. 6). The regional was a who's-who of great collegiate baseball coaches with Jack Leggett (Clemson), Pat McMahon (Old Dominion), Pat Murphy (Notre Dame), and, of course, Hal Baird.

Auburn opened play against the Hokies, and John Powell cruised, going the distance, pitching through almost two hours of rain delays and striking out 12 in the process. Auburn won the game, 7–0. Old Dominion defeated Notre Dame, and Clemson took care of business with The Citadel.

On the second day, top-seeded Clemson got a Notre Dame team facing elimination. The Fighting Irish pulled off the upset, 8–1, which meant the regional was wide open for Auburn and Old Dominion, who played the nightcap. The winner was in the driver's seat for a trip to Omaha.

Auburn jumped out to an 8–1 lead after four innings and things were looking good, but Old Dominion rallied against Auburn's Kevin Humphreys, and then Ryan Halla gave up seven unanswered to tie it at 8–8 going to the eighth. The game made it to extras…something Auburn was quite familiar with in postseason. However, this time it didn't take 17 innings to get the job done.

Robert Lewis singled, Jay Waggoner then reached on an error just trying to sacrifice Lewis to second—the throw into right field allowed Lewis to score. Then Mark Bellhorn finished a 5-for-5 day with an RBI single to score Waggoner, Dallan Ruch drove in Bellhorn, and it was a three-run tenth.

Halla then set 'em down in order in the bottom of the inning to preserve the 11–8 win. The Tigers were in charge of their Omaha destiny. They got a Clemson team the next day that had already played one more game in the loser's bracket. Auburn had Chris Morrison set to go on the hill, and we all felt good about our chances.

The Clemson game was never in doubt. Auburn led 7–0 after four, then 11–3 after six. The two through five hitters for the Tigers went 13–23 with eight RBIs. Chris Morrison and Ryan Halla on the mound combined to hold Clemson to five runs on nine hits. Auburn had beaten a Clemson team that had won 57 games up to this point and was ranked No. 1 in the nation. Auburn won the game 11–5, thus setting up a scenario that heavily favored the Tigers…a matchup with Notre Dame on Sunday. The Fighting Irish had already lost once, so they would have to beat Auburn twice to advance to Omaha. On top of that, Hal Baird had already made up his mind that he was going to put the ball in the hands of John Powell on just two days rest.

Notre Dame had no answer for two guys in the Championship Game… one being John Powell who had already blanked Virginia Tech…did the same to Notre Dame, going eight-plus innings and striking out 10. The other one was Frank Sanders, who was slowly but surely getting better as the season played out. He destroyed Notre Dame on this day, going 4-for-5 with a home run, two doubles, and four RBIs. That's all Auburn needed. Leading 7–0 in the ninth, Ryan Halla closed out another one to send Auburn to the College World Series for the first time since 1976.

Here I was, second year of doing Auburn baseball, and I was going to get to call one of the biggest spectacles in college athletics…the College World Series.

The first trip to Omaha was a bit of a blur. For whatever reason, I don't remember much. I do remember driving up for the first time to the original Rosenblatt Stadium. It sat on top of a hill, giving it the appearance as some sort of mecca. Yes, it was an old, antiquated stadium, but the blues, yellows, and reds of the ballpark popped out at you like neon lights. You could feel the history and tradition.

For Coach Hal Baird, it held a special place in his heart, too. He was a mainstay in the Kansas City Royals organization as a player. Coach Baird spent many years in Omaha in this stadium playing for the Kansas City Triple-A team. The stadium club located down the right-field line included photos and memorabilia from Baird's time in Omaha.

Auburn drew Oklahoma in the first round. I thought the Tigers were a little wide-eyed early in the game. John Powell got the start but wasn't his usual self. Oklahoma had a lot to do with that. Powell wasn't getting the usual number of strikeouts. His out pitch, the split-finger fastball didn't have the usual bite. The Sooners led 4–0 going to the eighth inning when the Tigers finally got it going. A three-run inning made it a one-run game, but in the bottom of the inning, the Sooners got a solo home run to make it 5–3. The ninth had some dramatics with Auburn getting one of the runs back. They had the tying run at third with one out and the number two and three hitters up, but back-to-back groundouts to short by Shawn McNally and Mark Bellhorn sent the Tigers to the loser's bracket to face Miami.

The game two days later was really decided in the first inning. Miami batted first as the visiting team. Their leadoff man was hit by a pitch, but a couple of groundouts to second quickly recorded two outs, and that man was at third. Danny Buxbaum skied a pitch into the bright sunshine that Mark Bellhorn lost in the sun. The ball fell to the ground, and a run scored. Unfortunately, Auburn could not overcome that miscue. The next batter singled, then Mike Torti blasted a three-run homer to make it 4–0 after a half inning.

While it set the tone, Auburn still battled their way back, tying the game at four thanks to a two-run double by Brandon Moore in the sixth. The momentum didn't last long. After two quick outs recorded by starting pitcher Kevin Humphreys, the wheels came off. A walk and a single chased Humphreys from the game. In came Morrison, which tells you the direness of the situation— Morrison was normally a starter. Coach Baird felt he had to get his next-best guy in. I'm not sure if it was in part due to the fact he wasn't accustomed to coming in from the bullpen or if it was simply Miami's hitters...probably a little of both... but the 'Canes picked up back-to-back doubles that scored three runs to go back on top 7–4. Auburn managed a run in the eighth but no more. Their stay in Omaha was a short one, but one that would serve the program well. They would be back sooner than we all probably thought.

1995—Oh, for a New Stadium

The following year almost everyone returned off the 1994 team. The biggest loss on the pitching staff was John Powell; however, Ryan Halla easily slid into a starter's role, while Auburn signed closer Finley Woodward, who would turn into arguably the best the Tigers ever had. In the field, shortstop Brandon Moore, catcher Robert Lewis, and outfielder Mike Killimett were the biggest losses. But all in all, much of the College World Series lineup was back.

The 1995 team started 37–4. In the league they began with a 15–3 record as they headed to LSU. Auburn was 44–6 and LSU was 40–11. The atmosphere all weekend was unbelievable. The series was played at the old Alex Box Stadium, an old ballpark with a 1920s feel to it. At the time it was considered to be the toughest place to win in all of the country. Another unique feature to "the Box" was the fact there was no press box. There was a press area at the very top of the bleachers with three rows for radio, media, etc. You were basically right in the middle of the fans. It was a feature my first-year broadcast partner Andy Burcham did not care for. I always thought it was quite charming.

All three games were sellouts. With more than 6,000 in attendance, game one was all Auburn. The Tigers scored 19 runs (10 in the fifth) on 21 hits. Six doubles, two triples, and a home run set the tone for the weekend. Chris Morrison was the Friday night starter and he cruised to victory as Auburn won the game, 19–7.

After the game, as we packed up the equipment (another drawback at the open-air press box, you couldn't leave your equipment up for the weekend) we watched LSU's Saturday starter, Brett Laxton, work on the mound. He was getting the mound to his liking. Something a bit unusual, he basically dug a hole out on front of the rubber and filled in it with clay. He must have spent 15-20 minutes working on that spot. The reason I tell you this is because that work on the mound would have an impact on the Saturday game.

Ryan Halla was the starter on that Saturday. Early in the outing, his plant foot landed right on the hole that Laxton had filled with clay. It must have been a little soft because Halla appeared to tweak his ankle when he landed on the spot. He was not the same the rest of the game and got roughed up in an 11–6 loss to even the series, setting up one of the most epic games I've ever seen on the diamond.

Auburn fell behind 4–0 after one inning. The Tigers didn't get on the board until the fourth inning on back-to-back home runs from Mark Bellhorn and Shawn McNally. It had become a running joke that I never could get any runs in my first three innings of play-by-play, but once I turned it over to Andy in the middle three we all of a sudden started scoring. In this game after the back-to-back homers, Kent Partridge (who was the media relations director for Auburn at the time) called the press box and asked to talk to our baseball media relations director Scott Stricklin (who is now athletic director at Mississippi State) and told him I was not to do play-by-play again. He was joking, I think.

After the two-run fourth inning, Auburn scored four in the fifth to take a 6–4 lead. That was the first of five lead changes over the final five innings. LSU scored three in the bottom of the fifth and it was 7–6. Three unanswered for Auburn followed to give them a 9–7 advantage, but it wouldn't last for long. In the bottom of the eighth, LSU's Eddy Furniss hit a three-run homer and the Fighting Tigers scored four total to make it 11–9 going to the ninth.

The ninth didn't exactly start with a bang as Mark Weeks flied out to center. Dallan Ruch followed with a double. David Dews pinch hit for Rob Macrory and struck out. So down by two runs with two outs it didn't look good for the visiting Orange and Blue. Catcher Kirby Clark was next, and he singled to left, putting runners at first and third. Ken Key stepped to the plate and drove in a run on a single to left, making it a one-run game. The tying run was now at second and the go-ahead run at first with two outs. You could feel the magic building because one of the best clutch hitters ever to put on an Auburn uniform was up...Jay Waggoner. J-Wag, as we called him, hit a ringing double to left field. Two runs scored, and the Tigers had taken the lead, 12–11. The fifth lead change of the day was the last as LSU got one man on in the bottom of the ninth but Finley Woodward closed it out by getting a double play and a fly out to end the game.

Auburn had not only beaten LSU...again...in Baton Rouge but they did it in the most dramatic fashion. The following week the Tigers were ranked No. 1 in the nation for the first time in program history. They should have hosted a regional that season, but because the new ballpark wasn't built yet, they couldn't. If Auburn hosted that season they would have gone to Omaha for a second consecutive season...I'm convinced of that. Instead, they were shipped to Oklahoma City as the No. 1 seed in a regional hosted by the University of Oklahoma. Auburn won the first two games of the regional but lost a heartbreaker, 9–8, to the Sooners to go to the loser's bracket. They did beat Texas the next day to get to 50 wins for the first time in school history but didn't have enough in the tank to beat Oklahoma twice in the championship round.

It's a shame that a team (arguably the best baseball team ever at Auburn) couldn't host. It was a team that was not only good enough to go to Omaha, but would have been good enough to win it all. Two years later, another Auburn baseball team would get a chance to go to Omaha.

1997—Hudson, Ross, and the Miracle in Tallahassee

1996 was a transition year in many ways. Hal Baird made a decision about halfway through the year he was going to play a handful of first-year (freshmen/junior college) players that he knew were going to be the nucleus of future success. Adam Sullivan, Chad Wandall, Casey Dunn, Tim Hudson, and Jamie Kersh all had to cut their teeth in the SEC. None of them had "great" years, but that 1996 season set them up to take a huge step forward the next season. Of that group, Tim Hudson would make the biggest impact. We started to see a glimpse late that season, but we had no idea what was to come.

Heading into conference play the 1997 team got off to the best start in school history at 17–0. The Tigers conference opening series was at South Carolina and Sarge Frye Field. There was no reason to think Auburn would lose in game one with Tim Hudson going on the mound...wrong. Huddy got drilled. Giving up six runs in two innings, we later found out he had suffered a really bad stomach virus leading up to the game. Reliever Patrick Dunham wasn't any better, giving up nine more over two innings. The hero of the night was little used reliever George Jones, who that night earned the nickname "the opossum" after the famous country music singer; he pitched the final four innings, saving the Auburn bullpen for the rest of the weekend. The final was 17–3 and a dose of reality.

The next game didn't start much better as South Carolina led 6–0 going into the seventh inning. I'm really not sure what happened after that, but a switch flipped, the bats woke up and 10 runs and four homers later the Tigers had come from behind to win 10–6. It was one of the most remarkable turnarounds in a single game I've ever seen. The next day South Carolina had nothing and Auburn took the series by winning 21–6.

Auburn finished the first half of the conference schedule 11–4; the second half was much more difficult, going 10–8 overall. They lost three of the final five series and to be quite honest limped into the SEC Tournament in Columbus. Pitching consistency and depth were the biggest issues in the second half. Outside of Tim Hudson, the rest of the staff had its ups and downs. Auburn could hit the ball with the best of them, but sometimes getting outs was difficult.

Still we were witnessing what is to this day one of the, if not the, best single season by an Auburn student-athlete. Only Cam Newton in 2010 would rival the season this kid from Phenix City, Alabama, was having. Tim Hudson on the mound went 15–2 with an ERA of 2.97. He struck out 165 over 118 innings. At the plate he hit .396 with 18 home runs and 95 RBIs. Those last two numbers still rank second best in school history for a single season.

Not that Auburn was in danger of not making the NCAA Tournament, but I really thought they needed some success in the SEC Tournament to help with momentum going into the postseason. Wins over Arkansas and Mississippi State did just that as the Tigers went 2–2 in the SEC Tournament that was held in Columbus, Georgia…the last time it was held someplace other than Hoover, Alabama.

The following Monday, Auburn found out it was headed to Tallahassee, Florida, as the No. 2 seed. The rest of the field consisted of the host Florida State, Central Florida, South Florida, Western Carolina, and Marist. Auburn drew Western Carolina in the first round. Tim Hudson got the start on the mound and only pitched into the sixth inning as the game itself wasn't much. Auburn easily won 11–3, but it's what happened late in the game that would impact the rest of the regional for Auburn. In the eighth inning, the game well in hand, All-SEC catcher Casey Dunn was hit by a pitch for the second time on the day… this one broke a bone in his wrist/hand. He was done for the rest of however long the season lasted. His backup was David Ross, a freshman who had played in 33 games, starting just 12. He was a highly recruited catcher out of Tallahassee, but with Dunn in front of him he had to bide his time. Ross was thrust into a starter's role beginning with South Florida the next day.

Auburn breezed through game two against the Bulls. Bryan Hebson pitched his best game of the season, going eight shutout innings as Auburn took game two of the regional 9–0 setting up the big winner's bracket game against host Florida State who was the heavy favorite to win their own regional. The winner of that game was 3–0 in the regional, while the loser had to win three more games to overcome the loser's bracket.

Auburn was the home team. It was an early game starting at 11:00 am EST. Kevin Knorst got the start on the mound for Auburn. Florida State started Randy Choate, who was still playing in the majors as late as 2015. The game felt a little like game two of the South Carolina series mentioned earlier. The game was tied at one when the Seminoles broke it open with four in the fifth and two more in the sixth. It was 7–1 'Noles going to the seventh inning. Finley Woodward had come on for Knorst in the fifth inning and given up the last two runs.

In the seventh, Jamie Kersh doubled in Adam Sullivan to make it 7–2. Woodward put up a zero in the top half of the eighth. Then in the bottom half Josh Etheredge led off the inning with a solo homer…the score was 7–3. Woodward put up another zero in the top of the ninth. The hill was still mighty big to climb for an Auburn baseball team that had shown the ability to come from behind throughout the year.

So many ninth inning rallies are reliant upon that first man getting on base. Rob Macrory did just that, singling up the middle. Jamie Kersh followed with a two-run blast out to right center field and all of a sudden it was 7–5 with nobody out and nobody on. Randy Choate's day was done as longtime FSU head coach Mike Martin went to closer Randy Niles. Niles walked Tim Hudson, bringing the tying run to the plate in the Tigers' leading home run hitter, Josh Etheredge. Josh struck out looking on an 0–2 pitch. A big first out for Florida State, now a double play gets them out of the inning. However, Derek Reif on a 2–2 pitch singled past the shortstop, putting runners on first and second for Chad Wandall, who already had three hits on the day.

You could feel the tension rising inside sold-out Dick Howser Stadium. Niles coaxed a fly out to right field from Wandall, and now the tension eased. After all, only one out to go and FSU was in the catbird seat where everyone expected them to be. The only thing standing in the way was backup catcher David Ross. Coming into the game, the Tallahassee native was hitting just .230 on the season. He had driven in 10 runs with one home run. Not exactly the kind of numbers that should strike fear in the hearts of FSU fans. To be honest, we weren't expecting much in the booth, either. We were thinking, *"Okay, get a hit here, get that runner home, and give Heath Kelly a chance to tie this thing up."*

The count got to 2–2 on Ross. Niles delivered the next pitch, Ross swung, foul tip, into the mitt of catcher Jeremy Salazar...I called it a strikeout...what I couldn't see was the ball popping out and onto the ground. "NO! He couldn't hold on!" One more breath of life remained, and the next pitch would give me my first signature call—one that will forever be among my favorites.

Rod: 2 and 2 the count, two outs, runner at second base means nothing. The tying run is on first. Here we go again the 2–2 pitch. He swings and there's a drive to deep left field! That one's gone! That one's gone! Auburn wins! Auburn wins! Auburn wins! Auburn wins! I don't believe it ... Ross, with a three-run homer! The Tigers win! Oh my goodness! Oh my goodness! 8–7!

Andy: Unbelievable! He hit it out of the ballpark! Ross...on a 2–2 pitch...he hit it over the left field wall, and the Tigers are going to play for the championship tomorrow!

Picture of David Ross touching home after a dramatic ninth-inning HR.

1997 SEASON REVIEW

"Ross swings and a drive to deep left field ... that one's gone ... that one's gone ... Auburn wins ... Auburn wins ... Auburn wins ... Auburn wins ... I don't believe it ... Ross, with a three-run homer ... the Tigers win ... Oh my goodness ... Oh my goodness ... 8-7 ... David Ross is mobbed at home plate ... I don't believe what I just saw."

— Auburn Network announcer Rod Bramblett following David Ross' game-winning homer against Florida State in the NCAA East Regional.

A bunch of us from the office took our co-worker on a Braves trip in 2011 for a "bachelor's day at the ballpark." We had a chance to visit with David Ross during batting practice. From L to R: me, Brad Law (the bachelor), David Ross, Steve Witten, Chris Davis, John Mitchell, Ben Harling, and Ryan Sullivan.

Think about the drama here. Beyond the two-out, bottom-of-the-ninth dramatics, the man who hit the home run was from Tallahassee. Ross attended Tallahassee High School that is just beyond the left field wall where he hit the line-drive shot. He was a backup for goodness sake! He would have never been up in that situation if Casey Dunn had not been injured in the first game of the regional.

There was much hugging and high-fiving in the booth. In the celebration at the plate head coach Hal Baird, who rarely got emotional, joined in and met Ross as he crossed home. In the process Baird broke his glasses. The emotion was unlike I'd ever seen or felt to that point in my broadcast career. Those are the moments you live for as a broadcaster. A T-shirt with the call hung in one of the local bookstores for years. It's now on the wall in my office at home.

The next day Auburn started freshman Brent Schoening. He and Josh Hancock battled but just didn't have enough as Florida State scored two runs in the eighth inning and won, 9–7. Because of rain earlier in the day the game didn't start until 5:00 pm EST, which meant the championship game didn't start until close to 9:00 pm local time. What would Auburn do? Like they did in 1994 with John Powell, they went with Tim Hudson, who had thrown well under 100 pitches in the opener on Thursday and was pitching on just two days rest.

Auburn was again the home team. In the first inning, FSU's J.D. Drew, who went on to have a good major league career, grounded into a double play for the first two outs of the game. Later at one of the college national player of the year award ceremonies, where both Drew and Hudson were finalists, Drew mentioned that he told the team as he walked back to the dugout after that first at-bat, "Boys, we're in trouble, we haven't seen sh*t like this all season!" He was right, in one of the most heroic pitching performances I've ever witnessed, Hudson went eight innings allowing one earned run and striking out 12 Florida State batters. Patrick Dunham came in to finish off the 5–2 victory. The game ended on a double play.

The game ended just shy of 11:00 pm local time, which meant we were looking at a four-hour drive home into the wee hours, but we didn't mind...we were going back to Omaha for the second time in four years.

We were among familiar company in Omaha as four teams from the SEC Western Division made it there. LSU, Mississippi State, and Alabama all won their respective regionals, and oddly enough, Auburn played none of them while we were there.

Although it had only been four years, you could tell the College World Series had gotten even bigger. We went out a few days before the actual games began. Andy Burcham, Scott Stricklin, Kent Partridge, and I had a wonderful time. Unlike 1994, I was able to soak in much of the ambience and tradition of Rosenblatt Stadium. One day, for what reason I don't know, we all drove to South Dakota...just to say we did.

Auburn played the first game of the CWS against Stanford. The Tigers were seeded sixth and Stanford third. Unfortunately, because of the 144 pitches Tim Hudson threw in the regional championship game the previous week on a Sunday, he wasn't available on Friday, May 30. Instead, Auburn looked to Bryan Hebson, who actually pitched very well, but Auburn's defense committed three errors in the game leading to four unearned runs in an 8–3 loss. The Tigers were headed to the loser's bracket, and it was up to Tim Hudson to keep the season alive.

Timmy didn't need much support, but he got it anyway. Auburn pounded Rice for 10 runs on 11 hits. Hudson pitched seven innings, holding the Owls to a run on four hits—oh and by the way, he was also 2-for-3 at the plate with a home run, double, and six RBIs. It was the climax of the season and solidified Tim Hudson as one of the greatest players to play the college game. There was also a little drama after the game that indirectly involved Hudson.

Earlier at the SEC Tournament in Columbus, Georgia, one of the longtime LSU beat writers had taken a personal shot at Tim Hudson, saying he didn't deserve the SEC Player of the Year honor over LSU's Brandon Larson. Don't get me wrong, Larson certainly could have won the award. When the season ended Larson had big numbers—he batted .381 with 40 home runs and 118 RBIs. But this particular writer was way out of line making it personal. I would have no problem with the argument being made, but not in the fashion in which he made it. I wish I had saved the column. Anyway…fast forward to Omaha…after Hudson's six RBI performance and eight innings of stellar pitching, head coach Hal Baird went looking for that LSU beat writer (remember LSU was in the College World Series with Auburn). Baird found him in the press box, and while I'm sure there was a little more colorful language than this…Baird basically told him, "That right there is why Tim Hudson is the SEC Player of the Year!"

Two days later Auburn fell to Stanford for a second time to end the season. Hudson would go on to win one of the major national player of the year awards. That team will always be one of my favorites. I'm also proud to say that I call Tim Hudson a friend. He and his family call Auburn home, they give back to the community here and children everywhere with their Hudson Family Foundation. Who would have thought a redneck from Phenix City would have the impact he's had on people. His major league career is worthy of the Hall of Fame. Tim Hudson is a true Auburn man.

Meanwhile, Auburn has not been back to the College World Series since, but there was another championship in the near future.

1998—SEC Tournament Champions and a New Bramblett!

The 1998 team is one of my favorites of all time. The freshman class of Casey Dunn, Chad Wandall, and Jamie Kersh were now juniors. In the off-season, Auburn had added a legacy in Mailon Kent (whose dad was one of Auburn's all-time greatest quarterbacks). Josh Etheredge was a senior and would leave Auburn as the program's all-time home run hitter. Transfer Scott Pratt filled in at shortstop and proved to be one of the best to ever play that position. That allowed Coach Baird to move Heath Kelly to second base where he flourished, having one of the best seasons ever at that position. Two other freshmen would have huge impacts, as well. Hayden Gliemmo played some outfield but also became one of Auburn's weekend starting pitchers. Then you had Dominic Rich, who played in every game in the outfield as a freshman. But quite possibly the biggest piece to the offensive puzzle that year was the signing of Todd Faulkner, who had started out at the University of Texas but transferred to Auburn his sophomore season. He went on to hit 20 homers his first season at Auburn. On the pitching side the emergence of sophomore Colter Bean as the closer and another freshman starter, Chris Bootcheck, gave the Tigers the complete package.

The 1998 season was also memorable for personal reasons. After years of trying, my wife and I found out we were going to have our first child, and there's a baseball story or two that goes with that life-changing news. As I said we had been trying to have our first child for about three years and for whatever reason it just wasn't happening. In fact, we had decided to quit trying and if it happened it happened. We were prepared to move forward without kids.

Paula traveled with me to Ole Miss for our March series. The weather was awful that weekend. It took us three days to play two games. The last day of the series Paula was feeling terrible. In fact, on the ride home we didn't even make it all the way back to Auburn. She was feeling so bad we had to stop in Birmingham to get a room. The next day she went to the doctor thinking she had the flu. The nurse asked her if there was any chance she could be pregnant...something they always ask before administering any medication. My wife said sure, but there was no reason to think things were any different than before. Well, one test later and we were going to be parents. Considering our difficulties in the past, our doctor told us to be prepared for the worst. Nine months later we got the best—a brand new baby girl, Shelby Grace Bramblett. She was a challenge to get into this world, and because she holds a lot of the same stubborn tendencies of her father, she's a challenge today. We call her our "angel baby" because we had all but given up on having children.

Looking back we joke about how all of this came to be. We say our baseball trip to Kissimmee, Florida, is what actually jump-started our miracle. Auburn opened the season in the same Olive Garden Classic where I called my first Auburn baseball game. Paula went on that trip, as well. When we arrived at the team hotel (separate from the team) and unlocked the door to what was supposed to be our room, there sat Todd Faulkner on the end of the bed with no shirt on. Let me stop here and say…Todd wasn't hurting in the looks department or the muscle department, either. We still say my wife walking in on that little surprise is what "put things in motion." Thanks Todd!

Auburn finished that season 39–15 and 16–12 in the conference, good for third in the west and a fifth seed in the SEC Tournament. The Tigers opened the tournament against Alabama. It was the fourth straight game against the Crimson Tide as Auburn had just dropped two of three in Tuscaloosa to close out the regular season. More than 14,000 were in attendance as Auburn used a five-run seventh inning to take a four-run lead and then held on to win, 11–8. Heath Kelly, Scott, Pratt, Chad Wandall, and Mailon Kent combined to go 11-for-19 with five RBIs to lead the way.

The next night (and I mean late night, the game didn't end until after midnight) Auburn played No. 1 seed Florida. An interesting note on this game: remember David Ross and his dramatic home run to beat Florida State the year before? Well, he transferred in the off-season. There was no bad blood, but he knew he would still have to sit behind Casey Dunn as catcher so he transferred to Florida. Ross was the Gators' starting catcher and picked up a couple of hits in this game, but it wasn't enough as Kevin Knorst and Colter Bean held the Gators in check. Little Hayden Gliemmo hit an eighth-inning home run to give Auburn some insurance, and the Tigers continued to advance in the winner's bracket with a 6–4 win.

Auburn got the next day off as Florida and Alabama played an elimination game. Alabama won the game, setting up a rematch with the Crimson Tide Saturday. Like the NCAA Regionals, it was double elimination and at this point Auburn had to lose twice not to advance to the championship game. Alabama won the first game 4–3, setting up an elimination game for both in the night cap.

Auburn went with Chris Bootcheck, who had thrown 90 pitches in relief in the first game against Alabama. Bootcheck gave way to Gliemmo, who baffled Alabama hitters over the last five innings. Meanwhile, the Auburn offense pummeled an Alabama pitching staff that was in its fifth game in four days. Auburn won the game 9–1 on a mercy rule. In those days, to help save pitching, the SEC had a mercy rule that if a team led by eight or more runs after seven innings then the game was over.

Freshman Mailon Kent went off on Alabama again, going 2-for-4 with two more RBIs. He made every play in the field. Like his father before him as a football player, the younger Kent was becoming known as "an Alabama killer." His best games that year and for the rest of his career came against the in-state rival.

At the Hoover Met, where the SEC Tournament is played, the radio booths are side by side with a clear window between the two. Again, I ask you to remember my story from 1994 in Tuscaloosa when the Alabama announcer had called the game-ending home run that never happened. The same guy was doing this game. After Kent's second double of the day (he had doubled in two runs earlier) to lead off the seventh, the Alabama announcer put up a piece of paper to the window for us to read. It said, "I hated his daddy when he played at Auburn, and I hate his son!" That was as great a compliment as could have been paid! Of course, he wrote the note in jest, and we are great friends to this day.

The win set up a championship game with Arkansas, which had played one less game than Auburn, so the Razorbacks should have been in much better pitching shape than Auburn. The Tigers started Eric Wood, who was making just his second start of the season. Coach Baird's plan was to hopefully get four or five out of Wood and then go to Colter Bean, who had the ability to go longer than just an inning or two as a closer. Bean had only thrown 24 pitches to close out the win over Florida on Thursday night. The plan worked to perfection. Wood went the first four and Bean the final five. Meanwhile, Arkansas struggled in the field with four errors that led to five unearned Auburn runs. It really was a good game until the very end. Auburn held just a 6–5 lead going to the ninth as the visiting team. An insurance run (one of the only two earned runs on the day) in the ninth wrapped things up, and the Tigers went on to win the SEC Tournament Championship Game, 7–5.

In the modern era it was Auburn's third SEC tournament title. Hayden Gliemmo, Heath Kelly, and Chad Wandall made the All-Tournament team. I'm still baffled how Colter Bean was left off after getting a save against the No. 1 seed and then winning the Championship Game. The Tigers returned home with a trophy in hand and expecting an NCAA tournament bid. They got one alright...to Tallahassee again. Again, I was baffled as to why the NCAA selection committee would send the SEC Tournament champion to one of the toughest places to play a regional...and a place where the memories of David Ross were still fresh in the Seminoles' minds.

Auburn couldn't repeat the magic and lost the opener to Rutgers to go to the loser's bracket. The team did reel off wins against Liberty, Rutgers, and Oklahoma only to fall to Florida State 16–10. Still, it was another great season with a bunch of great guys. With much of the 1998 team back, 1999 would be another special year with a big "first" for the program.

1999—Hosting a Regional

The freshman class of 1996 was now the senior class. Auburn lost very few players off the 1998 SEC Tournament championship team. The pitching staff was intact from the year before, but Auburn did add freshman outfielder Gabe Gross. Like Mailon Kent, Gross was a legacy player. His father, Lee, was one of Auburn football's all-time greatest centers. His son was a two-way player for a short period of time at Auburn as he was actually signed to play quarterback. As a freshman, Gross hit .363 with seven home runs and 65 RBIs. To tell you how good that team was, those numbers were third best on the team.

The team finished the regular season 41–15 and 18–12 in the conference. Since the new Plainsman Park opened in 1996, the goal was to always host a regional. This was the season to do that. Four SEC teams hosted regionals that season...all were from the Western Division. That year also marked the first year of the Super Regional format where you first played 16 Regionals that fed into eight best-of-three Super Regionals. Auburn and...you guessed it...Tallahassee were paired together.

In Auburn's Regional, the Tigers were actually the No. 2 seed. Tulane was No. 1, NC State No. 3, and Winthrop No. 4. It was generally considered one of the toughest regionals. Auburn opened with a 9–7 win over NC State, then an 8–6 victory over Winthrop, which had upset Tulane in the first round. That set up a "must lose two" situation for Auburn against Tulane on Sunday. The Tigers dropped the first one 7–5, but the Green Wave ran out of pitching in the final game and Auburn made history winning their first ever Regional at home.

It was off to Tallahassee, where Auburn came up short, losing the first two games of the series. It was time to turn our attention to 2000. For me personally, it was going to be an emotional one. Coach Hal Baird had announced that 2000 would be his final season at Auburn. This was going to be tough.

2000—Coach Baird's Final Year

The 2000 team was a good one…offensively one of the best I've seen, but unfortunately in Coach Baird's final season his pitching staff was deeper but inconsistent. It gave up 10 or more runs in 10 games, which was highly unusual for a Coach Baird staff. The 2000 Tigers were tough at the plate. The top four in the lineup—Dominic Rich, Mailon Kent, Gabe Gross, and Todd Faulkner— were as good as there was in the country. Those four accounted for 51 of Auburn's 65 home runs, 344 of the 507 RBIs, 306 of the Tigers' 558 runs, 387 of the 702 hits, and 71 of the 97 stolen bases. LSU's legendary head coach called Gabe Gross

Final postgame interview with head baseball coach Hal Baird. It took place at Georgia Tech in the NCAA Regional. From L to R: me, Hal Baird, and Andy Burcham.

and Todd Faulkner the best three/four combination in a lineup that he had ever seen.

As good as they were offensively the Tigers still limped a little down the home stretch, going 5–9 the last month of the season. The record was still good enough for an NCAA Regional appearance at Georgia Tech, where the Tigers went 1–2.

The Coach Hal Baird era was over. I'll always remember our final postgame radio interview with the man I still very much look up to. We had to wait a while…the NCAA makes all head coaches go through a 10-minute cooling off period before going to the regular media. We are last on the totem pole even though we cover the team throughout the season. But when he got to us he was not ready for it to be over. When asked how he felt about the season (and his coaching career) being done. His reply was, "I'm mad as hell. I didn't like losing when I started coaching, and I still don't like losing!" He was as fired up as I've ever seen him. I know he wanted to go out on a higher note, but his entire body of work is his high note.

Former Auburn football coach and athletic director Pat Dye had hired him from East Carolina to resurrect a baseball program. For his first 11 years he had to do it recruiting to one of the worst, if not *the* worst, baseball facilities in the Southeastern Conference. He did it with the likes of Bo Jackson, Frank Thomas, and Gregg Olson in the '80s. In the '90s, the foundation had been laid for young men like John Powell, Jay Waggoner, Mark Bellhorn, Tim Hudson, Gabe Gross, and many others. The Auburn baseball program was at its peak when he stepped down. Unfortunately, it did not stay there. It's hard to say why. The shadow cast by not only a great coach, but a great man has been long and deep. There have been a few highlights in the last 15 years since Hal Baird roamed the third base dugout at Plainsman Park, but not the consistent level of success we saw during the Baird era.

Auburn Baseball—2001–present

The time since Hal Baird was head coach has been for the most part very difficult. I'm not here to speculate why the baseball program went into a downward spiral, but there have been a few bright spots along the way. After Coach Baird, longtime assistant Steve Renfroe took over the program. He took the team to the NCAA

Tournament in three of his four years as head coach. Along the way, there were some memorable moments.

In 2001, Coach Renfroe's first year, Auburn started 0–9 in conference play. They then proceeded to go 11–1 over the next 12 conference games. Series losses to South Carolina and Florida put Auburn in a must-win series situation going to Baton Rouge. Basically conceding the Friday night game to save the best pitching options for Saturday and Sunday, the Tigers were blown out 20–5.

The Saturday night game was one of the more bizarre I've ever seen. LSU scored five (four unearned) in the bottom of the seventh to take a 5–1 lead. With two outs in that inning a monsoon of epic proportions hit Alex Box Stadium. Rain, wind, and dangerous lightning were all around us as we sat in the open-air press box. The rain delay lasted 2 hours and 15 minutes. During that time I was planning in my mind where I would go with the family Memorial Day weekend because we certainly weren't going to be in Hoover competing in the SEC Tournament.

Once the rain stopped, we got back to action as a fly ball ended the seventh. Auburn catcher Trent Pratt lined out to center followed by designated hitter Brett Burnham striking out. Well here we go…LSU is going to win the series and there will be no SEC Tournament for the Tigers. With two outs, shortstop Jonathan Schuerholz walked. Then right fielder Javon Moran singled, and Mailon Kent doubled in a run to make it 5–2. Gabe Gross followed with a two-run double and it's 5–4. You're kidding me right? Todd Faulkner came to the plate and tied it with yet another RBI double. Auburn third baseman Scott Schade was next. Schade had been okay at the plate that year and finished the season hitting .265. He had a little pop, but wasn't a home run hitter. On a 1–0 pitch he hit a line drive (very similar to the David Ross home run in Tallahassee in 1997) over the left field wall to give the Tigers a 7–5 lead. The air was sucked out of Alex Box. The LSU fans were in shock. Eric Brandon finished the game on the mound for Auburn to preserve the win. Auburn still had postseason hopes, but it would take a win on Sunday to get there.

The scenario going into Sunday was this—if Auburn won they would go to the SEC Tournament. They could also get in with an Alabama loss since they owned the tiebreaker over the Crimson Tide thanks to a series sweep in April. Alabama was going for a sweep over Arkansas in Tuscaloosa. Their game started about 30 minutes prior to the Auburn-LSU contest.

The game was much like Saturday in the sense LSU led for much of the game. Going to the eighth, LSU held a 6–3 lead. Auburn started to rally, but managed only a run and left the bases loaded. Looking back I should have known better than to doubt them but you had to wonder if that was their last chance. Meanwhile, Alabama had just beaten Arkansas 8–6…now Auburn must win to go the SEC Tourney.

After a scoreless eighth for LSU, the top of the ninth started auspiciously for the home team. Schuerholz reached on an error, Javon Moran singled, and then Mailon Kent came through again with a two-run double to tie the game at 6. Gabe Gross was intentionally walked then Justin Christian singled in a run to give the Tigers the lead, 7–6. Two more runs scored, and it was a five-run ninth for Auburn. They had come from behind in dramatic fashion twice on the road in that hostile environment. The final was 9–7.

Meanwhile in Tuscaloosa, Alabama was already celebrating their assumed trip to Hoover. They had just beaten Arkansas and Auburn was losing 5–2 going to the ninth. Fortunately for the Auburn fans, the celebration was cut short by another miracle finish for this Auburn baseball team.

In 2002, I had the honor of calling a perfect game. Eric Brandon threw a nine-inning perfect game against Murray State. In an "only in baseball" occurrence—Brandon hailed from Murray, Kentucky. Auburn won the game 9–0 on March 2. It's the only perfect game and no-hitter I've ever called.

Auburn played one of the toughest schedules in the country during the 2003 season, and it paid off. The Tigers went 18–12 in the league and were named a national No. 4 seed hosting a regional for the second time in five years. Unfortunately, they ran into a hot Ohio State team that beat them twice to take the regional.

Between 2004 and 2010 Auburn only went to a regional once. Steve Renfroe was let go and another Hal Baird assistant, Tom Slater, was hired. Slater was an outstanding recruiter, but in 2008 he was let go after failing to make more than one regional (his first season) during his tenure. In 2009, John Pawlowski was hired as the head coach. He had great success at College of Charleston. He inherited a pretty darn good Auburn team (from a talent standpoint). In his second season at Auburn, the Tigers had one of the most prolific offenses in school history.

The 2010 set a school record for home runs with 131. Hunter Morris hit 23, Brian Fletcher 22, and three others had double-digit homers. As a team they hit a school-record .348. They also set school records for slugging percentage (.591) and extra-base hits (293). It's one of the few teams that could just outscore you on a regular basis. The pitching was just okay, but most days it didn't matter.

The team swept two of the last three SEC series to claim the Western Division title and host another NCAA Regional. The field included Jacksonville State, Southern Miss, and Clemson. Auburn lost the regional, but the weekend included one of those iconic moments in a broadcaster's career—much like David Ross in 1997—Auburn had a hometown hero against Clemson in an elimination game for the Tigers late on a Sunday night.

Down to their final out, the team was trailing 9–8 to Clemson, which needed only to win this game to advance to a Super Regional. Backup outfielder Creede Simpson came to the plate with two on and two out in the top of the ninth. Simpson had come on to play center field in the seventh inning. Simpson had been a capable backup…in fact he had started 35 games that season so in reality he probably was more of a starter. On a 1–2 pitch, the Auburn native put his stamp in the Auburn baseball history books.

Now the 1–2 pitch…fastball DRIVEN–DEEP LEFT CENTER FIELD! THAT BALL IS…GONE! IT'S GONE! IT'S GONE! IT'S GONE! IT'S GONE! 11 to 9 Auburn! 11 to 9 Auburn! Creede Simpson's done it again!

Andy: David Ross, you have company! He hit it in his hometown in '97. Creede Simpson hits one in his home town tonight! Unbelievable! A two-strike jack over the monster! And this place is up for grabs! Oh my goodness gracious! I don't believe what I just saw! Oh ho ho ho ho…holy cow! Tigers lead by two!

Like all of the other unbelievable finishes I've called, it was bedlam in the radio booth. I've also never seen Plainsman Park like it was in that moment and that entire night. It was a football atmosphere inside that baseball park. Fans were climbing over one another, drinks were thrown in the air, and folks were jumping over rails. It was an amazing sight. Auburn won the game 11–10 but just didn't have enough pitching the following night as Clemson took the series with a 13–7 win.

If Auburn had won that regional, they would have been the host the following week against Alabama in a Super Regional. I would have liked to have seen what the atmosphere would have been like that week, but alas, that will have to wait.

Creede Simpson's homer against Clemson is still talked about to this day. Head football coach Gene Chizik told me later that he was at home watching the game on his porch. He said you could hear the roar from the stadium when Simpson hit the home run. As the crow flies…that's three miles.

That home run by Simpson proved to be the high point of the John Pawlowski era. He was let go at the end of the 2013 season when the reins were handed over to longtime Oklahoma head coach Sunny Golloway.

Eric Brandon's final pitch in his perfect game against Murray St. on March 2, 2002, alongside a picture of the scoreboard from the Opelika-Auburn News.

Golloway's resume was amazing. In his head coaching career he had taken a team to the College World Series, four Super Regionals, and out of his first 19 years as a head coach he's gone to 15 NCAA Regionals. In just his second season, he took Auburn to its second Regional appearance in a decade...a big step in the right direction. Auburn deserves to be among the nation's elite baseball programs. It's where they belong despite not having been there on a regular basis in quite some time.

But unfortunately, things did not work out. There were issues behind the scenes that forced Auburn to let Golloway go "with cause." It was a shame that it happened right after such a successful season, but in the long term, it was probably for the best. Golloway was let go during the fall of 2015...right in the middle of fall practice. After fall practice ended, Auburn moved quickly to hire its next head baseball coach. On October 22, 2015, athletic director Jay Jacobs announced Butch Thompson as the next man to guide the program. I'll admit, when the job came open, Butch was the first person who came to mind. He was an assistant at Auburn from 2006 to 2008. He helped orchestrate the class in 2010 set all sorts of offensive records. After Auburn, he became the top assistant at Mississippi State. His specialty is pitching and recruiting...he has been recognized as the top assistant in college baseball. His time had come and the time was right. Butch has assembled a superstar staff. On top of all that, he's an outstanding human being with the highest of values and the utmost care for the student athlete...something Auburn baseball needs and deserves. Great success lies ahead.

I'm not sure how much longer I will continue to do baseball. It's the sport that is closest to my heart because I've been doing it for over 20 years. I love the game, and I love the kids that play it. Sometimes I'm a little too attached to the game, becoming more of a fan on the radio than I should be. I still have great passion for the game. As I get older, I will probably eventually give up the baseball duties. Being gone for weekends at a time isn't nearly as easy or appealing as it once was, but until that time comes I will love it in many ways more than any other sport I do. Auburn baseball is where I truly learned how to be a college play-by-play man.

Chapter 3

Following Jim

Jim's Passing

Thursday morning May 15, 2003, started like any other at that time. My wife was working on getting our 4-year-old daughter ready for daycare. I was in the shower getting ready for work. Thankfully, Auburn baseball was home that weekend hosting Ole Miss, otherwise I would have been packing to go out of town for a baseball series. It was the last regular season series of the year.

Everything was "as usual" until my wife came into the bathroom and said Barry McKnight called. Barry was hosting (as he still does today) a morning sports talk show on the Auburn Network's Montgomery affiliate, WMSP. My wife said, "Barry was asking if you had heard about Jim [Fyffe] being in the hospital. Apparently he collapsed at his home last night and he is not doing well."

It wasn't five minutes later that Jon Cole called me and gave me the news that Jim had indeed suffered a brain aneurysm after speaking to the Prattville Quarterback Club. He had made it home before collapsing in the bathroom. The doctors at Jackson Hospital in Montgomery were not optimistic on Jim's survival chances, but there was still hope. They detected no brain activity although he was being kept on life support.

Continuing to get ready for work, I remember thinking, *"This can't be."* I had attended an event with Jim at Tommy Tuberville's house on Lake Martin just a few weeks prior. He just had a minor heart procedure but was looking and feeling great…and now this. Jim was severely diabetic. Maybe that had something to do with what happened, but to be honest the doctors said there was no real way to know.

By the time I got to work, it was official—the legendary "Voice of Auburn" was silenced when the family and doctors decided there was no need to keep him on life support any longer. Jim was gone. He was only 57. This man who was beloved by everyone he touched was taken from us way too soon…and way too suddenly.

For me, I immediately thought of his wife, Rose, who had been through so much with Jim. Jim was her second husband. I remember she always talked about how he quickly became like a real father to her children from her previous marriage. She listened to just about every broadcast. She came to almost every game. I also thought of his five children, five grandchildren, and then one great-grandchild.

Our first broadcast without Jim was the next day. As I mentioned earlier, Auburn baseball was hosting Ole Miss at Plainsman Park. It was a big series. Auburn was looking to finish the season strong. The Tigers would eventually be a

Jim Fyffe and me prior to an Auburn basketball broadcast.

national No. 4 seed in the NCAA Tournament and host their own regional, but that was not on anyone's mind that night. In the span of 24 hours everything was put in perspective. Jim was not a part of the baseball broadcasts but still it was emotional. Auburn lost that night but won the next two to take the series. We thought of Jim the entire weekend.

The funeral was an incredible celebration of Jim's life. The memorial service was held two days after Jim had passed. I'm not sure the First United Methodist Church in Montgomery had ever seen anything quite like it. Fellow broadcasters, coaches, and people from all over the region were in attendance. Dr. Karl Stegall gave a wonderful eulogy, but it was Coach Pat Dye and Coach Sonny Smith who stole the show. Coach Dye gave a heartfelt reflection on Jim's life and their relationship. Coach Smith was the comedy relief. When he was talking it felt a little more like a roast than a memorial service. However, you could hear the sadness in Sonny's voice. He and Jim were very close.

"How Great Thou Art," "It Is Well With My Soul," "Shall We Gather at the River?," "Because He Lives," and "The Lord's Prayer" were the hymns of choice. They were Jim's favorites. Our entire broadcast crew had the honor of being the pallbearers. Beau Benton, Jon Cole, Joe Dean Jr., Paul Ellen, Daymeon Fishback, Mike Hubbard, Quentin Riggins, Phil Snow, Charlie Trotman, and myself couldn't have been more honored. It was clear to all what James (Jim) Williams Fyffe meant to so many. Born on November 20, 1945, the 57-year-old Paintsville, Kentucky, native was the "Voice of the Auburn Tigers."

I didn't know that much about Jim's background. I knew he was from Kentucky, but admittedly, I didn't realize how his roots were in radio at a young age. A few days after his passing, I started receiving clippings from the Kentucky area in which he grew up. One of them, *The Big Sandy News*, a regional newspaper that covered five counties in rural Kentucky, had a column in it written by Jim's nephew, Tony. My appreciation for Jim grew even more after reading the column:

> *Jim was "The Voice of the Auburn Tigers," Auburn's equivalent to Kentucky's late Cawood Ledford. In fact, Jim was mentioned as a possible replacement for Ledford when Ledford retired several years ago [Something I did not know].*
>
> *Jim was born and raised in Johnson County and got his career started here, thanks to my dad, Paul Fyffe. Dad at one time owned and managed WISP in*

Paintsville, where Jim cut his teeth in broadcasting. A lot of people got their start there.

Several years ago, Jim did something I have always wanted to do—write a book. Titled, Touchdown Auburn!, *the book was Jim's "memories and calls from the announcers booth." Although the book dealt mainly with Jim's career as the voice of the Tigers, it did contain a chapter titled, "From the Hills of Kentucky," that discussed his Keaton roots and his family. He mentioned my dad frequently, admitting that Dad had a better voice than him and saying my father "could have been 10 times better than me if he had wanted to."*

Jim never forgot his roots and would occasionally come to his Flat Gap High School reunions; in fact, I am told he was planning a trip to the next reunion next month.

This is just a small part of the column that made me appreciate Jim even more. Other than being a terrific broadcaster, the characteristic that always impressed me the most about Jim was his ability to remember names and faces. I saw this happen on numerous occasions. He could have met you 10 years ago, spoke to you for five minutes, not seen you since and still know your name. Jim would always make people feel special. He was one of those old-school broadcasters. A breed that is just about extinct. That's a shame...we could use more of those guys today. I try...but fail miserably. People like Jim Fyffe are a rare breed.

The Search for the Next Voice

Once a few days had passed after Jim's memorial service, Mike Hubbard (president of the Auburn Network) began the search. I'm not really sure how the whole process worked, but I do know this—Mike didn't have to go beyond the current broadcast crew to find Jim's successor. Paul Ellen had already served as Auburn's play-by-play guy for a few years in the '70s and to this day is still our pregame, halftime, and postgame host for football along with being a fill-in for numerous other on-air duties on the network. Andy Burcham had served as the voice of Southern Illinois before moving to Auburn in the late '80s. He is the dean of women's basketball play-by-play announcers in the SEC, having done it now for over a quarter century. Either one of these guys would (or maybe should) have been the choice.

I'm sure Mike was inundated with hundreds of resumes and tapes from broadcasters with vast experience to the pharmacist who just knew he was meant for this job. Mike could have gone in a hundred different directions, but Paul, Andy, and I always felt it would be one of us. The three of us rarely talked about it, but there was always this understanding if one of us was picked to take over it wouldn't affect the on-air relationship…and it didn't.

When Mike called me to his office on Monday, June 23, to tell me that he had made his decision, I wasn't sure how to react. I was certainly grateful. I was most definitely terrified. We went to then athletic director David Housel's office to get his final approval. The meeting didn't take long. David's advice was simple: "Be yourself." The official announcement came the next day.

I bet you'll never guess who the first congratulations came from. I'm still not sure how he found out since his call came before the official release went out…but it was longtime Alabama play-by-play man Eli Gold. My phone rang. I didn't recognize the number. On the other end of the line came an unmistakable booming voice, "Rod…Eli Gold here…I just wanted to congratulate you on your new position. I know you will do a great job, and I look forward to seeing you at this year's Iron Bowl."

Like David Housel, he gave me the same advice: "You are part of a special fraternity now, just be yourself, don't listen to the critics, because there will be plenty, and you will be just fine."

I was shocked and impressed. What a classy move by Eli. Jim and he had a tradition of riding to each year's Iron Bowl together. They were friends. Eli reaching out to me is one of the coolest and classiest gestures I've ever experienced.

The next 48 hours were a whirlwind of interviews on radio, TV, and newspaper. It wasn't until later in the week before I could catch my breath again. My dream job had come to me in tragic fashion. It was time now to earn my keep. It would be more difficult and more rewarding than I ever imagined.

Aftermath of the Announcement

The next two months were, to say the least, a little crazy, but the outpouring of support was humbling. Shortly after the announcement letters of encouragement began to flood in. There were several members of the media who also chimed in on the changing of the guard. One of my personal favorites was from the then sports editor of the *Opelika-Auburn News,* Joe McAdory. For someone who was, to say the least, a little unsure of whether he was up to the task…this meant a lot to me.

Bramblett is a Good Choice for the Job

Rod Bramblett paid his dues.

It wasn't too long ago when Bramblett spent Friday evenings calling high school basketball games with his sidekick, Bob Pelham. Whether it was a remote location from a cramped gymnasium deep inside central Alabama on a cold December night or the spacious quarters of the Birmingham-Jefferson Civic Center during the 6A Final Four, Bramblett enjoyed filling us in on the basketball exploits of Jimmy Vickerstaff, Aubrey Smith, or Dudley Smith.

That was seven years ago.

Monday, Bramblett was named the lead announcer for Auburn's football and men's basketball teams. He'll assume the void left by the legendary Jim Fyffe, who left us all too soon a month ago.

Bramblett can't be Jim Fyffe. There will never be another Jim Fyffe. He was one of a kind. For what Bramblett has to offer—a strong voice, unbiased play calling (perhaps with an Auburn lean) and a knack for keeping the listeners well-educated on what's happening—I'm sure you won't be disappointed.

Though Bramblett called high school games in the past, many know him more recently as Auburn's baseball play-by-play man, along with veteran broadcaster Andy Burcham. Not only does Bramblett's new assignment make him perhaps Auburn Athletics' voice nearly for all seasons, but it makes him an incredibly busy person.

Football, men's basketball, baseball, wow! That's a bunch.

Bramblett's new assignment was a safe one for Auburn Network president Mike Hubbard.

I would assume that Auburn people want to hear a familiar voice on the airwaves and would be more comfortable with what's familiar with the football program's history.

Not only is Bramblett an insider, he's from nearby Valley, so he's been a lifelong resident of east central Alabama.

He's one of us.

Auburn's football season kicks off two months from now on a hot August afternoon. Jim Fyffe will forever be missed, but the microphone has been left in good hands.

Joe is no longer in the newspaper business; instead he works in Auburn University's College of Business. I need to remind Joe how much that column meant to a still relatively young broadcaster who was about to embark on what hopefully would be his final job.

A Note from Rose

After the announcement I spent most of the summer visiting various Auburn alumni clubs. For the first time I was a wanted commodity on the "rubber chicken" circuit. I traveled all over the state but the most emotional trip was the visit to the Montgomery Auburn Club. It was their kickoff event late in the summer. I was not the main attraction, but they did want me to come and say a few words. I knew it would be very emotional—after all this was Jim's town, his club, and his people.

There was a touching tribute to Jim. His wife, Rose, was there in attendance. A few weeks earlier Rose sent me a handwritten note. It was actually dated the day I was announced as the new lead announcer for Auburn football and men's basketball, but it was delayed getting to me because of an incorrect address. I know it must have been extremely difficult for her to write, but what she wrote I still go back and read on a regular basis, particularly when the rigors of the job start to get to me...when I get a little jaded and forget what a great opportunity I was given. Considering I really didn't know what to say at the club meeting that I hadn't already said before I thought the crowd in attendance (a couple hundred at least) would love to know what the "first lady" to the Voice of Auburn had to say:

Dear Rod

Congratulations! You will be great, I'm sure. Jim has certainly left you big shoes to fill, but don't let anyone tell you, you can't fill them.

Jim has left you a legacy. When he got the job (in 1981) he and I were thrilled. But there certainly weren't any front page stories or pictures! As a matter of fact, I can't remember a little bitty blurb in any newspaper, anywhere.

Jim has made yours an important job. Grab the brass ring!

Love & War Eagle,

Rose

Needless to say, many tears were shed by me, Rose, and the Auburn fans in attendance. I didn't read the note to make these people like me. I read it because it meant so much to me. Here was Jim's wife who was still mourning the untimely passing of her husband, taking the time to wish me the best. I grabbed the brass ring…and I've been holding on for dear life ever since.

Rose passed away on June 5, 2011, from various health complications. One of my biggest regrets since I took over for Jim was not staying in touch with Rose. It's one of those things you can't go back and undo…but I wish so desperately I could.

Other Notes of Encouragement

There were many…too many to mention here…notes and emails sent to me in the days following the announcement. It was quite overwhelming. Sometimes you forget how many people you actually develop relationships with over time. First, there were notes from professionals in the business and even elected officials:

Dear Rod,

It was with pleasure that I learned you were chosen to be the lead announcer for Auburn football and basketball. This honor demonstrates the determination and dedication that you have put forth.

I know your friends and family are happy and proud of you. This recognition is an indication of the respect you have earned from your peers and you take great pride in this honor.

My congratulations to and best wishes to you.

I wish for you much happiness in the future.

Sincerely,

Kay Ivey, State Treasurer

P.S. War Eagle! Class of '67!

Kay Ivey is currently (2015) the lieutenant governor of the state of Alabama.

Then there was this short but meaningful email I received about a week after the announcement from another Auburn legend:

Rod...CONGRATULATIONS on your new position as play-by-play football announcer for AU! I was on vacation all last week and returned home last night and learned you had been selected for the job. Jim will certainly be missed. But, you'll do a great job. See you soon.
CARL STEPHENS

Mr. Stephens at the time was Auburn's longtime public address announcer. He retired in 2005. He is a legend himself. The University of Alabama graduate... that's right, he went to that other school...was also the longtime host of the Auburn football coach's TV show with head coach Shug Jordan. He was so good at what he did the Southeastern Conference asked him to be the PA man for the first 15 Southeastern Conference Championship games and 14 Southeastern Conference men's basketball tournaments.

Here is another one from someone I probably should have included in the list of those who influenced me:

Dear Rod,
Congratulations on being named as the new Voice of the Auburn Tigers. You are very deserving of this opportunity and I know you will do a great job on the Network, as you have for so many years.
Rod, again congratulations and best wishes!
Joe Dean
Athletics Director, Birmingham Southern

Joe, of course, was also Jim's longtime color partner on Auburn basketball radio broadcasts. Now he is one of the best color analysts on television. He and I actually called a few games together when Jim had a football conflict with basketball. I regularly see Joe now as he does color for the SEC Network's coverage of men's basketball. Fans of Joe when he was our color analyst I'm sure remember his "dramatic" reading of the "disclaimer." For those who don't know, that's what you hear on every broadcast that says something along the lines of "any rebroadcast is strictly prohibited under right granted by..." blah, blah, blah. Joe's version was much more entertaining.

Then there were those notes that were more personal in nature whether they were from old colleagues who had become friends or old teachers from high school. Their kind words were much appreciated and quite overwhelming, starting with my college roommate all four years at Auburn:

Rod,

I know by now you are probably inundated with calls, emails, and all kinds of well wishers so I will keep this short. I just wanted to say congratulations and to tell you that I am so happy that this has happened for you. I couldn't be more happy about it if I tried. We have been friends for a long time and all of those years and those memories have been good ones. We never really said one way or another how we felt, we just were what we were. But that doesn't mean the thoughts and the prayers and the hopes aren't there. You are a very good friend, a confidant and one of the best straight up people I have ever known. You and Paula have always meant the world to me and I wanted to say that out loud. I think Auburn made the best choice they could possibly make. Please know that when you sit down for the first time and broadcast that first game and for every game after that I will be among your biggest cheerleaders.

Take care & War Eagle!

Jeff

P.S. What happens if Paula delivers on a football Saturday? (Thankfully that didn't happen)

Jeff is now living in the New York City area. He has a very lucrative daytime job, but on the weekends he is pursuing his lifelong dream of becoming a standup comedian. We both used to joke about how our "dream jobs" weren't exactly easy to obtain. I know he will make it someday.

There was also a lengthy letter I received from my government teacher back in my senior year of high school. Mr. Logue was one of those teachers you never forget. He taught me how I needed to go about my studies in college. He also provided guidance/advice on a number of topics. I was so proud when he reached out to me. The note was too long, but here are some excerpts to give you an idea of what kind of mentor he was not only to me but to many of his students:

Dear Rod,

Congratulations! I look forward to hearing you announce the Auburn University football games for many years to come…

In your interviews after the announcement you indicated you would probably be nervous for your first game. I want to tell you my Ethel Merman story.

For 26 years at Valley High School I was the teacher responsible for preparing the valedictorians and salutatorians for their speeches. Virtually all of those students were nervous at graduation, so just before we went out I told them this story. When asked in interviews if she ever got nervous performing on Broadway, Merman always said no, because not one person in the theater audience could do what she did, so why should she be nervous. I used to tell my students that the same was true for them at their graduation. And it's true for you, Rod, only on a much larger scale. Not a single football fan in your broadcast audience could ever do what you will be doing this fall, and deep down, we know it.

Hemingway wrote that the essence of great writing was determined by how much the author was able to leave out. He claimed that most all the great writers were able to say more with less, that the ability to do this is what gave their work depth and resonance (read his short story, "The Short Happy Life of Francis McComber")…

Rod, to me this has always been your greatest strength as a broadcaster— saying more with fewer words—which is simply remarkable in an auditory medium such as radio…your economy of words. I don't know how you do it, and you literally do it better than anybody that I have ever heard on the radio, and while never having any dead air. With your exact accuracy, you in fact are always able to paint that picture. It's truly a gift, obviously augmented by preparation and hard work, which constantly provides your listeners with solid, dependable information that is filled with "depth and resonance."

Mr. Logue, if only I could live up to half of what you wrote in this note. I still go back to this day and read it. His words remind me of what's important in this job—great advice from a great man.

Another one that meant a lot to me came from a former student. Yep, that's right, I was a graduate teaching assistant in Auburn's political science department. I taught Intro to American Government and Intro to State and Local Government. It helped pay the bills while my wife finished Auburn, and I really enjoyed it. Anyway, this one came from a former student who was doing something much more important than I was…he was protecting our freedom as a staff sergeant with the 386th Force Protection Element stationed at Ali Al Salem Air Base in Kuwait.

Dear Rod,

Congratulations on becoming the new Voice for Auburn football. Everyone likes to say they knew famous people before they were famous, and I guess you fall into that category for me. I'm sure you don't remember me at all, but I was a student in your State and Local Government course back in the fall of 1991...I really enjoyed your course and I'm very excited to hear you call the games this season. Hopefully, I'll be back from this war in time to catch the webcasts. My home unit is in Missouri, so if all goes well I could bump into you at the Arkansas game in October. Good luck this season and War Eagle!

I didn't see him at the Arkansas game that year. I hope he made it back okay...very grateful he took the time to send me that email.

There were hundreds of these that came to me over the next two months. I saved every one. But as August rolled around it was time to focus on the task at hand. I had a football season to get ready for...ready or not, here we go.

Chapter 4

The First Season

There were high expectations going into the 2003 football season—like I needed any added pressure. Auburn had finished the 2002 season with an impressive victory over Penn State in the Capital One Bowl in Orlando, Florida. The score was 13–9. Sophomore tailback Ronnie Brown took over the game by rushing for 184 yards and a score. He, along with Carnell "Cadillac" Williams returned to the squad in 2003. Williams had been injured but was ready to go as 2003 began. Couple that with quarterback Jason Campbell gaining another year of experience and a defense led by linebackers Dontarrious Thomas and Karlos Dansby, and it looked like the Tigers were poised for a championship run.

Auburn opened the season at home versus the USC Trojans. The date was August 30. It was hot and humid by even Deep South standards. Temperatures in the low- to mid-90s and a heat index of above 100 made for an even more exhausting day for everyone at the game.

Both teams were ranked in the top 10. The Tigers came in at No. 6 and the Trojans were ranked eighth. USC was led by a first-year starting quarterback by the name of Matt Leinart. It was 10–0 Trojans after the first quarter. Turned out they could have ended the game then. USC went on to win 23–0. They also went on to finish No. 1 in the AP poll at the end of the season but were left out of the BCS National Championship Game…Oklahoma and LSU got to play for the national title that season.

Reading my first open (or tease as we call it) as lead announcer. Auburn lost the game to USC 23–0.

Because of the national hype surrounding this first game, I think it actually took some of the spotlight away from the debut of a new Auburn play-by-play guy. The week leading up to the game was a blur to me. I do remember my co-workers staying out of my way, which I appreciated. Looking back, I believe it was intentional. I'm sure my eyes were as big as saucers all week long.

One of my first priorities that week was to write my first column as Auburn's lead announcer. I could have gone in several directions, but I chose to make it a "thank you note" of sorts:

Where do I begin and what do I write about in this first column? It's something I've toiled over for the better part of the last two months. Should I spend my time introducing myself to the Auburn fans? Should I talk about the most highly anticipated football season in 20 years? Or should I just take the time to say thank you, thank you to all those who've congratulated and wished me well as I take over the role of Auburn's new lead play-by-play announcer? I chose the latter. So here goes...I'm sure I'll forget someone:

THANK YOU TO:

Jim Fyffe and family…Jim you made this job what it is today. It's the best play-by-play job in the country and it's because of what you did. For 22 years I listened to you as a fan and a co-worker and there's no way I can equal your performance on the air. I pray every day that I can be half as good as you were on the air. If I can, then I'll consider my career a success. And thanks to the Fyffe family. In particular Rose Fyffe, we never got to know each other very well while Jim was still with us but in the last two months your support and love has been quite humbling. Rose, thanks for handing me the brass ring.

The Auburn family…the support has been overwhelming. Over the course of this summer I received hundreds of e-mails, calls, and congratulatory notes; all of them positive, all of them advising me to develop my own style and be my own man. Fans would point out that no one will ever replace Jim (and that is so true) but they had confidence that my love for Auburn and professionalism in the booth would shine through, leading to a long and memorable career as Auburn's play-by-play announcer. I hope they are right. Simply put…Auburn fans are the best.

The Auburn Network and Auburn Athletic Department…for showing the confidence in me to be the next lead announcer. Thanks to my boss, Mike Hubbard, who's set a standard of excellence at the Auburn Network that is unmatched in the country. Mike took a chance on me in 1996 when he hired me full-time. Seven years later that chance has turned into a dream come true for me. Thank you to David Housel and Hal Baird. Thanks David for also having the confidence in me to get the job done. Thanks to Coach Baird for being himself; he is one of the finest human beings (and not a bad baseball coach, either) I've ever known. You've had more influence on me than you'll ever know.

Thanks to Auburn Media Relations. Meredith Jenkins, Kirk Sampson, Chuck Gallina, Mendy Nestor, and Dan Froehlich and staff are the best around. The inside access they've given me has helped me become a more informed and certainly a better announcer. They are pretty good friends, too. Meredith, or as I like to call her now, "Mama," don't forget the lipstick on those high speed chases leaving the Grand Canyon. And Kirkie…truly one of the funniest human beings I've ever been around…please never change. By the way, both of you keep your sons away from my daughter.

And last but not least…the two ladies in my life. Paula…the most understanding and patient wife known to mankind. When she signed up for a lifetime contract with me 14 years ago I know she never in a million years thought my career would go in the direction that it did. However, she never once had a discouraging word, even when I was barely bringing home a paycheck. Happy Anniversary (August 26) baby…I love you more than you'll ever know. You're going to make a wonderful mother again.

And to Shelby…my little piece of Jesus. On November 5 of 1998 you were sent down from heaven, and I count my blessings every day that you're my little girl. You're going to make a great big sister.

I apologize to those who I haven't mentioned, but you certainly haven't been forgotten.

Now…bring on the Trojans…ready or not here come the Tigers…and ready or not here I come!

Picture taken by Todd Van Emst on the photo deck of Jordan Hare Stadium the week leading into my first game as lead announcer.

Once that was done, it was time to focus on the game itself. By the time Saturday rolled around I was more than ready to get this day done. It was one of the rare times my family attended a game with me. None of them are big sports fans, so this was more a requirement than a desire. At the time my daughter was just shy of five years old and my wife was almost eight months pregnant with our second child. Couple that with the fact it felt like it was a million degrees and we were walking between the stadium and our pregame location and then back to the stadium…needless to say they were more ready for the day to be over than I was.

On top of that, we had a newspaper writer following us. Mike Marshall of the *Huntsville Times*, who I had known for several years, asked if he could "shadow" me on my first day as lead announcer. I agreed, so we had him following us wherever we went.

We arrived at the stadium approximately four hours before kickoff. To be honest, I was expecting a lot more pomp and circumstance than actually occurred. Looking back and comparing it to a typical gameday now it wasn't much different other than Mike trailing us.

Me holding my five-year old daughter, Shelby, with my wife, Paula. She was eight-months pregnant at the time with our second child, Joshua. He was born October 1, the week of the Tennessee football game.

Two hours before kickoff it was time to go on the air. Our pregame show, for those who don't know, is called the "Tiger Tailgate Show" and is hosted by Paul Ellen. It had been tradition with Jim Fyffe to allow him to leave after the first 40-45 minutes. It would be the same for me. I was more nervous at the beginning of the broadcast than I was when it was time for me to start the game. I don't even remember who the guests were that day. The show took place at that time in front of the old Beard-Eaves Memorial Coliseum. There was a big crowd on hand, although nothing unusual.

We went on the air at 3:00 pm CST, so I was done around 3:40. While I don't remember who the guests were that day, I will never forget the walk from the "Tailgate Show" location to the stadium. Again, I expected more people to speak, wish me luck, pat me on the back, etc. But that wasn't the case at all. I'm guessing it was the deer in the headlights look I had, but I don't believe anyone had the courage to talk to me.

With my wife and daughter in tow...and Mike Marshall...we made the trek to the west side media entrance. I was more concerned about my eight-month-pregnant wife suffering heat stroke than I was actually making it to the press box. She was a trooper, though, and we finally arrived at the home radio booth. Many pictures were taken. A few interviews done with local media about my first game and then it was time to get to work.

In the booth when we arrived were our engineer, Patrick Tisdale, and longtime spotter, Beau Benton. It was at this point in time I thought to myself, *"What do I do now?"* For the past four years I had sat to Jim's right as his statistician...now I was "Jim."

Once I was done with the "Tailgate Show," the nerves had pretty much disappeared...that lasted until about 10 minutes before it was time for me to utter my first words from Jordan-Hare Stadium as the lead announcer. When the nerves kicked in...they kicked in hard. For the next 10 minutes all I could think about was not screwing this up, could I do it, was I worthy of one of the best play-by-play jobs in the country. Since that first game, the only other time I was remotely close to being that nervous...no...scared...was prior to the 2010 BCS National Championship Game.

It was time. The music played...we still called it the "Fyffe Tease." It was the lead-in to what is still my favorite part of the broadcast to this day. We still call it the "tease" or "scene setter." As the music started, everyone gave each other our "traditional" fist pump and away we went.

In a book Jim wrote about seven years before he passed away, he also said this was his favorite part of the broadcast. It's a chance to prepare the listener for what is about to happen...to add some drama to an already dramatic event. It's not always super dramatic, sometimes it's humorous or even educational, but it's something that I still take pride in sitting down and writing during the week prior to every football game. In fact, you will see more of these here in this book to "set the scene" of some of Auburn's biggest football games that I have called.

As you can imagine, this one was an important one, yet it was one of the easiest ones I've ever written. As the music faded out, the nerves went away. This sounds corny and maybe a little self-serving, but it was as if Jim Fyffe was in the booth with us. It almost felt like he put his hand on my shoulder saying, "You've got this Rod, it's what you've always dreamed of doing, now go be yourself." And this is what I said to start a new era in the broadcast booth:

Do you remember that feeling when you were about six years old...that feeling on Christmas Eve when you couldn't go to sleep in anticipation of what was to come the next morning...that feeling that made it so hard to sleep the night before?

Well if you don't remember that feeling, then you must not be an Auburn fan, because those are the exact emotions that Tiger faithful have had all summer long in anticipation of one of the most highly touted seasons in the history of Auburn football. Well, guess what Tiger fans, Christmas morning is here, and it's time to open the presents...

Hello again, everybody, and War Eagle...I'm Rod Bramblett, along with Stan White, Quentin Riggins, and Andy Burcham, and this is the Sherwin-Williams Countdown to Kickoff. We're coming to you from a sold-out Jordan-Hare Stadium where we're just under a half hour away from the start of the 2003 season.

All those feelings of excitement and anticipation have been tempered this past off-season as we lost a dear friend and legendary broadcaster Jim Fyffe. His 22 years as Auburn's play-by-play announcer were cut way too short this past May, but thank the Lord above that his great calls will live forever and never be forgotten. But as I'm sure Jim would say, the broadcast must go on, and it's with that thought in mind that all of us here on this Auburn Network crew press on today. Jim, we dedicate this one to you and to your family. I hope we can do you proud.

That is certainly our goal today as sixth-ranked Auburn plays host to No. 8 USC. Last year, the Tigers went to La-La Land and came out with a 24–17 loss. Both teams would go on to finish the seasons strong. USC finishing fourth in the nation, while Auburn had three wins over top 10 opponents down the stretch including a bowl victory over Penn State that catapulted the Tigers into the national spotlight going into this year.

Oh, and let's not forget about the weather today. It's hot, it's humid, it's August in Alabama...feels like the start of another football season to me...

By the time I had finished reading the "open," the nerves were mostly gone and we were off and running with the game. Unfortunately, this one was over quickly. We didn't realize it at the time, but it was.

Quarterback Jason Campbell threw an interception on the first possession that led to a quick USC touchdown. The Trojans followed up two possessions later with a field goal to make it 10–0 going into halftime. USC methodically pulled away with two second-quarter field goals to take a 16–0 lead going to the fourth. A Jason Campbell sack led to a fumble deep in Auburn territory, and one play later the Trojans had scored another touchdown to make it 23–0. That would end up being the final score, and the Tigers faithful left the stadium in a little bit of shock.

Auburn's offense never got on track. The Tigers managed only 163 yards of total offense. In the off-season, Coach Tuberville had named co-offensive coordinators in offensive line coach Hugh Nall and tight ends coach Steve Ensminger. Bobby Petrino, Auburn's offensive coordinator in 2002, had left for Louisville to provide the opening. Unfortunately, for whatever reason, the offense never clicked that 2003 season. As the season wore on, things did get a little better but they never met expectations that were perhaps too high to begin with.

The following week I still tried to paint a rosy picture while thanking those that made my first broadcast as smooth as possible:

Alright everyone...nobody panic...just calmly step away from the ledge... everything will be just fine. Boy oh boy! What a way to make your broadcasting debut. Believe me, I felt like all was lost, along with many Auburn fans, immediately following Saturday night's game. But like all bad things...you start to forget about them with time. Hopefully, the majority of the Auburn faithful have realized that this season is not lost, in fact, there isn't a single goal that isn't still intact. Look back to 1983 when the Texas Longhorns came to town and put a 20–7 whooping on a very good Auburn team. Of course, that Tiger team went on to finish 11–1 and should have won a National Championship…so it is possible.

But that's not what I wanted to talk about this week. Instead I wanted to write about the people that made my first broadcast as Auburn's lead announcer so great. People would be surprised at how much goes into each football broadcast. It takes a lot of manpower to put together a seven-hour broadcast. Kudos to the many student workers and others behind the scenes that make it happen each week.

However, I want to spotlight my fellow broadcasters and those in the booth Saturday. Let's start with Paul Ellen…a true professional and one of the most witty guys I know. He scripts out exactly what he wants to cover during the "Tiger Tailgate Show." Many times that script is thrown out the window by the time we're five minutes into the show, but he still covers all the information before the show is up. I was as nervous as a cat in a room full of rocking chairs at the beginning of the "Tailgate Show," but Paul's laid back style got me into the flow of things and really settled me down for the rest of the day.

Then there's Andy Burcham…one of my best friends in the world. His support over the past two months has meant as much to me as anybody's. Andy or Paul would have been excellent choices as the new play-by-play announcer, and I'm thrilled that they were also considered. When the announcement was made that I was fortunate enough to get the job those two guys were among the first I heard from. Andy and Paul are great broadcasters but above all else they are great people. Andy returns this season in his role as host of the pregame and postgame interviews. Andy is 10-times the interviewer I am. He knows all the right questions to ask in some of the most difficult situations. You need to make sure you tune in early enough to hear his interview with Coach Tuberville…it's well worth it.

That brings us to the guys in the booth and of course I have to begin with my sidekick Stan White. Over the last couple of months I've been asked if Stan and I planned to do what I guess would be called a dress rehearsal. My answer to that question was no. I knew Stan and he knew me…we both knew that wasn't necessary and hopefully that came across during the USC game. I personally thought we had an immediate chemistry that will only get better with time. Stan knows the game backwards and frontwards and it shows on the radio.

Someone who isn't in the booth but is just as important on the air is sideline reporter Quentin Riggins. Over the past eight years Quentin and I have become good friends. Here is a guy who was one of the meanest, nastiest linebackers ever to play the game, but you would never know it talking to him. What a great family man who loves Auburn with every ounce of his being. I can guarantee you when Auburn loses there is no one hurting more than "Q." This past Saturday when asked by a photographer on the sideline, "How's Rod doing?" Quentin's response was, "He's been the only bright spot of the day." My response to that is, "Thanks Q, that means a lot."

There are several people behind the scenes in the booth that are key to a good broadcast. Jon Cole is the producer. He is the one that keeps me straight. There are a ton of little things that I have to say at certain times of the broadcast that I couldn't if it weren't for Jon. Little things like what to say when we go to commercial or when to send it down to Quentin Riggins. When your thought is "Boy this sure is a smooth broadcast" it's because of Jon.

Beau Benton is the spotter. Beau's spotting abilities are nothing short of amazing. My main concern when calling a game is to make sure I get the offensive side of things right. That means I can't always pick up who made the tackle or who recovered a fumble. Beau is the one telling me who did what when but he's able to do it for both sides of the football even when I don't need it. And he's able to relay the information to me in such a fashion that it never breaks the flow of the play-by-play description. In many ways, Beau is the most important person in the booth for me.

Chris Hines is the statistician. Chris is another person that I consider to be a good friend. He feeds the numbers to me. If I give out a stat on the air, it's coming from Chris. He's the one who came up with the stat this past weekend that I gave out along about the third quarter. You know the one…Auburn was averaging a quarter of a yard on first down…nobody can say we always paint a rosy picture.

Patrick Tisdale is the man who makes sure we're actually on the air. As our engineer, he is there the day before setting up equipment and there four hours before we go on making sure everything is working properly. Without him the Auburn Network would never make it to your radio or computer.

So as you can see there is a whole lot more than meets the ears to an Auburn Network broadcast. I wanted to make sure these folks got their props…they are the reason why the Auburn Network is one of the most respected radio networks in the *country. My whole-hearted thanks to everyone on the Auburn Network team that made my first broadcast so enjoyable (despite the outcome of the game).*

Most of these folks are still on the broadcast team today. The only change to the team now is that Gene Dulaney serves as our statistician. Gene does a great job. Another Auburn graduate, Gene is high up in one of the local banks and serves on the city council. My producer has changed numerous times over the years. After Jon Cole, it was Sam Brumbeloe, who passed away all too soon in 2009, then it was Jessi Duval. Jessi actually served as producer for one year before leaving to have her first child; she came back and is our producer today. Another Auburn graduate, she's the member of the team that actually has been on a major network. As an intern at FoxNews in New York she was allowed to appear in her own story. We kid her that she's made it bigger than any of us. When she came back she followed Brad Law. Brad is an incredible broadcast talent himself. He was with us for the 2010 National Championship. Brad deserves to be the "Voice" somewhere…I hope he gets that chance. But I digress, back to the 2003 season and the question…when would Auburn actually score a touchdown?

Curse or No Curse? You Be the Judge

After the 23–0 loss to USC, the team had to put it behind them quickly as they traveled to Atlanta to take on Georgia Tech. It was a big deal. These two teams were old rivals that played every season even when Tech left the SEC to become an independent and later joined the ACC. When the SEC expanded and split into divisions the annual rivalry ended, so when the two got together at Grant Field in downtown Atlanta it drew a lot of attention.

When the series ended in 1987, Auburn had won nine in a row. Coming into this one the Tigers had fallen to No. 17 in the country after the opening-week loss. Things wouldn't go much better on this day than they did the week before.

The Tigers went almost six quarters without scoring. Not until 33 seconds to go in the first half did Auburn crack the goose egg. A field goal made it 10–3 Georgia Tech going to the locker room. With the offensive struggles continuing, the Yellow Jackets' touchdown late in the third quarter gave them more than enough as they went on to win 17–3 and send Auburn to its first 0–2 start since 1984.

The Tigers only managed 40 yards of rushing offense as they once again failed to get in the end zone. Eight quarters had come and gone and I had yet to get the monkey off my back…not to mention the growing angst among Auburn fans with the coaching staff and the season thus far.

Jim Fyffe always told the story of Auburn fans coming up to him and wanting him to say his signature "Touchdown Auburn!" Whether it was a quarterback club he was speaking to, a group of fans he would see on his way to the stadium, or just some random folks on the street, he would always refuse…saying it was bad luck to say it out loud unless an Auburn touchdown actually occurred.

In fact, the only time that I know of Jim saying "Touchdown Auburn!" when the Tigers didn't score was the time he actually decided that it needed to be his signature call.

Jim's story goes like this: he was playing golf in Montgomery in a charitable tournament. Jim made a long birdie putt and he let loose a big "Touchdown Auburn!" Over on the next tee, there was a foursome about to hit. One of the golfers, all decked out in his Alabama gear, came running over to Jim. He was steaming mad and let Jim know he was number one…if you know what I mean. Apparently, Jim yelling out what became his (and Auburn's) signature phrase caused the guy to dribble one off the tee box. Jim thought, *"Man oh man, if yelling 'Touchdown Auburn!' makes an Alabama fan that crazy, then it's something I'll do all the time!"* I'm pretty sure that's the only time Jim ever said that phrase outside of Auburn actually scoring a touchdown.

Now back to the "bad luck" scenario. I became a firm believer in the "curse" or whatever you want to call it after those first two games. At the season opener versus USC, as a tribute to Jim the Auburn cheerleaders had one side of the stadium say "Touchdown" and the other side say "Auburn." This was done as part of the pregame ceremonies. The thought crossed my mind that Jim was a little uneasy with the crowd screaming those two familiar words, but didn't give it much more thought than that afterward…until Auburn had gone (eventually) nine quarters without a touchdown.

The Drought Finally Ends

One-hundred thirty-seven minutes and fifty-seven seconds of football had passed in the 2003 football season before Auburn scored a touchdown, before I was able to pay tribute to Jim, before I was able to get the "what will Rod say" question behind me. It was on Auburn's fourth offensive possession. On the fifth play of the drive, Jeris McIntyre caught a pass from Jason Campbell in the right flat. As he caught it, three Vanderbilt defenders converged and collided. Jeris, whose dad was a pretty fair Auburn Tiger himself, spun to his right and outran everyone to the end zone for 31 yards and Auburn's first touchdown of 2003:

So another big third down play for the Tigers here...third down and a little less than five yards to go...they need somewhere between the 26 and the 27...the ball is spotted on the 31...Obomanu goes wide out to the far side...McIntyre and Taylor to the near side...Campbell under center, to throw...fires—caught...at the 25...still on his feet, McIntyre...to the 20, to the 15, to the 10, 5, GONE! Touchdown Auburn!! Thirty-one yards—Campbell to McIntyre!

To this day, that was probably the most awkward "Touchdown Auburn" I have called. It didn't matter to me. It was done. As the play ended, I remember looking to my right to the visiting athletic director's booth. There was David Housel looking back at me. He grinned then wiped his brow as if to say, "Sheesh, glad that's finally over." He then gave me a thumbs up.

I was still in the "I need to prove myself" mode, so I didn't say "Touchdown Auburn" the rest of the game or the rest of the next few seasons. There were plenty of opportunities to figure out what that signature call would be on Saturday, September 13, in Nashville, Tennessee. The Tigers went on to win 45–7, scoring six touchdowns. McIntyre had another one for 67 yards. Tre Smith rushed for two, while Carnell "Cadillac" Williams and Ronnie Brown each had one.

With the first touchdown behind me, it was time to move on and do my best to become Auburn's announcer. That first season there would be more chances. By the end of the season, there would be signs of things to come.

Back-To-Back Wins Over Top 10 Teams

After dropping the first two games that season, Auburn bounced back with two wins. The victory up in Nashville and then a blowout of Western Kentucky put Auburn back at .500 on the season. It set up the Tigers' first true test after the rocky start against the folks from Rocky Top Tennessee. The Volunteers came to Jordan-Hare Stadium unbeaten and ranked No. 7 in the country.

Auburn's rush defense was stifling, holding Tennessee to just four yards on the ground. Meanwhile, the opposite could be said for the Tigers' ground game. Ronnie Brown got things started with an eight-yard run on Auburn's first possession. Wide receiver Ben Obomanu scored later in the first quarter, catching a 29-yard pass from Jason Cambpell to make it 14–0. The Tigers never trailed in the game, leading at one point 28–7. Tennessee quarterback Casey Clausen kept them in it with 355 yards of passing and two scores, but the Volunteers never had much of a chance with Carnell "Cadillac" Williams leading the way offensively with a 185 yards and a touchdown. On the other side, the two men who were on the cover of *ESPN the Magazine* prior to the season led the way for the Tigers' defense as Karlos Dansby and Dontarrious Thomas each had eight tackles.

The final score was 28–21, and things seemed to be looking up as the Tigers were over .500 for the first time in 2003. It was the end to a successful week as my son was born Wednesday, October 1, just three days prior to the game.

As the old saying goes, "No rest for the weary," and the team had very little time to catch a breath. Yes, it appeared that the ship had been righted, but it could easily start taking on water again if Auburn went to Arkansas the following week and lost. It would not be easy, for the second straight Saturday the Tigers were facing a top 10 team. The Hogs from Fayetteville had supplanted Tennessee as the No. 7 team in the country.

A Reynolds Razorback Stadium record crowd of more than 74,000 was on hand to see their undefeated team host unranked Auburn. It was a beautiful day and an early start, something that always concerns you if you are the visiting team. For whatever reason, it has been tradition the road team has a little trouble getting "up" for those early kicks. That wasn't the case in this one as both teams were ready to go...particularly on defense.

It wasn't until 29 seconds to go in the first half that either team scored, and it was Auburn on a six-yard run by Williams. The two teams swapped field goals, and that was it for the scoring. Auburn won the game 10–3. Arkansas had its chances. A long touchdown run by quarterback Matt Jones was called back due to a penalty. The Razorbacks also fumbled inside the 20. Both plays occurred with the score 10–3, but it was Auburn's defense that got the last shot, literally. Karlos Dansby came up with a big fourth down sack of quarterback Matt Jones.

Dansby's 12 tackles and his one and only sack pretty much iced the game. It is still one of the hardest hits I've ever witnessed. The following week Auburn re-entered the top 25 at No. 19. They had won four in a row, and the next Saturday they would make it five on a record-setting day.

Cadillac Being Cadillac

On what was a flawless weather day in Auburn, the Tigers played an almost flawless football game against Mississippi State. No question the Bulldogs were struggling. Jackie Sherrill was under fire, eventually retiring after the season concluded. Auburn, on the other hand, had momentum. Winners of four in a row, the Tigers continued to click on all cylinders.

While it was a team win, the day belonged to Carnell "Cadillac" Williams. He set an Auburn record for rushing touchdowns in a game with six. His first went for 70-plus yards, coming on the second play of Auburn's second possession.

The score gave Auburn the lead for good, but Carnell wasn't done. He proceeded to score four more times before the half and the rout was on with the Tigers leading 38–7. Coach Tuberville took the foot off the pedal in the second half but not before Williams picked up number six.

Campbell under center…and the give to Williams, he's around the corner at the five…looks for the end zone…he's in! Touchdown…Tigers, I think, or they say he was down at the one foot line…no, he's in—touchdown for Carnell Williams…that breaks an Auburn record!

It is still one of the greatest individual performances in Auburn football history. However, little did we know it would be a while before Auburn fans could get excited. Another rough patch was on the way.

Punched in the Gut

After Mississippi State, Auburn suffered a blowout loss at LSU then came back for a homecoming win over Louisiana-Monroe to start the month of November. While not great, a chance at the division title was still there, but the margin of error was zero. That meant the game on November 8 versus Eli Manning and the Ole Miss Rebels was huge.

Ole Miss rolled into Auburn ranked No. 20 in the country. To be honest, they probably deserved a higher ranking than that. Early season losses to Memphis and Texas Tech hurt their national outlook, but by the time they came to Jordan-Hare they had found their groove, having won five in a row.

It really was a classic game. There were five lead changes and a great quarterback duel between Eli Manning and Jason Campbell. The lead changed for the fifth time when former Auburn Tiger, now Ole Miss Rebel, Brandon Jacobs, powered his way in from one-yard out with 2:39 to go to give the Rebels a 24–20 lead.

The Tigers had one more chance. On six plays they had driven to the Ole Miss 3-yard line with 45 seconds remaining. Ben Obomanu had a big catch of 50 yards to keep the drive going, but now it was third down and goal to go. Campbell rolled to his right and found his favorite target, Obomanu, wide open—the ball hit him right in the hands and fell to the ground. Jordan-Hare Stadium let out a collective moan. One of Auburn's most sure-handed receivers dropped the ball that would have given Auburn the lead. It happens to the best of them, and Ben was certainly in that category.

Auburn had one more shot, but the Rebels defended an intended pass to Jeris McIntyre and the game ended in a 24–20 loss.

I would be hard pressed to think of a loss that left me with a more intense sick feeling in the pit of my stomach than did that heart-breaking defeat at the hands of Ole Miss. It left Auburn with no championship to play for (other than the state championship), just pride.

After the game was over I wanted to be mad at someone, something, anything that would help me vent the frustration felt after that loss. Over and over in my mind I saw the pass to Ben Obomanu...he had it...heck, I even got out, "Touch..." on the radio call only to sink to my knees in disbelief when the ball went to the ground. *How could he drop it?* was the first thing that went through my head. Although the Tigers had one more opportunity, I already had a bad feeling that it just wasn't meant to be.

I'll be honest with you, there was a part of me that wanted to blame Ben Obomanu for the outcome; however, it didn't take very long for me to realize how asinine that was. A thought that was reconfirmed when I got home and saw what Miami tight end Kellen Winslow had to say after Miami's loss at home to Tennessee. Compare Winslow's comments to those made by Obomanu, and I can say with great confidence that I'm glad we have Ben on our side and not Kellen.

For those of you who might have missed it here's a portion of what Winslow had to say after the game. "It's war. They're out there to kill you, so I'm out there to kill them. We don't care about anybody but this U[niversity]. They're going after my legs. I'm going to come back right at them. I'm a [expletive] soldier." He also made reference to the officiating saying, "I hate refs." The son of the former NFL great later apologized for his comments...as well he should have. However, the disrespect shown should have never happened to begin with. Winslow is a supposed leader for one of the most successful college football programs in the country. Comments like he made are not ones of a leader.

Compare that to the comments of Obomanu after the Ole Miss game. "I was wide open in the back of the end zone. It was kind of like I misjudged the ball. I thought I was going to have to jump for it, and it just came down. I guess it hit me in the wrong place...the hands...and I dropped it." Here's a kid who could have easily refused to talk to the media after the game, instead he met it head on like a man...no whining, no blaming anyone, no foul language in the heat of the moment. In fact, the youngster was able to have a sense of humor about the whole thing.

All of us were disappointed in the way the season had transpired, but I believe after that game we all developed a newfound sense of pride—a pride for individuals like Ben Obomanu who we watched grow up on that Saturday night. He learned how to deal with responsibility and adversity. We also saw a young man, along with his teammates, give Auburn a chance to win in the final seconds...this time it just wasn't meant to be. Yes, the loss was disappointing, but our young men handled it with pride, grace, and respect.

Ben Obomanu went on to have a nice career with the Seattle Seahawks. The Selma, Alabama, native is still one of the most impressive student-athletes I've ever encountered in my time at Auburn. His adult life has been lived with the same type of class and maturity that he showed after that devastating loss to Ole Miss.

The next week Auburn was about to face their fifth top 10 team of the season in Athens, Georgia. It wasn't much of a game. The Bulldogs took control early and won, 26–7. It was on to the Iron Bowl. We didn't realize we were headed for a crazy two weeks that changed the course of the Auburn football program and the career of Tommy Tuberville.

Go Crazy and JetGate

The 2003 season was an adventure to say the least. Being a first-year guy I was just trying to hold on for dear life. The season was also an adventure outside of the broadcast booth. That wild ride culminated in the craziest two weeks I've ever seen. At the time, it was controversial and embarrassing, but in the long run, what became known as "JetGate" was a good thing for the Auburn football program and Auburn athletic department.

I don't want to go into the details here, because to be honest I don't know all of them. But basically here's what happened. Members of the board of trustees were concerned about the direction and performance of the football program. That concern heightened following the Georgia loss (the third in a row in SEC play). According to stories, members of the board and athletic director made a trip to Louisville, Kentucky (or someplace in the area), to gauge the interest of former offensive coordinator Bobby Petrino, who was the head coach at Louisville. The trip somehow got out to the press and it became the story of the week in college football. All the while, Auburn was trying to prepare for its biggest game in any year...the Iron Bowl.

What happened next was fascinating to watch. After the Georgia loss, I truly believe a majority of fans probably shared some of the same opinions as those in charge, but after word got out of this meeting, the fact that it took place the week of the Iron Bowl, and the way it appeared the whole situation was being handled, completely changed the emotional tide (sorry for the pun) of the Auburn fan base. Add to that the way Tommy Tuberville handled it once it got out—which was with a calm professionalism—and the court of public opinion swung fully to his favor.

By the time the Iron Bowl rolled around on that Saturday night in late November, the game became secondary to the soap opera off the field. The stadium was at a fever pitch and totally behind the head coach.

I've often wondered what the week of practice was like. Players had to know what was going on. The way Auburn came out that night you could tell they too were ready to play. Looking back at what and when everything happened off the field and in the press that week, I'm not sure Alabama really ever had a chance that night, and after the first play from scrimmage I knew they didn't:

Carnell Williams at the tailback, they'll hand it off to Williams up the middle...25, cuts it inside, 30, 35, 40—there goes Cadillac! To the 50, to the 40, to

*the 30, to the 20, to the 15, 10—go crazy, Cadillac, GO CRAZY! TOUCHDOWN
AUBURN!! 80 yards!*

*STAN: First play from scrimmage, Carnell Williams—he's been waiting for two
whole years to do that right there...a heavy set, handoff on the draw...thank you and
goodbye, Carnell Williams, 80 yards down the sideline. Rod, how about these fans?*

Unbelievable...absolutely unbelievable!

You know how you pop a cork to a wine bottle and it all comes foaming
out...that was the crowd at Jordan-Hare Stadium at that moment. A week of
embarrassing news about the football program, an embattled coach they now
wanted to embrace, and a rival they all so dearly hated...it all came pouring out
on that first play. The final score was 28–23, but the game was never that close.

On top of it all, I had what was my first signature call. To this day, there are
many that believe I copied the "Go crazy" portion of the call from the late, great
St. Louis Cardinals broadcaster, Jack Buck, who used those words on an Ozzie
Smith home run versus the Dodgers. Actually, I got the idea from "Cadillac"
himself. In talking to the media at some point that season, Carnell mentioned
part of his pregame routine was to scream out to the team, "Time to go crazy, let's
go crazy!" So yes, I did copy the phrase, but it applied to this moment perfectly
don't you think? It was my first call of an Auburn win over Alabama. The first of
many, but the first one was certainly a doozy.

By the end of the following week, Tommy Tuberville was well on his way to
being retained as head coach. His team was preparing for a bowl trip to Nashville
to take on Wisconsin.

Setting the Table for 2004

If you can't win a championship then the next goal is to always play in a bowl
game. You obviously want to win the game, but in most cases, you also want to
make sure your team (and fans) have a great experience to cap off the season.
Every once in a while, a bowl game is much more than that...it's a chance to
build for next season. After all that occurred around the Iron Bowl, the Music
City Bowl became a mission of vindication for Coach Tuberville and the Tigers.
To win this game would further solidify the future into 2004.

Points were hard to come by in the first half with Auburn leading 7–6 going
to the locker room. The second half didn't start much different until Carnell

Williams scored with a little over 90 seconds remaining in the third quarter to give Auburn a 14–6 advantage.

The final nine minutes of the game had all of the action. The Badgers tied it up on a touchdown and two-point conversion with 8:52 to play. Auburn came back with an 87-yard drive to take the lead. The drive ended with Ronnie Brown's second touchdown of the day. Wisconsin still had 2:16 to stage a final drive to send it to overtime, but two plays later Karlos Dansby and Reggie Torbor made the big defensive play of the day on a tackle and forced fumble that set up two plays later a Carnell Williams touchdown—his second of the day—and the game was done, 28–14 Tigers. A season of unrealized expectations, controversy, and, most important, a season of growing up was over. My first football season as Auburn's lead announcer was done. It had a little bit of everything, but the best was yet to come.

Chapter 5

2004—Undefeated and Left Out

O nce the dust settled after the roller-coaster ride that was the 2003 football season, attention quickly turned to 2004 and two big questions. One, who would be Auburn's new offensive coordinator? It was obvious the combination of Hugh Nall and Steve Ensminger just wasn't working. Coach Tuberville went out and got Al Borges from Indiana. A man who had an outstanding record developing quarterbacks, Borges brought his Hawaiian shirts and pro-style offense to Auburn. Two, would Borges have his two starting running backs at his disposal? On January 19 he got his answer: both Ronnie Brown and Carnell Williams decided to come back for their senior seasons. Defensive back Carlos Rogers had also considered moving on the pros. He too decided to come back. All three will tell you today they made the right decision.

The next challenge for Al Borges…how do you utilize two running backs that could start for any team in the country? More important, how do you keep them happy? It helped that Ronnie and Carnell were truly good friends. Never once during that 2004 season was there a sense of jealousy among the two. Because of that they were on their way to a very special season as were the rest of the Tigers.

The LSU Game

Auburn entered the season ranked No. 17 in the country. Not many knew what to expect. If memory serves me correctly there was quiet confidence. Other than road trips to Knoxville and Tuscaloosa, the schedule appeared to be manageable. The season opened with two easy wins. Auburn handled Louisiana-Monroe without having to show much at all, winning 31–0. A trip to Starkville followed and another easy victory, 43–14. Both Carnell and Ronnie rushed for more than 100 yards.

Week 3 would provide Auburn's first test of the season. We would all find out how good this team could be as Nick Saban and No. 5-ranked LSU came to Jordan-Hare Stadium. Auburn had climbed three notches to No. 14 but was still the underdog to the defending national champions.

This game turned into one of the most physical games I've ever witnessed. In doing my research on this one, I was surprised that both teams actually eclipsed 300 yards of offense. Statistically, it was even across the board.

LSU scored first midway through the first quarter, but missed the extra point—boy, would that turn out to be big. The two teams traded field goals over the next two quarters to make it 9–3 going into the fourth. On the first play of the final 15 minutes Carnell Williams fumbled a punt return at the LSU 43-yard line. *"Uh-oh, this isn't good, if this game gets to a two-score difference Auburn is in trouble."* Points had been so hard to come by, a nine- or even 13-point margin would have been insurmountable. However, Auburn's defense rose to the occasion. LSU had to punt it away and disaster was avoided. The two sides traded punts. In a game of field position, Auburn won the final battle, getting the ball at its own 40 with 6:37 to go in the football game trailing by six.

A 20-yard run by Ronnie Brown put Auburn into LSU territory at the 39. A few plays later Jason Campbell scrambled for four yards and a first down. Then it was LSU's turn to turn up the wick defensively. Cadillac lost two yards, and two incomplete passes set up the biggest fourth-down play in Jason Campbell's career up to that point. The Auburn quarterback rolled to his right, floated it up, and there was Courtney Taylor to come down with it for the first down at the 12-yard line.

The pass wasn't exactly a bullet, but it got the job done. Taylor came back to get it with authority and the drive was still alive. Two plays later, Campbell completed a six-yard pass to Anthony Mix, but Mix fumbled the ball and Auburn fell on it at the LSU 16—just one of those good bounces you get when you are on your way to a championship. Facing third-and-12, the 2004 Auburn football team found a way.

Ball is spotted actually back at the 16 so third down and 12 to go with a minute and a half to go...Campbell steps up under center now, steps back in the shotgun with 8 on the play clock...lot of precious time wasting away...he clears out the backfield... five wide receiver set...on third down. Campbell into the end zone–CAUGHT! Touchdown Auburn!! Touchdown Auburn!! Touchdown Auburn—Courtney Taylor! Oh my goodness!! Wide open–back of the end zone! 9–9, a minute-14 to go!

With the game tied the drama wasn't quite over yet. John Vaughn's extra point was no good. It was a bad snap, but wait, a flag was on the play. One of the LSU's players had climbed the back of his teammate to try and block the PAT. You can't do that. Vaughn got the second chance, and he nailed it to make it 10–9.

LSU still had time with a little over a minute to go. All they had to do was get in field goal range, but Junior Rosegreen intercepted a JaMarcus Russell pass at the Auburn 38 to seal the victory.

I was most happy in this game for Jason Campbell. When he came to Auburn the expectations were high...probably too high. So much pressure was laid on his shoulders. Follow that with four different offensive coordinators in as many years...no wonder he had not performed up to his or anyone's expectations. But in this game, he joined the club of great Auburn quarterbacks as I wrote in a column the week after.

Getting What He Deserves

Parade All-American...Gatorade Player of the Year in Mississippi. As a high school senior, he passed for 2,884 yards, 24 touchdowns, and rushed for over 500 yards and six touchdowns. As a junior he threw for 33 touchdowns and won a state title. He was rated the second-best quarterback and the seventh-best player coming out of high school.

These are the credentials that Jason Campbell brought to Auburn out of high school. From the day he walked on campus everyone was in Jason Campbell's corner. He was the second coming of _____ (fill in the blank with your favorite quarterback). This was the guy who was going to lead Auburn to title after title during his, what was sure to be storied career...my how quickly things change.

The tide of public opinion began to turn on September 22, 2001, when Campbell went into the Carrier Dome against Syracuse. His numbers...11–20, 155 yards, 1 interception, and one rushing touchdown. Not terrible, but he spent most of the game fleeing defenders. Oftentimes he did not escape. From that point on Jason had his detractors. I was never one of them. I got to know Jason from talking to him before and after games. I could tell this kid had character, class, and talent. What he didn't have was an offensive system that he felt comfortable with. It's taken a long time, but I believe he now has that system.

But first let's consider the numbers he's put up. They are pretty amazing for a kid who's been through four different offensive coordinators. To this point Campbell is Auburn's most accurate passer in history. He is second on the career list for yards per attempt, fourth in touchdown passes, fourth in passing yardage, and fourth in pass completions. More important, Auburn is 21–9 in Jason's 30 starts. Not bad for a kid who some probably still think can't lead Auburn to a big win.

Now everyone is entitled to their opinion. Heck, that's what I do each week in this column. So if you're still one of those that feels Jason isn't the quarterback for Auburn...all I have to say is this...I think you're dead wrong. Or maybe blind. You didn't see what I saw this past weekend in the fourth quarter. I've seen it happen here before. I've seen Pat Sullivan, Randy Campbell, Jeff Burger, Reggie Slack, Stan White, Dameyune Craig, and Ben Leard all do it. They look their teammates in the eye, tell them to follow, they do, and they win. That's what happened on Auburn's final drive Saturday. A team that couldn't move the ball all day against the vaunted LSU defense, all of a sudden could. There's no doubting it was a team effort, but on that drive Campbell led and his offense followed.

For his efforts, Jason Campbell was recognized as the SEC Offensive Player of the Week. The numbers weren't through the roof. Completing 16–27 passes for 170 yards and 1 touchdown typically won't raise many eyebrows, but under the conditions it was phenomenal. Jason finally got what he deserved...recognition.

Who knows what will happen the rest of this season. As we sit here today the sky is the limit for Auburn. All because Jason Campbell did what he does best... be a leader. I wish I had half the leadership qualities that Jason brings to the table. He may be just a quiet young man from Taylorsville, Mississippi, but let me tell you this. When my kids are old enough to understand and appreciate it, I'm going to tell them to look at what Jason Campbell achieved while at Auburn. It's one of the best examples of perseverance and character you'll ever see. He represents Auburn University with the best of them.

Here's to you Jason…lead on!

The 12-play scoring drive that gave Auburn the victory catapulted that team to one heck of a season. It gave them full confidence they could play and beat anyone. I still say this game lit the fuse, but it wasn't until a few weeks later in Knoxville that the nation really took notice and the fireworks began.

Blowout on Rocky Top

College GameDay was there, the eyes of the college football world were on Knoxville, Tennessee, and Neyland Stadium. The talking heads were heavily on the Volunteers' side. Erik Ainge and his offensive mates…Jason Allen and the Tennessee defense would be too much for Auburn to handle. After all, this was eighth-ranked Auburn's first real test on the road, right? The crowd of more than 100,000 inside Neyland Stadium would be more than the Tigers could stand.

I'll never forget sitting in our room at the team hotel watching *GameDay*. Charles Barkley was on the show and he boldly picked Auburn to win the game, saying, "I think Jason Campbell is going to have a great game, cause they [Auburn's defense] are gonna slow down the running game. And for Tennessee, there's a light at the end of the tunnel but it's a train coming…get off the tracks!" Uhhh…he was dead on. Auburn scored on five of their first six possessions. The only one where they failed to score, the Tigers fumbled at the Tennessee 1-yard line.

The first half was something special. Auburn scored time and time again, keeping the pedal to the metal.

It was 31–3 at halftime. Before the Tennessee Marching Band could finish their show, Neyland Stadium had emptied. There were just as many Auburn fans as there were UT faithful. Speaking of the Tennessee Marching Band, we kept track of how many times they played the school fight song, "Rocky Top." On average it was in the 30 to 40 range for a normal Tennessee win. On this night, they played it only 17 times, and Auburn won 34–10…to be honest, it wasn't that close.

Auburn took them out early and made a statement to the rest of college football they were a special team. The Tigers would roll through the next four games with an average margin of victory at 29 points.

Halloween in Oxford

The fourth game in that stretch was at Ole Miss. On the day before Halloween the Tigers had an opportunity to clinch the Western Division before the month of November rolled around. Now there wasn't much remarkable about this win, but I did have one of my favorite openings to the broadcast:

> On this eve before Halloween, there are children all across this land donning their favorite costumes in preparation for their trick or treat journey. For the Auburn football team they will be playing for one big treat…a Western Division championship and a berth in the SEC Championship Game.
>
> Hello again everybody, War Eagle and Happy Halloween, Rod Bramblett with Stan White, Quentin Riggins, and Andy Burcham broadcasting to you from Vaught-Hemingway Stadium and Hollingsworth Field on the campus of the University of Mississippi.
>
> It's hard to believe, but the Tigers have a chance to clinch the Western Division before the month of November even arrives. A win by the Tigers would ALMOST completely exorcise the demons of high expectations from a year ago. ALMOST but not quite…with Auburn's version of Freddy Krueger and Michael Myers still lurking in the shadows there is still plenty of work to do.
>
> Meanwhile, the Ole Miss Rebels are still haunted by the ghost of Eli Manning. Head coach David Cutcliffe has tried everything and everyone to get the offense going…including a three-headed quarterback system.
>
> Sure, when you compare the two teams it doesn't look like this one is a real thriller, but it is the night before Halloween, there was a lunar eclipse this week…and the Boston Red Sox won the World Series…strange days indeed…
>
> So watch out Rebels…there's someone knocking at the door…open at your own risk…on the other side are an angry bunch of Tigers who aren't leaving until they get what they've come for…what they feel rightfully belongs to them…the Western Division and a trip to Atlanta.

Like I said, the game was a blowout, 35–14 in favor of the Tigers. Auburn kept it going.

However, despite dominating everyone they played they could get no higher than third in the BCS rankings. USC and Oklahoma started the year at the top and never lost. When the Deep South's oldest rivalry came around on November 13, it was Auburn's best chance to prove they deserved to be in the top two. No. 8 Georgia was coming to town with ideas of playing the spoiler, Tommy Tuberville's Tigers knew they had something to prove.

What Else Can We Do

Up to this point, Auburn and Georgia had met well over 100 times. The series to this day is about as even as it gets. As I prepared for this game, it was hard for me to believe that these two hadn't met as top 10 opponents much at all. I wrote this about the rivalry as the week started and the excitement was building:

Top 10s Meeting In The Deep South's Oldest Rivalry Is A Rare Thing

Since 1893, Auburn and Georgia have met 107 times. It's hard to believe in this great rivalry that Saturday's game at Jordan-Hare Stadium will mark only the third time in the series' history that both teams are ranked in the top 10. That's right...while there have been numerous games where both were in the top 25 only three have taken place with both among the nation's elite. I thought it would be fun to look back at the two previous games.

The first time it happened was November 13, 1971. The game was a matchup of unbeatens at Sanford Stadium in Athens. The Tigers were ranked sixth and the Bulldogs were ranked seventh in the nation. The Bulldogs had allowed only 28 points in their last eight games, including four shutouts. This game would be a different story for the vaunted Bulldog defense with Pat Sullivan coming to town.

Auburn scored two touchdowns in the first quarter. One was a one-yard run by Tommy Lowry that capped off Auburn's opening drive. Then Pat Sullivan hit Terry Beasley on a 34-yard strike to make it 14–0. Already the Bulldog defense had given up as many points as it had allowed in its previous five games.

Georgia would bounce back with two touchdowns of its own. One to close out the first quarter and then another in the second. But the Tigers regained the lead before the half on another Sullivan touchdown pass, this one a 15-yarder to Dick Schmalz.

The defenses would take over in the third quarter. Neither team would score. However, the Bulldogs would close the gap to one with a two-yard touchdown run by Andy Johnson that followed an Auburn fumble at their own 13-yard line. The extra point was no good.

Auburn would take over from there. On the first play of the ensuing kickoff Pat Sullivan hit Terry Beasley on a 70-yard touchdown bomb. The play took the wind out of the Bulldogs' sails. Auburn would then ice the game with a five-yard touchdown toss from Sullivan to Schmalz. Final score: Auburn 35–Georgia 20.

Pat Sullivan finished the game with 248 passing yards and four touchdowns. The following week (prior to the Alabama game) he was announced as the winner of the Heisman Trophy. Auburn would finish the season 9–2. A disappointing finish that saw the Tigers get dismantled by Alabama and then lose to Oklahoma in the Sugar Bowl.

That's game one. Game two took place 12 years later on November 12, 1983. Like 1971 the game took place at Sanford Stadium. Fourth-ranked Georgia was looking for its fourth straight Southeastern Conference championship and second national championship in four years. Their only blemish an early season tie with Clemson. After an early season loss to Texas, the Tigers had climbed to third in the polls and had thoughts of a conference and national championship themselves.

Auburn scored in the first quarter on a four-yard touchdown by Lionel James and in the second quarter on two Al Del Greco field goals, a 21-yarder and a 41-yarder. Auburn would not score again but the Tiger defense would prove to be too much for Georgia. Auburn held Georgia scoreless until the last two minutes of the game when quarterback John Lastinger threw a 13-yard touchdown pass to Herman Archie for the Bulldogs only score. Final score: Auburn 13–Georgia 7.

The Tigers would finish the season 11–1 with their first Southeastern Conference championship since 1957. Auburn defeated Michigan 9–7 in the Sugar Bowl and should have won a national championship.

You look at both of these games and see a lot of similarities to this year's matchup. But this game is unique. I expect the atmosphere at this game will only be overshadowed by the one on December 2, 1989, when the Crimson Tide came to town for the first time. However, I would make an argument that this is the biggest game ever to be played at Jordan-Hare Stadium. With all that's on the line for Auburn and Georgia this one has the national implications unlike any other game played here.

Not since I was announced as the successor to Jim had I had such a busy week. Numerous radio talk shows, several television interviews, and even an appearance on ESPN made it an interesting lead-up to the game. As I wrote in the column, I couldn't remember a game outside of that 1989 Iron Bowl that had more hype and attention, at least not one at Jordan-Hare Stadium.

Driving into the game you could see it. There seemed to be more tailgaters than usual. Normally, for the Auburn-Georgia game you see a lot of red and black milling about amongst the fans clad in Orange and Blue. Not on this day. It wasn't due to the fact there were fewer Georgia fans in attendance, but instead because there were so many more Auburn fans. The ratio of Auburn to Georgia people was much higher in favor of the Tigers' fan base. I'm sure there were many who didn't have a ticket but just wanted to be there. The day had the same feel as the 1989 Iron Bowl in the sense you got the feeling there was no way Auburn was going to lose that game. This Auburn football team had come too far to be turned away. This was their chance to make the case that they deserved to play for a national title.

In the long and storied history of the Auburn-Georgia rivalry it's hard to believe we've never had one of these...one of these types of games at Jordan-Hare Stadium...a top 10 matchup between the Tigers and the Bulldogs. Sure it's happened before but only twice and those two games took place in Athens. This afternoon the college football world is watching a small town in East Alabama...waiting to see what happens in the 108th edition of the Deep South's oldest rivalry as third-ranked Auburn and fifth-ranked Georgia square off once again.

Hello again everybody and War Eagle, Rod Bramblett with Stan White, Quentin Riggins, and Andy Burcham. The sky is blue and the stands are full of orange on a beautiful day for college football in Auburn, Alabama.

I'll go ahead and say it...this game today is the biggest ever to be played at Jordan-Hare Stadium. It's an issue that has been discussed all week long, but I challenge anyone out there to find a game played in Auburn with as much national ramification. Today...Auburn knows and Georgia believes that a win puts them into position to vie for the top spot in all of college football and they're right.

So today 18 seniors will lead their team on to battle in this great rivalry. A rivalry that has only been stopped by two World Wars. These are truly hard fighting soldiers in their own right...and it's time for all who wear the Orange and Blue to walk right, talk right, sing right, and pray right...this might not be a battlefield, but today Jordan-Hare (Auburn's house) is certainly not a place for the weak of heart. There's an angry pack of dogs in the backyard, now the question is...what are you going to do about it?

The day was cloudy and just a touch on the cool side with temperatures in the low 60s. All things considered, very good weather for mid-November. The atmosphere was, to say the least, electric. The fans understood the magnitude of this game and they brought their A-game.

After a missed Georgia field goal, Auburn, like they had done so many times that season, scored on their first possession to get the early lead 7–0. The two teams traded possessions three times before midway through the second quarter, Tommy Tuberville reached into his bag of tricks to give Auburn what would turn out to be a lead Georgia had no chance of overcoming. A toss sweep to Carnell Williams turned into a halfback pass from Cadillac to a wide-open Anthony Mix for the touchdown.

It was 24–0 before Georgia scored a meaningless touchdown late in the fourth. The stars for Auburn were the usual suspects on offense. Campbell, Williams, and Brown all did their thing behind that stout Auburn offensive front. On the defensive side, Georgia quarterback David Greene was sacked four times. Carlos Rogers had an interception and Junior Rosegreen knocked out Georgia receiver Reggie Brown on what was a clean hit in those days...today it probably would draw a penalty and ejection. It is still one of the hardest licks I've ever seen. As the clock wound down, the Tigers had done all they could do...this was their best opportunity to show they deserved to be in the top two of the BCS. Yet another win over a top 10 opponent in the best conference in America:

Auburn 24, Georgia 6...put this in your BCS pipe and smoke it! The Tigers defeat Georgia—dominating the Bulldogs at Jordan-Hare Stadium, 24-to-6!

STAN: And this Auburn team has put its mark on the nation—GameDay coming here—the whole national spotlight here in Auburn, Alabama, and they put a mark on this, 24–6 in a dominating—a DOMINATING—performance by the Tigers!

Of course, Auburn never moved any higher than three over the next two weeks. The Tigers went out and picked up two workmanlike victories over Alabama (third in a row by the way) to complete an 11–0 regular season, followed by a 38–28 win over Tennessee in the SEC Championship Game. USC and Oklahoma kept winning so it was a Sugar Bowl trip for the Tigers to take on Virginia Tech.

The week after Auburn captured its sixth SEC title I received an email from a loyal Auburn fan. I thought it captured the emotions we all felt. After all, the 2004 season was the culmination of a lot of hard work on the part of the players and coaches. It also marked the end of a couple very interesting and emotional seasons for those that care so deeply about Auburn athletics and football in particular. I felt the need to write about it…make one more case for this Auburn football team and recognize a particular fan who summed up emotions shared by many.

My Feelings Exactly

What a weekend…what a game…what a team. The 2004 Auburn Tiger football team capped off what has to be the most special in modern history for Auburn fans. The best team in the country will not be playing in Miami. And when I say the best team, I'm not talking about just the team on the field. I'm talking about the team on AND off the field. I'm not talking about just the players. I'm talking about EVERYONE involved with the football team. You people are what make this the best team in the nation. No computer poll can change that.

Every now and then I get e-mails or letters from fans that are truly inspiring. I received this one Monday morning after the championship game. This one e-mail crystallized my thoughts exactly about Saturday's game and this football team. Here it is:

I Believe in Auburn, and love it!

I have two admissions to make. The first is that I actually cried because of a football game today. I've never done it before, and can't imagine doing it again, but… more on that later. The second is that I wasn't a big fan of Tommy Tuberville when he first arrived at Auburn. He seemed a little cold, a little distant, and I wasn't ready for Auburn to become one of "those" schools—the ones that trade coaches on a whim. I didn't dislike him—I just didn't like him much, either. All of that changed, however, when word got out about that little plane trip last year. Coach Tuberville showed his true colors then, and they weren't the shades that I expected. In the midst of the storm, he stood strong and proud, and in those dark moments became the personification of the Auburn I have always believed in. While a few dark and powerful figures proudly boast of their love of Auburn, they need only to look to this man to know what Auburn was, is, and should always be, and see that they themselves have fallen well short of the mark. One has to only read the words of George Petrie in The Auburn Creed to see that Tommy Tuberville understands Auburn:

I believe that this is a practical world and that I can count only on what I earn. Therefore, I believe in work, hard work.

I believe in education, which gives me the knowledge to work wisely and trains my mind and my hands to work skillfully.

I believe in honesty and truthfulness, without which I cannot win the respect and confidence of my fellow men.

I believe in a sound mind, in a sound body and a spirit that is not afraid, and in clean sports to develop these qualities.

I believe in obedience to law because it protects the rights of all.

I believe in the human touch, which cultivates sympathy with my fellow men and mutual helpfulness and brings happiness for all.

I believe in my Country, because it is a land of freedom and because it is my own home, and that I can best serve that country by "doing justly, loving mercy, and walking humbly with my God."

And because Auburn men and women believe in these things, I believe in Auburn and love it.

Tommy Tuberville has done many things for Auburn men and women—he has given us our pride, and he has given us not just something to talk about, but also something to cheer about. For many of us, though, the benefits will be temporary. We will go back to our lives with a little more bounce in our step, but we will be largely unchanged. For Coach Tuberville's players, however, things will be different. He has taught them the value of true teamwork—a value that's been all but lost in an era of "me" sports. He has taught them the value of integrity—a value that's becoming more and more difficult to detect in our "me" society. He has taught them the value of faith—a value with eternal implications. He has taught them to value their fellow man—one of the most valuable lessons of all. The lessons he has taught them will last them for the rest of their lives, and benefit them in ways that polls, computers, and sportswriters never can.

They won't be playing for a national championship this year. Yes, they deserve it. Yes, they've earned it. Yes, they're being cheated by a faulty BCS system. And yes, we're definitely disappointed. With a national championship under their belts, they *would be known as a great football team. I have faith, however, that these young men and the coaches that lead them will, even in disappointment, continue to show the world that they are more than players. They are "hard-fighting soldiers" on the battlefield of life. As I watched the final moments of the SEC Championship Game tonight with tears in my eyes, I realized that I'm not crying tears of sorrow for a national championship lost, but tears of joy and appreciation for those men who have restored my faith in Auburn men, women, and values. The 2004 Auburn Tigers are a great football team, but more than that, they are, in a word, Special.*

Special fans like this one are what make Auburn special. I'm honored to be a small part of it.

The Sugar Bowl versus Virginia Tech had a different vibe to it. Coach Tuberville, players, and fans had all come to the realization that there was no scenario in which Auburn could claim the No. 1 spot. I don't want to go as far

From L to R: Quentin Riggins, Stan White, me (with a New Orleans flair), producer Chad Cleveland, and engineer Patrick Tisdale at our special "Tiger Talk" prior to the Sugar Bowl versus Virginia Tech.

as saying Auburn went through the motions in that game, but you could tell it did not have the same energy as most did during that very special season. The Tigers finished off the Hokies methodically with three John Vaughn field goals and a Devin Aromashodu touchdown catch. Auburn held a 16-point lead in the fourth quarter. Frank Beamer's squad scored a couple touchdowns, but they were meaningless and Auburn won the game, 16–13.

Three days later USC dismantled Oklahoma 55–19, causing many to finally agree it should have been Auburn in that game. The BCS system had failed. A little more than five years later USC was stripped of that title over the Reggie Bush controversy in which he received improper benefits while playing for the Trojans.

Although it was of little solace to Auburn fans, some good did come out of the controversy. The new College Football Playoff system was developed using the 2004 season as an example as to why a four-team playoff was needed. I thought it a bit ironic, too, that Auburn played in the final BCS National Championship game in 2013 against Florida State. The poster child for why change was needed helped usher out the BCS era.

Chapter 6

The Rest of the Tuberville Era

L ooking back, it's somewhat remarkable what the Tigers did on the football field considering what they lost from the previous season. Ronnie Brown, Carnell Williams, Carlos Rogers, and Jason Campbell were all taken in the first round of the NFL draft, and defensive tackle Jay Ratliff was taken in the seventh round. Those are major pieces to the puzzle of an unbeaten team. Couple that with breaking in a new quarterback in Brandon Cox and a 9–3 season, 7–1 conference record, and another Western Division Co-Championship, it was a good season that also had its great moments.

The season got off to an all-too-familiar start with Georgia Tech coming to town. It was the return trip after Auburn had gone to Grant Field in Atlanta and failed to score a touchdown for the second straight game to start the 2003 season.

It was a tough night for new starting quarterback Brandon Cox, who was intercepted four times. More concerning was the fact that Auburn only managed 50 rushing yards—the fewest yards on the ground for the Tigers since Georgia Tech held them to 40 in 2003. Trailing only 17–14 going into the second half, Auburn couldn't get out of their own way with turnovers and penalties ending potential scoring drives. The loss ended the nation's third-longest winning streak at 15 and caused great consternation among the Auburn fans. However, as we quickly found out, it was a wake-up call more than anything.

The Tigers proceeded to outscore their next four opponents 176–24. The team went 28–0 over Mississippi State, 63–3 over Ball State, 37–14 against Western Kentucky, and dished out a 48–7 thrashing of South Carolina. All the games were played at home inside Jordan-Hare Stadium, but the first real road test was coming up as the Tigers traveled to Arkansas on October 15. The Razorbacks were off to a tough start at 2–3 but featured two of the best freshman running backs in the country, Darren McFadden and Felix Jones.

A rare, rare thing is taking place tonight...no it's not the fact the weather is absolutely perfect in Fayetteville, Arkansas...it's the fact an Auburn Southeastern Conference game is not being televised live...anywhere...like the old days...fans are having to belly up to the radio, or in this day and age, the computer to follow their Tigers. So welcome...to all our new listeners we have with us tonight and all our regulars...join us as we hopefully paint a picture with our words...the old fashioned way...on the radio.

For the first time this season the Tigers are on the road. Auburn travels to the westernmost outpost of the Southeastern Conference...Fayetteville...to see what they're made of. No longer with the luxury of playing in the friendly confines of Jordan-Hare Stadium...Auburn must defend their SEC title in hostile territory...with four of the final six games away from home.

Houston Nutt's Razorbacks have already been wounded pretty bad a couple of times this year...however, they seemed to be on the mend. With two of the most talented freshman tailbacks in the country, the Razorbacks will provide Auburn with a challenge they really haven't faced this season...a physical team that can smash you in the mouth with its running game.

Not since 1993 have there been so many people glued to their radios listening to the adventures of an Auburn football team...so whether you're listening on your radio at home, in your car, on your computer, or even here in the foothills of the Ozarks on this cool mid-October night ...we all hope we can say the same thing that we did at the end of the 1993 season...the Auburn Tigers are most definitely the best team on the radio.

That's how the broadcast started. It was very strange in 2005 that a game was not on television. Auburn wanted to broadcast the game via pay-per-view but athletic director Frank Broyles said no. Never could quite figure the logic, but all of us on the radio crew were thrilled. We were the only source for Auburn fans to follow the game.

We all were a little anxious because we had seen (and would see again) Arkansas ruin a perfectly good Auburn football season...particularly one where the head coach was Tommy Tuberville.

Arkansas led at the half 10–6, but the second half belonged to Auburn, outscoring Arkansas 28–7 and winning the game, 34–17. Kenny Irons, who had been replaced that week as the No. 1 tailback by Brad Lester, got the call when Lester went down with a strained hamstring. Irons re-established himself as the No. 1 guy, rushing for 182 yards. Auburn's offensive attack was balanced: rushing for 233 yards and passing for 203. Arkansas entered ranked third in the nation with 286 yards rushing per game, but the Razorbacks only managed 148 in this one.

Auburn had won five in a row since the Georgia Tech loss and had climbed back into the rankings at No. 16 with a road trip to Red Stick on the horizon the following week.

For a series that's been played only 39 times...the Auburn-LSU rivalry has quickly become one of legendary proportions...anytime a series has earthquakes, hurricanes, fires, and magic as part of its lore...you know it's a special one. Today another chapter will be written in the series—the winner, if history holds true, will be the frontrunner for a trip to Atlanta and the SEC Championship Game...

The Tigers of Auburn passed their first road test of the season last week with a dominating second half in Fayetteville and a 34–17 win over Arkansas. At the same time, LSU was holding it's own here in Baton Rouge against Florida...despite turning it over five times, the Fighting Tigers found a way to win, 21–17.

They say Auburn has been under the radar since the Georgia Tech game...no flying in under the radar tonight...just flying in day of the game.

Here in the bayou they like their football like their food...with a lot of spice... so have your antacids ready...there's no reason to think you won't need them before this night is done.

The winner can call destiny its own in the SEC Western Division...the loser, while not out of it, will need to bring back the magic to have a shot.

Tiger Stadium was sold out with a record crowd of 92,664. It would witness one of the most thrilling games in the series—and one of the most heartbreaking losses in Auburn's football history.

The previous season John Vaughn got a reprieve on his extra-point attempt in the game at Jordan-Hare Stadium. He took advantage of the penalty on his first PAT try to make his second. Sometimes you wonder if there are football gods out there, because on this night the junior from Brentwood, Tennessee, would miss on five field goals, including the one that would have won the game in regulation and the one that would have at least extended the game into a second extra period. The first one was 49 yards and went wide left. The second one of 39 yards hit the upright, and the ballgame was over.

Not since Ben Obomanu dropped the touchdown pass against Ole Miss in 2003 have I felt simultaneously angry and sorry for a player. Vaughn was, and is, one of the best kickers in Auburn history, but on this night the football gods struck him down and struck down Auburn despite the fact Kenny Irons ran for a career-high 218 yards. The final was 20–17, and the Tigers lost control of their own destiny in the SEC West.

Facing four straight conference games to close out the season, one would have to wonder how Auburn would respond. Well, they responded like champions. Easy wins over Ole Miss and Kentucky set up a meeting between No. 15 Auburn and No. 9 Georgia and a chance for Mr. Vaughn to redeem himself.

Minnesota and Wisconsin have Paul Bunyan's axe, Kansas and Missouri play for the Indian War Drum, farther west you have Washington and Washington State playing for the Apple Cup and USC and UCLA competing to see who takes home the Victory Bell...what do Auburn and Georgia play for?...no bells, cups, jugs, axes, or cocktail parties here...like life in the Deep South, it's pretty simple...good old fashioned braggin' rights are what's at stake tonight...

Actually, bragging rights aren't the only thing on the line tonight. Both teams are still in the hunt for division titles and a trip to Atlanta. The route is pretty plain for Georgia...wins over Auburn and Kentucky and they're in. For Auburn...they too need two wins to close out the season, but they also need a loss by LSU to have a chance to defend their title.

Yep...in the Deep South we like to keep things simple...we like our tea sweet, our biscuits drowned in gravy, our porches on the front and the back, and our football like what we have tonight...two honored foes getting ready to do what they do best...play 60 minutes of hard-nosed, slobber-knockin' football...on the line...championship hopes and what really matters around these parts...good ol' fashioned braggin' rights.

It was a cool night at Sanford Stadium with temperatures in the mid-50s. Perfect weather conditions for this big rivalry game. It was a classic. In fact, you could make an argument that it was the greatest and most dramatic Auburn-Georgia football game ever played—that is until 2013.

There were seven lead changes over the course of the contest. It was a game that featured great offense from both sides. For Georgia, quarterback D.J. Shockley returned from a knee injury and threw for more than 300 yards. Meanwhile, Auburn's Kenny Irons ran for 179 yards and two touchdowns in his home state. On top of that, Brandon Cox threw for more than 270 yards.

However, it was a big defensive play late by Auburn that gave them what they hoped would be their final lead of the game. Auburn linebacker Karibi Dede picked up a fumble and ran it in from 14 yards for a touchdown. The extra point gave Auburn a 28–27 advantage.

Still better than nine minutes to go and this one was nowhere near done. Georgia responded a couple possessions later with a field goal to give them a 30–28 lead, leaving the Auburn offense a little over three minutes to pull off the upset.

Starting at their own 20, Brandon Cox completed a nine-yard pass to Ben Obomanu, followed by a six-yard Kenny Irons to set up first-and-10 from their own 35-yard line with just under three minutes to play. Three plays later, they were still sitting on their own 35-yard line facing fourth-and-10...and then chaos ensued.

2:05 to go and here's your ball game for Auburn...they've GOT to make a first down to keep this drive goin'...they need the 45 and this Georgia crowd makin' some noise like, (chuckle) tell you what, I think this might be louder than Tiger Stadium in Baton Rouge right now...four wideouts—two left, two right...fourth down and 10 and a half...Mix in motion from left to right...Georgia showing blitz...low snap, Cox picks it up...looks, fires downfield, wide open Aromashodu, at the 35–30, 25–20, there goes Devin, there goes Devin, all the way down...and...is he in? is he in? TOUCHDOWN!!

To this day, this is one of my least favorite calls. I couldn't see anything that was going on down around the goal line. The play went from our left to right down the near sideline. All I knew was the official signaled touchdown, but there was clearly a mad scramble in the end zone for the football that I completely missed. Georgia defensive back Paul Oliver had knocked the ball out just prior to Devin making the end zone. The ball went forward into the end zone where Courtney Taylor recovered it for Auburn. Devin was quoted after the game about that last play, "When it's fourth down you just cross your fingers and hope." The officials placed it at the 3-yard line with a 1:52 remaining in the game.

This actually worked to Auburn's advantage as they were able to run out the clock and set up a chip-shot field goal for John Vaughn who erased those terrible memories of Baton Rouge.

Auburn won the game 31–30, moving up to No. 11 in the rankings. However, the time for celebration was short-lived as Alabama was coming to town and the Tigers were looking for their fourth in a row over their archrival.

What is your favorite Iron Bowl memory? Is it 1972...two improbable punt blocks giving Auburn the win...or is it 1982...the streak finally broken. How about 1989...the first Iron Bowl game at Jordan-Hare Stadium? Or it could be 1993...Nix to Sanders...or even just two years ago Cadillac goes crazy for 80.

Maybe it's one I haven't mentioned but the lore, the tradition, the hatred behind this rivalry has been built on memories and moments like the ones just mentioned. It's no different today as almost 88,000 cram Jordan-Hare Stadium and a national television audience watches the 70th renewal of college football's fiercest rivalry...

Just two weeks ago, the so-called experts were already looking at this game and expecting the Crimson Tide to come into Jordan-Hare Stadium with a chance to go 11–0 and punch their ticket to the SEC Championship Game. Last week, the dream of an unbeaten season and a very slim chance at a national title ended in overtime versus LSU.

Just two weeks ago, the Auburn football team was still looking for respect and those same so-called experts really didn't expect the Tigers to gain that respect what with two games to close out the season against top 10 opponents. Last week in Athens, Auburn showed they hadn't gone anywhere and now are knocking on the door of the top 10.

I believe it was one of those northern sportswriters that once called this rivalry Gettysburg South...boy did he get that wrong...the participants of that battle eventually made peace. There's no peace in this rivalry, and there will certainly be no peace for the loser of today's game.

Slowly but surely, Auburn had built the best offense in the SEC, but on this day it would be the defense that made the headlines. Alabama came in 9–1 and off a heartbreaking overtime loss to LSU in Tuscaloosa...something Auburn was all too familiar with against the Bayou Bengals. Alabama also came to Jordan-Hare Stadium with a young and battered offensive line. Tommy Tuberville found that weak spot and pounded it time and time again with a relentless pass rush. Stanley McClover, Travis Williams, Antarrious Williams, T.J. Jackson, Quentin Groves, Wayne Dickens, and Marquies Gunn all combined to sack Brodie Croyle and backup John Parker Wilson eleven times in the game. McClover was in on four of those sacks.

This one never lived up to its billing. It was complete domination from the outset. Auburn led 21–0 after the first quarter and the Tigers went on to win 28–19 thanks to a couple of meaningless scores.

Coach Tuberville said after the game, "I am really proud of this football team. When we started, most people thought I was crazy when I said we had as much talent as last year. When you have to earn respect, for some reason we have had to earn it the last couple years. There is no doubt who was going to win that football game tonight after about the first five or six minutes. Our guys made a statement. I'm proud of our seniors. I'm proud of our coaching staff. It has been just an excellent year for us. We were just a couple of plays away from something that a lot of people didn't think we could do two years in a row. I'm really excited about tonight and winning the state championship again for four years in a row."

I had the great pleasure of writing this column the following week:

Four In A Row

I don't think I've ever seen a more dominating performance than the one we witnessed last Saturday in the first quarter of the 70th Iron Bowl. Auburn's defense had eleven sacks on the day, but the first quarter, heck the first two series, gave us clear indication who was the better football team and who was going to win on that November afternoon. Yes, the offense performed almost flawlessly, but it was thanks to Auburn's defense giving the offense a short field to work with that they were up by 21 in the blink of an eye.

With its fourth win in a row and fifth out of the last six against Alabama, Auburn can officially say they are dominating this series. And to be quite honest for the next couple of years, I don't believe there's an end in sight. Auburn fans should and I'm sure will handle this new era of the Iron Bowl with class. Now I'm not saying don't get that friendly little jab in on your Alabama friends, but let's act like we've been there before.

I guess it was one of Alabama's players who said after the game, "You can't say Auburn is a better program. They played a hell of a game. But you're going to put Auburn on a pedestal ahead of Alabama? That will never happen in this state." There is probably one part of that statement that is true…in the state of Alabama there will more than likely always be a few more Alabama fans than Auburn fans. It's only natural for a majority of college football fans who do not attend a particular college to gravitate toward the state school, although I think even that trend is slowly changing with each Auburn victory in the Iron Bowl.

That's the only part of that statement that is accurate. Here are the facts. Auburn has now won 24 of its last 26 games dating back to the 2003 season. The Tigers own the best record in the SEC since 2000 at 36–12, meanwhile, Alabama over that same period of time is 24–24…sixth best in the league. Another fact, Auburn owns a 55–20 record over that same time for a winning percentage of .733…13th best in the nation. Alabama doesn't show up in the top 20…pretty convincing stuff.

Now I'm not saying Alabama won't be back on the national stage…they had their brief moment and possibly a preview that they are on their way back this season. However, Auburn is on the verge of becoming one of the nation's elite programs. Will they do it? We'll have to wait and see…I personally think they will. Kevin Scarbinsky of the Birmingham News *put it best in a column he wrote after Auburn's 28–18 win, "This year is proving that last year wasn't a fluke. It was a warning."*

At the time, things seemed to be on the upswing. Despite the Tigers losing their bowl game to Wisconsin down in Orlando, the outlook was good. In fact, Auburn would be ranked in just about everyone's top five going into 2006.

2006—The Best of Times, The Worst of Times

The 2006 season was certainly one of "what could have been." Auburn started the season ranked fourth in the country. They rose as high as second and finished the season as high as No. 8.

A 5–0 start included the most physical football game I've ever witnessed. A September 16 matchup against No. 6 LSU reminded you of one of those old-school games when the defenses dominated and offenses had no chance. Coach Tuberville described it as "a very violent game." It was. It was also the lowest-scoring game in Jordan-Hare Stadium since 1973 when Auburn defeated Houston, 7–0.

Auburn's only score came in third quarter when Brandon Cox ran it in from one yard out. But the stars in this one were on the defensive side of the ball... in particular Eric Brock. The senior safety from nearby Alexander City came up with two big plays late. Brock broke up a fourth-and-8 pass attempt by JaMarcus Russell. Interference was initially called but was overturned by officials who said the contact occurred after the ball was tipped. I think Auburn got one there. I remember replay showing that wasn't the case.

Brock came up big again with a game-winning play deep in Auburn territory with less than three seconds to go. He came up with a tackle at the 5-yard line that preserved the victory. It was one of the greatest defensive struggles I've ever seen.

The final score was 7–3, and I believe we all had the same kind of feeling in 2004 after the LSU game...this season could be special.

Two weeks later Auburn improved to 5–0 with a win at South Carolina on a Thursday night. Steve Spurrier was still building the program in Columbia, but his team almost pulled off the upset.

What I will always remember about this game was the third quarter. Auburn held the ball for the entire quarter! I've never seen it happen before and haven't since. The Tigers opened the second half with a long 17-play drive for a field goal. The drive lasted almost nine minutes. On the ensuing kick, Tuberville elected to try an onside kick...risky to say the least considering Auburn only led 17–10 at the time. But the Tigers recovered it and kept the ball the remainder of the quarter, and on the first play of the fourth quarter Kenny Irons scored from one yard out to make it 24–10. After the game, Tuberville was asked about the onside kick: "The wind was blowing real hard in their face. Eddie Gran did a good job in designing the play and looking at it. Our kicker did a good job with it. It just worked. Sometimes they do. I could also be sitting here explaining why it didn't if it didn't work. Good for television, but not very good for the heart." It makes for pretty good radio, too.

Still, Auburn needed a big play at the end as Patrick Lee deflected a pass away from South Carolina's Sidney Rice in the end zone to preserve the win, 24–17. The win lifted Auburn to No. 2 in the nation with a thorn in the side coming to town the next weekend.

Remember those two freshmen tailbacks we mentioned? Well, they were even better as sophomores at Arkansas. Darren McFadden and Felix Jones came into Jordan-Hare Stadium and ran roughshod over the Tigers as the Razorbacks made it look easy with a 27–10 win over the second-ranked Tigers. It wasn't the first time Arkansas had put a beating on Tommy Tuberville's team. In 2001 and 2002, the Hogs from Fayetteville defeated two ranked Auburn teams by a combined score of 80–34.

This Razorback team was playing with confidence coming off a double-overtime win against Alabama. Offensively, they were much better than the year before…oddly enough their offensive coordinator was Gus Malzahn. In his first collegiate position he helped lead that Arkansas team to what would turn out to be a 10–4 season. Four years later he would win a national championship as Auburn's offensive coordinator and three years after that a national runner-up as Auburn's head coach.

But back to this game. It was a loss that all but dashed Auburn's national title hopes, but there was still plenty to play for. The western division title was still in sight but the margin of error had been greatly reduced, particularly when you consider No. 2 Florida was next on the agenda.

Like Mr. Balboa in the third Rocky movie…the Auburn Tigers were knocked from their perch near the top of the rankings last week when the Arkansas Razorbacks pulled a Clubber Lang…giving the Tigers a knockout punch, sending them into the ropes reeling in the Western Division race. Today they look to bounce back in another heavyweight bout against the second-ranked Florida Gators.

Hello again everybody and War Eagle…I'm Rod Bramblett, along with Stan White, Quentin Riggins, and Andy Burcham at Jordan-Hare Stadium as we approach darkness on the plains and the start of tonight's main event.

> *Auburn comes in with their national title hopes all but dashed, but they are still a force to be reckoned with in the SEC. Florida, on the other hand, has replaced Auburn as that No. 2 team in the nation and the front-runner in the Southeastern Conference using a stingy defense and a two-headed offensive monster in Leak and Tebow.*
>
> *The Tigers have returned to their roots this week...focusing on being tougher both mentally and physically...hoping to make a comeback in the SEC and re-enter the national picture.*
>
> *This week Clubber Lang returns for the rematch...this time wearing the Gator Blue trunks instead of the Cardinal and White. Cue the music boys...let me hear a little Survivor...like they said...don't lose your grip on the dreams of the past...you must fight just to keep them alive.*

I remember this being one of the few times Coach Tuberville was truly upset with his team. He blistered them at halftime. He was extremely animated with our sideline reporter, Quentin Riggins, coming out of the locker room at the half. Saying he called out his defense in particular for their first-half play. Auburn only trailed 17–11, but the head man wasn't happy.

The defense played better in the second half but it was a spectacular play by the special teams that gave Auburn the lead for good. Florida punter Eric Wilbur dropped the snap, tried to pick it up but couldn't get the punt away. Tre Smith picked up the loose ball, somersaulted into the end zone, and the Tigers tied it at 17.

The Tre Smith score is still one of those highlights you see played over and over. Auburn never did anything on offense...in fact, did not score a touchdown. Outside of the blocked punt Auburn's scores came on four John Vaughn field goals, a safety, and a fumble return for a touchdown by Patrick Lee to end the game.

Somehow they found a way to win the game 27–17 and hand Urban Meyer a very difficult defeat. It marked the fourth straight Saturday that a No. 2 team fell. However, Florida would go on to win the BCS national title that year. The Gators would also go on to win 11 straight until they lost to Auburn again, but more on that later.

Tulane, at Ole Miss, and back home against Arkansas State were all wins... coupled with more upsets and Auburn had moved back up in the rankings and appeared to be heading for one of the big bowls with unranked and struggling Georgia coming up next.

The Bulldogs were 6–4, losers of four of their last five games and toughing it out with freshman quarterback Matthew Stafford. They had nothing but bragging rights to play for. Meanwhile Auburn was in a group of one-loss teams that all still felt had a shot at a BCS national title. This one was over early. Like the Arkansas game, Auburn didn't appear ready to play. Brandon Cox had three of his first eight passes intercepted by Georgia's Tra Battle…one of them went for a touchdown. It was 30–7 at the half. We were all in shock. How could a team look so ill-prepared with so much to play for? There's still no answer to that question. Of course, you have to give a lot of credit to Georgia for coming in with a great plan. They let the defense do the heavy lifting then turned loose their freshman quarterback.

The game put a damper on what had started as a promising season. All that was left was to hopefully put "the fear of the thumb" into archrival Alabama.

Friends and Enemies

It is here…Iron Bowl week. For one of the rare times in its history and for the first time since 2003 both teams are coming off losses. Alabama played hard but came up short at LSU 28–14, while Auburn got blasted at home by Georgia in one of the most disappointing losses in that series in a long while.

It will be interesting to see how both teams respond this week. Alabama probably feels they have the momentum. The way they played against LSU was encouraging despite losing the game. Meanwhile, Auburn must find a way to bounce back from a terrible performance against the Athens Bulldogs.

I don't think either team will have difficulty getting ready for this one. Both sides should feel good about their chances. And that typically means we're in for a close, low-scoring game in Tuscaloosa Saturday.

This week, more than any other, I get the question, "So, how do you get along with your peers at Tuscaloosa?" Of course, we're talking about the guys who do the radio broadcasts for Alabama. Now don't get me wrong, having grown up in a town that was 50-50 Auburn-Alabama and having graduated from Auburn, I still fully appreciate the rivalry and the passion that goes along with it. But I must say I am probably closer to the guys in Tuscaloosa than any other broadcast crew.

I guess our good relationship is attributable to the fact we empathize with each other to the highest degree. Both sides realize how, on a personal level, we despise the other school. And yet, on a professional level we must raise ourselves above that and put on a broadcast that somehow manages to stay above the passion of the rivalry. We don't always accomplish that goal, but we do try.

Of the members of the Alabama broadcast crew, I've known Chris Stewart and David Crane the longest. We go way back because of our work with baseball. Chris hosts their postgame show on football and does play-by-play for men's basketball and baseball. David is their weekly TV show host. He also does play-by-play for women's hoops and baseball. Both terrific guys and I consider them both friends. Again, however, we never like to lose to the other one...and I mean never!

Sure the rivalry gets in the way sometimes. We (being the Auburn broadcast crew) would love to make it five in a row this weekend in Tuscaloosa and on the other side I'm sure Eli Gold and the gang would love to take their thumb and stick it where...well you get the picture. But at the end of the day we'll all still be friends... peers in a business that has given us our dream jobs.

I can't speak for Eli, but I'll be tight as a tick on a bloodhound come Saturday. That's the fan in me. But when it's time to turn the headsets on we're there to do a job and describe another chapter in college football's greatest rivalry.

You can keep your No. 1 versus No. 2 Ohio State and Michigan. I wouldn't want to be anywhere else Saturday afternoon at 2:30. So have a good broadcast my friends down on the other end of the Bryant-Denny press box, I know we'll have one. Stan, Quentin, Andy, Paul, and me...we're bringing our "A" game...just like we do every week.

The game didn't have the same emotion at the beginning like most Iron Bowls. Auburn was ranked No. 15 in the country, and Alabama came in unranked. The Tigers, in a very workmanlike manner, made history winning the game 22–15. The go-ahead score came on a Brandon Cox to Prechae Rodriguez 22-yard pass in the corner of the end zone.

David Irons ended any hope Alabama had with an interception late in the fourth quarter. Auburn had done something it hadn't done since 1958 (Bear Bryant's first year as Alabama's coach) and that was beat Alabama for the fifth straight year.

The previous year in Orlando, Tuberville had appeared with a T-shirt that said "Fear the Thumb." Obviously in reference to Auburn going for their fifth straight win in the Iron Bowl. Needless to say, Alabama fans did not care for that little jab. But on that chilly November night in Tuscaloosa, the "fear" became "reality."

The Tigers earned a bid to the Cotton Bowl in Dallas where they defeated Nebraska 17–14 in another defensive struggle. Outside of the BCS National Championship Game trips, the Cotton Bowl in Dallas is the best bowl experience I've had. They do a great job in Dallas…and still do from what I understand.

So the 2006 season had come to a close. The Tigers produced an 11–2 record and a No. 8 ranking that left most with a good feeling going into 2007.

2007—Up and Down Season with a Gator Chomp in the Middle

Auburn never quite got on track in 2007. There were clearly some issues on the offensive side of the football. In conference play the only time the Tigers scored more than 30 points was against Vanderbilt. But defensive coordinator Will Muschamp had it going on the defensive side of the football. In six games, the Tigers held the opposition to less than 14 points.

Auburn started 1–2 with back-to-back losses at home to South Florida and Mississippi State before defeating New Mexico State to get back to .500. Auburn's first road game of the year was next…and it was at No. 4 and defending national champion Florida. The Tigers were huge underdogs to say the least, but it wasn't the first time. Sometimes in this business you guess right. Whether it's predicting the next man up is going to hit a home run or the next time down the floor your guy is going to hit a big three. Most thought I was crazy, but I had this strange feeling going into this football game. This was the type of game that Auburn and Tommy Tuberville live to play as I wrote in the week leading up to what most were calling a blowout waiting to happen.

An Unusual Auburn-Florida Experience

It's really hard to believe that Auburn has been dubbed an almost 20-point underdog to the Florida Gators this weekend. However, I guess when you look at just the big picture and not the details you can see why. The Tigers are just 2–2 and even though they seemed to have turned things around, they still haven't played anyone the likes of Florida this year. For that reason and others the so-called experts have pretty much said Auburn has no chance this Saturday night.

You know, Auburn was a 16-point underdog some 13 years ago (1994) when the 6th-ranked Tigers traveled to Gainesville for an October 15 showdown. We all remember the circumstances...Florida was No. 1 in the nation, while Auburn had reeled off 17 straight wins. The Tigers were still for the most part under the radar thanks to being on probation and off television for the entire 1993 season...getting very little respect from the national media.

The game turned out to be one of those classic games, with Patrick Nix hitting Frank Sanders on a touchdown catch for the ages. It to this day is one of those games where you will always remember where you were when it happened. Many of you attended the game. Most of you probably listened to it on the radio while watching the game on television. I was neither...it is to this day one of my favorite stories I tell related to Auburn football.

Months earlier, my wife and I planned a trip to visit my old college roommate and his wife. At the time, the two lived in Taunton, Massachusetts, which is about 45 minutes south of Boston. This was prior to my working with the Auburn Network full time, so I had no specific duties on weekends when the Tigers were away.

We arrived in Taunton right at noon. We hoped to watch the game on television when we got there, but the game was not being shown on a national basis by ABC... in fact, I think Boston College was playing Temple that day. Since we couldn't watch the game, we thought...let's get out and do some exploring. Our destination? Cape Cod and the National Seashore. We routinely called (using one of those fancy cell phones in a bag) my friend's parent's house to get updates.

Early in the trip...oh along about Middleboro...we checked in. Good news! Auburn was up 10–0 midway through the first quarter. We drove on. About 30 minutes later we placed another call...uh-oh...Florida had scored a couple of touchdowns and had taken the lead 14–13. At the time, we thought, "Okay, maybe this was it, the streak was coming to an end."

Let's fast forward, in another hour we call back...halftime had come and gone. It was early fourth quarter. Just as we placed the call, Florida scored on a Danny Wuerffel pass to Ike Hilliard giving the Gators a 26–22 advantage. It was at just about this time we arrived at our destination...the Cape Cod National Seashore.

Holy cow, I had never seen anything quite like it. The high cliffs, the rocky beaches, the lighthouse overlooking the Atlantic Ocean and the crisp sunny, October day really took our breath away. So please forgive us as we forgot about football for the moment...just a moment, however.

Despite being a good 100 yards from the car, we could hear the faint ring of the cell phone. We thought the game was over and we were getting the bad news. My friend and I ran to his 1983 AMC Spirit to answer the phone only to hear screaming in the background. Not only was the game not over, but Auburn and Florida had exchanged scores once again. Florida was on top 33–29, but Auburn had the ball back and they were driving.

So picture this...here we are four Southerners on the location of one the most beautiful sights in the world, and we're huddled around a bag phone listening to Jim Fyffe's call of that final drive.

When Sanders caught the touchdown that won it, my friend responded like you would expect...with cheers and high fives, we made so much noise, one of the locals walked over and asked what was going on. "We're listening to a football game over the car phone," we told him. "Who is it...Boston College and Temple?" they asked. "No," we responded. "It's much bigger than that. It's Auburn and Florida." I don't quite remember the response, but it was along the lines of, "Florida and who?" followed by a look of disbelief.

We laughed and headed back to the edge of the cliff, took one more deep breath of that chilly salt air. It wasn't the same as the Gulf of Mexico, but at that time it really didn't matter. Auburn had beaten Florida...again...just like the year before when they weren't supposed to. The Tigers beat the odds against the Gators...sound familiar? It should.

Now I have no idea how this game is going to play out. All I know is that Auburn seems to play better when no one gives them a chance. All I know is over the past five years only USC and Boise State have a better record on the road than Auburn (17–5). And all I know is this team has never quit believing in itself, believing they are good, believing they have the talent to compete in this league.

Saturday night, we'll see two very young teams. We'll be watching the future Saturday night with one eye on the past and hoping lighting strikes twice in "the Swamp."

Lighting did strike twice...but it took two times for it to hit the mark. With the game tied at 17, Florida punted to Auburn with 3:38 to go. Plenty of time to get down in field goal range, but it would be a freshman, Wes Byrum, kicking. Lord knows how he would respond. The drive was the Ben Tate show...of the nine plays leading up to the field goal attempt, seven went to Ben Tate out of the backfield. With three seconds to go, Auburn was at the Florida 26-yard line. The Tigers called timeout and out trotted the freshman from Fort Lauderdale, Florida, trying to pull off one of the biggest upsets in recent memory right there in his home state.

This one to beat the third ranked team in the nation...will Florida use its timeout? Doesn't look like it...here's the snap...coming up to Motley...place, kick, it's up, it's long enough...is it good? YES!! TIGERS WIN!!!! Oh my goodness...oh my goodness, they...did they call the timeout? How did they get that timeout off in time?

STAN: They called time-out...Urban Meyer was sitting there at the line judge.

Oh! Oh my goodness! Timeout called by the Gators! Oh my goodness gracious.

STAN: Well that's exactly what Urban Meyer and company wanted to do.

How about that! Alright...well let's hope its déjà vu all over again.

The snapper is Robert Shiver, a sophomore out of Thomasville, Georgia...the holder is Matthew Motley, a senior from Opelika...and Wes Byrum, a freshman out of Fort Lauderdale, trying to put it through to give Auburn the win...here's the snap, the place, the kick is up, the kick is long enough...the kick...is good!!

STAN: GOOD, GOOD!!

See ya later, alligator...Tigers win, 20–17!

The stadium was stunned, and so were we.

Auburn went on to go 4–2 over the next six games. If the offense got enough done, typically the defense would do its job and Auburn would win, but that wasn't always the case. The Tigers were 7–4 heading to the Iron Bowl, where they were going for their sixth straight against first-year Alabama coach Nick Saban.

Once again it was Will Muschamp's defense that was the real story. The Tigers held Alabama to just 225 yards of total offense. Brandon Cox, playing in his final Iron Bowl, scored the final touchdown that put it away, making it 17–7. Alabama tacked on another field goal, but Auburn's defense wasn't giving more than that, and the Tigers had set a new school record with six straight Iron Bowl victories.

Nationally it wasn't a huge story, but in the state of Alabama it was a big deal. Everyone knew that it wouldn't last much longer (and it didn't). Nick Saban is a great recruiter and coach. You knew the rivalry would even back up, but for six years Auburn dominated the series. The balance swung back the other way over the next few years, but the Iron Bowl will never be lopsided again. When Coach

Pat Dye came to Auburn as the head coach in the early 1980s, the days of the series not being competitive were long gone.

Rocky times were ahead for the Auburn Tigers, however. After the regular season, Coach Tuberville fired offensive coordinator Al Borges. Tuberville had always been a conservative coach (despite his moniker as the "Riverboat Gambler"). When it came right down to it he would let the air out if he got a big lead. He preferred the pro-style offense, and that's what made his hiring of Tony Franklin as the new offensive coordinator so surprising. You could describe Coach Franklin many ways, but "conservative" was not one of them.

Franklin coached Auburn's bowl game in Atlanta against Clemson. The Tigers won 23–20 in overtime. You saw glimpses of the wide-open offense that was coming, but what you couldn't see was what came next. The 2008 season turned into one of turmoil and the end of an era.

From L to R: producer Sam Brumbeloe, me, and my color analyst at the time, former Auburn great Daymeon Fishback, prior to an Auburn-Kentucky basketball game at Rupp Arena.

2008—A Lost Year

The 2008 season sucked. Yep, simple as that it sucked—and it had very little to do with what occurred on the football field, basketball court, or baseball diamond. It sucked because of cancer and what that horrible, unfair disease did to a beloved member of our crew. I'll talk about many of these people before the book is done, but this one fits here because it was one of the most difficult things to deal with. When a co-worker is a close friend it's a wonderful thing, when you lose that co-worker it makes work and life a living hell.

I'll never forget while we were setting up the radio equipment in Gainesville, Florida, at Ben Hill Griffin Stadium. It was the day before Wes Byrum ripped Florida's heart out making not one but two game-ending field goals. Our producer, Sam Brumbeloe, complained of some back pain. At the time he thought it was a pulled muscle or a nerve issue. None of us thought much of it. That was October 2007. Just nine months later we said goodbye to Sam…a victim of a rare form of childhood cancer. Forgive me, I don't remember the name. All I know is the cancer was in the brain and spine…basically "dripping" tumors down his spine.

Sam and I had become good friends. We were both geeks at heart, sharing our opinions on our favorite superhero movies or our favorite TV shows. It was a tough, tough spring and summer watching Sam's health deteriorate every day. I'm not going to lie to you, I was in denial. No way was this happening—however, it did. Sam passed away around July 30 or 31, his memorial service was a few days later just weeks before the start of another football season. As we prepared for what would turn out to be one of the worst seasons in a long time, I felt compelled to put things in perspective with my first column leading into that 2008 football season.

Perspective—Saying Goodbye To a Friend

Normally, I really look forward to getting back in the saddle. Normally, there's an air of excitement and anticipation with the start of football practice, but forgive me if I wait just a little while longer before I get wrapped up in the "pageantry" and "tradition" of Auburn football. You see for the second time in the last three summers I've had to say goodbye to someone who meant a great deal.

A few summers back, my grandfather passed away at the age of 86. It was a tough time as he was like a father to me. However, "PePaw" had lived a long life and really the family had some time to prepare mentally and physically for his passing.

What happened this summer is simply not fair. Sam Brumbeloe, our producer on the football, basketball, baseball, and "Tiger Talk" broadcasts, lost an all-too-quick but courageous battle with a rare form of cancer last week. It happened fast... less than a year...and he was gone. He passed away just four days before he was to turn 32 years old.

His memorial service was this past Sunday (August 3) and what a wonderful thing it was. You see Sam had a knack for fitting in any social circle...that was evident by the diverse group of people that gathered to assist his wife, Kelly, four-year-old son, Luke, and one-year-old daughter, Lily, celebrate their husband's and father's life.

I was honored to speak at Sam's service—it was honestly the toughest thing I've ever had to do in my life. I will remember Sam for many reasons, but it was his ability to laugh and make others laugh that sticks out the most.

I'll never forget the first time I saw Sam Brumbeloe. I guess it was around the year 2000. He walked in one afternoon looking for any sort of work he could get. He was decked out in a very professional looking button-down shirt and slacks. I could tell he wasn't real comfortable in that sort of get up.

My first impression was, well interesting...he comes in...jet black hair with some nice sideburns going...skinny...kind of a cross between Elvis Presley and Steve Urkel.

I quickly discovered though that he was a hard worker, cared about his work, his co-workers, and he was very reliable—traits that are often hard to come by in our business these days. Sam graduated from Auburn and still taught part-time in the communications department. He loved his Tigers. Being from Tampa, Sammy also loved his Buccaneers. He was also an avid Atlanta Braves fan.

Over his time he did a number of things, but radio was his passion. One of those jobs was studio producer. This is the person during a radio broadcast who is back in the studio making sure the broadcast runs properly and gets on the air. Quite often, Sam was that person during our baseball broadcasts. This person has the ability to talk to us (the announcers) without it going out on the radio. Again, if you knew him—Sam and talk were synonymous—we got a good bit of it during a broadcast; however, what Andy Burcham and I didn't know on one particular broadcast...was that Sam also liked to sing...or at least attempt to sing.

Now we make it a point to be in a commercial break when the National Anthem is being played...it's just a radio thing. Now at Plainsman Park they play a beautiful version of the anthem as performed by the Auburn University concert choir. So Andy and I are standing there in the booth...hands over our hearts, headsets on...when we hear in our ears...Sam...low at first and then louder and louder...it was his personal version of the anthem.

It was awful. Imagine Ethel Merman, a whale's mating call, and fingernails across a blackboard all rolled into one...that's what it sounded like.

It was so bad, that Andy and I couldn't help but start laughing, and it was one of those times, where you start laughing and can't stop. The problem was...we were back on the air...the anthem had stopped and we had to start talking again. I know listeners wondered what in the world was our problem...more so than usual!

We couldn't catch our breath much less give the starting lineups...and all I could do was picture Sammy laughing back in the studio.

Laughing...Sam made us all do that. His favorite targets were the ladies in the office.

Like the trick of walking into the front office and conveniently dropping his keys in front of Tracy Ledbetter our administrative assistant and bending over with his you know what pointing right in her face.

Another example...he had a favorite line...as he walked up front. He typically did this when there was more than one female in the room. He would hike his pants up...Barney Fife style...and say, "Sorry ladies...this one's already taken."

Speaking of being taken...Kelly, his wife...when Sam first told us he was married...we were a little skeptical...but when he showed us a picture of her...I can honestly say there were some of us who thought the boy had just gone down to the local picture shop and purchased a frame and just left the picture in it.

To say the boy outkicked his coverage would be an understatement.

Over the last few years, he was our producer on the radio for the football and basketball broadcasts...which meant the two of us spent a lot of time together not only here in Auburn, but all the exotic places that make up the Southeastern Conference.

We've seen a lot of Auburn wins, thank goodness not a whole lot of losses, but most important had fun. We loved what we did, and believe me when you're losing at Georgia by three touchdowns or getting beat by 40 in basketball at Starkville...you better love what you're doing. The easy stuff is when you're winning.

When I first wrote this, I thought I would end with the things that I'm going to miss about Sam...but, you know what, in a way I'm not going to miss him, because

I'll always have him…in my heart, in my head, in his family, and every darn time I hear that National Anthem at Plainsman Park.

And so we close, with a healthy dose of perspective…I ask that you think about Sam and his wonderful family the next time you find yourself a little too wrapped up in the lives of 18- to 21-year-old college football players. I know I certainly will.

Now, as we get closer and closer to what hopefully will be an exciting and winning football season, I think it's only appropriate that I finish with the words Sam would utter into my ear before every broadcast, "Alright guys, let's make history!"

The memorial service was amazing. Hundreds of people attended. I was especially impressed with Auburn's recently hired baseball coach John Pawlowski. He never met Sam, but I shared Sam's story with him. Coach Pawlowski's daughter was fighting for her life against a similar type of childhood cancer. Coach Pawlowski signed a jersey and delivered it to Sam while he was in hospice. He also attended the memorial service. Despite the fact he did not have a very successful run as Auburn's head baseball coach, I've always respected him greatly for embracing a young man he never really knew.

Now we had the difficult task of putting the loss behind us and move forward with the upcoming broadcast season. It would be one to remember, but not for very good reasons.

Auburn opened the season ranked No. 10 in the country. There were certainly high hopes and things got off to a good enough start with wins over Louisiana-Monroe and Southern Miss, but it was a trip to Starkville, Mississippi, where the first red flag was raised.

In quite possibly the most inept offensive game I've ever seen, somehow Auburn won the game 3–2…that's right 3–2.

The teams combined to go 3-for-30 on third down and punted a total of 17 times. Offensive coordinator Tony Franklin's spread offense was obviously not clicking, and it wouldn't for his short time at Auburn. The following three weeks, the Tigers scored 21, 14, and 13 against LSU, Tennessee, and Vanderbilt going 1–2 in that span. It was becoming clear that Tony Franklin was not a good fit philosophy-wise or personality-wise with the rest of the staff.

It was after the Vanderbilt game that Coach Tuberville made the decision to let Franklin go. Many of you I'm sure remember the scene of Franklin walking out the front door of the Auburn Athletic complex with boxes and boxes of his belongings. That was almost definitely for show as coaches typically departed out of the back of the complex on a daily basis since that was where their parking spots were located.

Nevertheless, it made for good TV, and Auburn's season spiraled even more so after that. Only one win was left on the schedule for the Tigers that season—a 37–20, way closer than it should have been, win over UT-Martin. The writing was on the wall. The Tuberville era was coming to an end.

Auburn's last game that season was on November 29. The speculation immediately began on not if, but when, Tuberville would be dismissed. I'll always remember where I was when I received the news. As is the case most of the time when a coach is hired or fired…I was out of town. In this case I was in Cincinnati, Ohio, with Auburn basketball. It was Wednesday, December 3. Chuck Gallina (men's basketball media relations director), Chad Cleveland (radio engineer), and myself were back at the team hotel after having just enjoyed some Skyline chili for lunch. We were literally boarding the bus to go to the game when I got the call that Tuberville had been let go. By the way, Auburn lost the basketball game that night to Xavier 81–74, despite a monster second half by freshman guard Frankie Sullivan.

It was probably time. I'm not sure Tuberville had ever truly forgiven the way "JetGate" all played out. I also feel that at the time the Auburn fan base was ready for a change. They had grown tired of those one or two games every season where Auburn seemed ill prepared…or the constant turnover in offensive and defensive coordinators.

Even though it was time, Tommy Tuberville is now generally beloved by the Auburn fans. It's amazing how the phrase "time heals all wounds" is true in this case. Tuberville's son, Tucker, walked on as a quarterback when Gus Malzahn became head coach at Auburn in 2013.

For me personally, I'm glad to see that. Coach Tuberville was and always will be one of my favorite coaches to work with. It's good to see him welcomed back to Auburn with open arms and tremendous gratitude.

Now the search began for the next head coach, and the decision would change the course of Auburn football history in dramatic fashion.

Chapter 7

2009—Gene Chizik's First Year

The Hiring of Gene Chizik

It was during the final exam period at Auburn when Gene Chizik was hired as Auburn's 26th head football coach. During that period the students on campus are focused on final exams. That also means an almost complete halt to the athletic activities, as well. After our trip to Xavier for basketball, the Tigers returned home on December 6 to play Louisiana-Monroe. That would be my last scheduled broadcast for 11 days. But behind the scenes there was plenty of activity as Auburn looked for its next head football coach.

I'm not sure when exactly it was...seems like just a few days after Coach Tuberville had been let go when my phone rang at the house. It was Quentin Riggins. I knew something was up because it was relatively late in the evening. Quentin informed me that he had been asked by athletic director Jay Jacobs to be on the search committee. I could tell "Q" was excited and a little bit nervous. I also knew that I probably would get a little bit more inside scoop as to what was going on behind the scenes.

I told Quentin he shouldn't feel the need to keep me informed, but he insisted on giving me as much information as he could through the process. It never was too much, but just enough for me to keep up with the various candidates being interviewed.

The process took place in Atlanta and New York. That is where the interviews were conducted. The top candidates that did not get the job were Turner Gill, the head coach at Buffalo, Todd Graham at Tulsa, Brady Hoke at San Diego State, and Gary Patterson at TCU. There were others but those were the ones that got a little deeper in the interview process. However, in the end, the committee decided to go with a familiar name, someone who had put together some of Auburn's best defenses in recent memory. But also someone who had not proven himself at all as a head coach in his short time at Iowa State—Gene Chizik.

Quentin kept me up to date over the 10 days it took to make the decision. Like when Tuberville was let go…I was out of town when I got the call from Quentin that Chizik was going to be the man. My wife and I were in Las Vegas on an early 20th anniversary trip. We were preparing to go in and see standup comedian Bill Engvall when I received the call from "Q." It was shocking because Chizik had not been discussed all that much in the days leading up to the hire. I'll admit I was surprised. So were fans—while some were vocally positive most were the opposite. They couldn't get past Chizik's 5–19 record at Iowa State—a place where many coaches have gone and failed. There were fans waiting at the Auburn airport when Jacobs and Chizik flew to Auburn for his introductory press conference. The most vocal were not happy, yelling disparaging remarks at both Auburn's athletic director and new head football coach.

Thankfully, I missed all of this. Needless to say Coach Chizik had a lot to prove on top of turning a program around that had nosedived the previous season. He immediately earned "brownie points" with the fans with the staff he put together, led by up-and-coming offensive coordinator Gus Malzahn and defensive veteran coach Ted Roof as the coordinator on the other side of the ball. That was a big step, particularly for the offense. The 2009 season was a harbinger of things to come…some very special things.

The Season

There was much excitement surrounding the start of the 2009 season. Mainly because fans were anxious to see what a Gus Malzahn offense really looked like. I think most realized that not all the tools or weapons were in place…yet. But still, the thought of having one of the best offensive minds on the staff was something Auburn had not had in a very long time.

The Tigers opened with four straight at home. Louisiana Tech was first on the docket and Auburn dispensed with them, 37–13. Mississippi State came in next, and Auburn took care of business again, winning 49–24. The team had scored 86 points in the first two games. The previous season the Tigers had gone a five-game stretch and didn't score 70 combined. It was indeed the dawn of a new day as I wrote the week going into the third game of the season against West Virginia.

Reaching into the Record Books

First-year radio broadcast producer Brad Law was gassed...wore out...he had paper cuts all over his fingers. Why? Well part of his duties as the producer during our broadcasts is to update us on any records broken or first-time occurrences. Following Auburn's 49–24 victory over Mississippi State Saturday night he was suffering from hand cramps from reaching into the record books so much...okay, that's an exaggeration, but you get the point.

The first two weeks have been fun. There's no other way to describe it. We all realize that much tougher hurdles await this football team, but it's been fun to watch a team come together with two convincing wins. Saturday night was another example of how good things could be in the future.

It truly was a night of firsts. Ben Tate and Onterio McCalebb both went over 100 yards rushing for the second consecutive game. Believe it or not, even with Auburn's rich tradition of running backs...that's never happened. Never have the Tigers had two 100-yard rushers in back-to-back games. Rarely I'm I truly shocked at records being broken or "first-times," but I was genuinely taken aback when Brad gave me that little tidbit.

McCalebb also established a first for a freshman at Auburn. He became the first Tiger freshman ever to run for 100 or more yards in each of the first games of the season. Could Auburn actually have two 1,000-yard rushers in the same season... well, at this current pace the answer is yes.

We're not done. Darvin Adams came up with a career-high 116 yards receiving, marking the first time in the school's history that there were two 100-yard rushers and a 100-yard receiver in the same game. Auburn came very close to having it happen in the first two games as Terrell Zachery had 104 yards receiving at one point during the Louisiana Tech game, but he lost six yards on his final reception to give him a total of 98 yards.

Now all of this makes great "water cooler" talk and it certainly makes it a more interesting broadcast. The real question is...can Auburn continue this torrid offensive pace as the season goes on? It will be tough, but offensive coordinator Gus Malzahn has a track record that indicates it will continue, and if that's the case then we'll need a new record book before the season is done.

We'll find out a lot this Saturday night when a very good West Virginia team comes to Jordan-Hare Stadium. The Mountaineers have a stout defense that returns seven starters. Like Auburn, the defense really hasn't received a whole bunch of love, but they are fast and they are good. It will be Auburn's toughest test from an offensive standpoint. By the end of the night, we'll know if this offense is ready for the grueling SEC schedule that awaits.

West Virginia has a five-game win streak against SEC schools; however, since 1976 the Mountaineers have played only twice on the campus of a SEC school...2006 at Mississippi State and 1976 at Kentucky.

So let's give them the typical dose of Auburn hospitality and then kindly show them that a night game at Jordan-Hare Stadium is a little more, shall we say, "intense" than anything they've seen in their travels across the Big East.

West Virginia Game

Little did we know this game would turn into one of the more surreal games I've ever witnessed. The game itself was delayed by more than an hour due to a severe thunderstorm that included lighting and torrential downpours. The stadium was cleared, however, the students stayed in throughout it all and basically had the Auburn version of Woodstock in the stands. When I say downpour I'm talking about rain so heavy you could barely see the other side of the stadium.

On a Thursday night in late October last year...Auburn found out what it was like to play in one of the Big East's loudest and most intimidating venues... the experience and outcome did not leave Auburn folks with the best feeling about Mountaineer country. Tonight, a little southern hospitality is in order as the folks from Morgantown come to the land of the SEC.

Here in the south, we typically welcome folks with open arms.

Not from around here? That's okay. We invite them in...have 'em take a seat and treat them to some sweet tea...and maybe a slice of pecan pie.

Here in the south we always make our new visitors feel right at home…that is… until game time. And…it is game time.

There's no denying the success of the West Virginia program…a perennial power in the Big East…they've also won five straight against Southeastern Conference opposition, but only one of those victories came at an SEC venue…Starkville…in 2006.

A West Virginia player was quoted earlier in the week that they weren't too concerned about the atmosphere…saying that a "stadium is just a stadium." Yea right…welcome to the SEC…welcome to Jordan-Hare…where the southern hospitality ends just about…now.

When the game finally got underway, West Virginia jumped out quickly with a 14–0 lead. Auburn came, back scoring 20 of the next 27 points, and just before halftime it was a 21–20 lead for the Mountaineers. The previous two games Auburn had done their damage on the ground, but in this one quarterback Chris Todd showed what the Tigers could do through the air, throwing for almost 300 yards and four touchdowns. His 17-yard touchdown pass with just over 12 minutes to go gave Auburn their first lead of the day, 34–30. However, it was Auburn's defense that came up with the game-clinching play on a day where Auburn took as much as they gave. Linebacker Craig Stevens picked off a West Virginia pass and ran it in. It was the fourth turnover of the day for the Tigers' defense.

Auburn won the game 41–30 and went on to a 5–0 start to the season. A season where the expectations weren't very high, but the good start got them into the top 25 at No. 17. The trip to the Fayetteville the next week would be a wake-up call for the Tigers as the Razorbacks won easily, 44–23. It was the first of three straight losses. Auburn was reeling when Ole Miss came to town on Halloween Day.

Ole Miss and a Fallen Soldier

All across the land tonight, ghosts and goblins will head out in search of various tricks or treats. Some will welcome the frights that await, while others will have nightmares as their heads hit their pillows…All Hallows Eve has a way of doing that to you…no matter what your age.

Here in the middle of the day, the Tigers are hoping they can exorcise the demons of the past three weeks...freeing themselves of the curses that have haunted them.

Like a good horror flick gone bad, the Tigers seem to be in a never-ending cycle of bad sequels...with each one worse than the last.

Today, a chainsaw-slinging Texan with the last name Snead comes to town hoping to massacre the Tigers, just like he slaughtered a bunch of hogs last week in Oxford. He has help too...there's this guy named Dexter, a serial offender who has proven that he can gash any defense.

But not so fast, lurking in the underbelly of Jordan-Hare Stadium the mad scientists Malzahn and Roof have been hard at work on a potion that they hope will return Auburn to the beast that it was the first month of the season.

Every nightmare must come to an end...Auburn is banking that today is their time. If it is...watch out...it's very doubtful these Tigers will wake up in a very good mood.

And pity the poor soul that awakens this creature from its slumber...because it will happen...it's just a matter of when.

The real horror story in this game would occur late in the first quarter. With about three minutes to go in the first period Ole Miss led 7–0 and was starting another drive when Rebels tailback Rodney Scott ran up the middle for just one yard. The end of the play saw Josh Bynes, Antonio Coleman, and Zac Etheridge all converge. Coleman and Etheridge collided, causing Zac to fall on top of the runner. He lay there motionless and face down on top of Scott. It was one of the scariest scenes I've ever witnessed. Zac later said he was conscious and awake throughout the eternity it took to get him on a cart and out of the stadium.

Etheridge had suffered a cracked fifth vertebrae and severely torn ligaments in his neck. We also found out later that if Scott had moved at all following the play it could have caused irreparable damage and paralysis. Scott said he really wasn't sure why he didn't move at all. All he could tell you is that God was speaking to him. Whatever it was, it saved a young man from suffering an even more terrible injury.

The game itself was tight at halftime with Auburn holding a slim 10–7 lead, but a 23-point third quarter highlighted by a Walter McFadden interception return for a touchdown essentially put the game out of reach.

The game's final score was one you don't see very often as Demond Washington ran back a missed extra point attempt for a score.

Auburn had stopped its three game slide with a 33–20 win. One more win over Furman and then it was time for the Tigers to serve notice to their two archrivals.

The Georgia Game

The game in Athens was a battle between two unranked teams. Auburn traveled to Athens and jumped out quick. The Tigers held a 14–0 lead going into the second quarter, but the Bulldogs answered with 17 unanswered points and then the game settled in to quite the matchup. Even though both teams were not ranked I remember it as being a very good football game.

Auburn tied it at 17 before Georgia took the lead on a Caleb King 11-yard touchdown run. However, the Georgia lead didn't last for long as Demond Washington returned a kickoff 99 yards for a touchdown.

After exchanging possessions, Georgia scored quickly on a four-play drive to take a 31–24 lead with just over six and a half minutes to go. The Tigers drove to the Bulldog 35 before failing on a fourth-down attempt with a minute to go. Georgia won the game, but Auburn once again showed it wasn't far away from returning to championship form. The team would prove that again 13 days later in Jordan-Hare Stadium when No. 2 Alabama came to town.

The Alabama Game: "It's Great To Be an Auburn Tiger!"

Alabama was on its way to a national title. Auburn was a double-digit underdog at home. The game marked the 20th anniversary of "The First Time Ever" game— Alabama's first trip ever to play a game on campus at Jordan-Hare Stadium. There had probably been more talk about that game in 1989 than the game itself in Auburn. After all, it was a foregone conclusion that Alabama would win big.

For years it was said...it will never happen...no way would the great University of Alabama agree to play a game...at Auburn...two consecutive Alabama coaches said the same thing...not their watch...they were wrong.

Twenty years ago it did happen...and today it will happen again...for the 10th time...Alabama comes to Jordan-Hare Stadium.

Hello again everybody and War Eagle! I'm Rod Bramblett with Stan White, Quentin Riggins, and Andy Burcham. We are counting down to kickoff of the 74th renewal of the Iron Bowl.

Where were you 20 years ago on that historic day...maybe you were listening on the radio...who could forget the words "and this one my friends is history."

Maybe you were in the stands...where just before kickoff, a blue haze hung somewhere between the upper and lower decks...never in my life had I seen anything like it...and I don't think I ever will. Or just maybe you had the fortune of playing in this game...like our own Quentin Riggins...part of history.

On that historic day...December 2, 1989...Alabama came to Auburn on track for a shot at the national title...unbeaten and ranked No. 2 in the country. We all know the outcome.

Fast forward 20 years and it's another Alabama team that comes to Jordan-Hare Stadium with the same credentials and the same goals.

There are differences, however, for this Auburn team...they are not deep in talent like the 1989 squad...in fact, unlike that day two decades ago...very few are giving Auburn a chance.

But that's okay...let 'em keep saying, "It's never gonna happen." We've heard that before from the other side of the state. They were wrong then...and I don't see any reason why history can't repeat itself today.

Like the Georgia game, Auburn jumped out to a quick 14–0 lead...and like the Georgia game...the opponent came back. Alabama scored twice in the second quarter to tie it at 14 at halftime.

Auburn struck first in the second half, showing they were in for the long run on this day. Chris Todd out of the shotgun hit Darvin Adams for a 71-yard touchdown play to get the lead back early in the third quarter.

The stadium was at a fever pitch. Auburn's defense played inspired football, holding the vaunted Alabama running attack to less than 100 yards on the day. The Crimson Tide settled for a couple of field goals to get the game to 21–20. After Auburn failed to do anything with two possessions, Auburn's defense was asked to make one more stop against Alabama, but I give credit to the Crimson Tide. They did what championship teams do—find a way to win. And 15 plays later, Greg McElroy dumped off a pass to Roy Upchurch from four yards out for the touchdown. The two-point conversion failed, but Alabama had the lead for good, 26–21.

Just like the Georgia game, Auburn managed to get into Alabama territory, but simply ran out of time. The teams left the field, but the Auburn crowd did not leave the stadium. Instead, they stayed—they stayed because they didn't want to leave. They had just witnessed an undermanned Auburn football team go toe to toe with the eventual national champions. Now this is where I truly believe Auburn fans are different than most. Most fans would have left the stadium ticked off, disappointed, down on their team for coming so close, but not Auburn fans. Instead they remained in the stadium and chanted, "It's great to be an Auburn Tiger!"

Over and over the cheer rang out. The players in the Auburn locker room could hear the chants and so could the head coach. He told the team this after the game, "I just told them that we are not walking out of here with heads down. We are a family. We are a family when we win. We are a family when we lose. Nobody has to like the outcome of this game, but everybody in that locker room who played did what we asked them to do. They fought for 60 minutes in a game that was really, really tough, and I said that we were going to build on that from there. Unfortunately for the seniors, it is the last home game ever that they are going to play here, but we have a bowl game, and we are going to have another good opponent to play. We have one more game together as a team, and our aim is to go win that game. Again, we are not walking out of this building today with our heads down, but we are going to know right now that the future is bright."

Someone else also took notice of the way the crowd supported a team that had just lost to its rival and finished the season at 7–5—the Outback Bowl reps that were at the game. Normally, a 7–5 team doesn't get the honor of playing in a New Year's Day bowl, but due to the Auburn fans, the folks down in Tampa knew they would get a good crowd and a good game if they invited Auburn to take on Northwestern. They were certainly correct.

Outback Bowl and a Glimpse Into the Future

There were thousands and thousands of Auburn fans descending upon Tampa, Florida, the last week of December as the Tigers prepared for the Outback Bowl versus Northwestern. It was expected to be a wide open offensive shootout. The radio crew gathered on New Year's Eve to do a special edition of our weekly coach's show, "Tiger Talk." We had set up in the team hotel restaurant/lounge. It wasn't the biggest place we'd ever done a show, but it was good enough. It was packed, and we had several special guests lined up for the two-hour show. But it was what happened before the show that I will never forget.

Let me take you back a few weeks first. Chuck Gallina and I were driving to Tallahassee, Florida, for an Auburn basketball game against Florida State. The date was December 17. On the way down, my good friend Jason Caldwell who works for Inside the Auburn Tigers, a website dedicated to covering Auburn athletics and mainly recruiting, sent me a text asking if I had seen the junior college quarterback Auburn was looking at. If memory serves me correct, I in turn sent our producer Brad Law a similar text (or maybe I called him) to take a look at this kid. His name was Cameron Newton. He was listed at 6'5", 245 pounds. I didn't know much about the young man because I don't follow recruiting as much as others, but I did know he had gotten into some trouble at Florida then transferred to Blinn College in Brenham, Texas. I started to dig deeper, and I looked at his numbers in junior college and was amazed. Auburn desperately needed a quarterback, and this guy had the look of something special.

The Tigers were competing against Mississippi State for Newton's services. Head coach Dan Mullen and Newton had a relationship dating back to his days at Florida. Auburn assistant coach Curtis Luper, who was recruiting Newton, actually had to convince Auburn's Gene Chizik to take a look at this kid. I'm sure there were some concerns about his troubles, but Chizik was soon convinced to give the go-ahead and put the full-court press on Newton. I don't know, but I'm sure offensive coordinator Gus Malzahn was more than onboard in getting the quarterback out of Texas and on Auburn's campus.

Fast forward to December 31, just about an hour before we were to go on the air with our show, word was released that Newton had signed at Auburn and would be able to enroll in January. Only minutes before the show started, we announced his signing to the couple hundred Auburn fans there for the show. Well, by this time even the most casual Auburn fan knew who Cam Newton was so the place went nuts. Auburn had found its quarterback for 2010. It made for a great way to kick off the show. What we didn't know at the time was that announcement also marked the first step toward a national championship.

"Tiger Talk" prior to Outback Bowl in Tampa. From L to R: me, Stan White, Quentin Riggins, and former AU football player Richard Shea. It was prior to the show that we announced to the audience that Auburn had just signed a junior college quarterback by the name of Cam Newton.

However, there was still a game to be played, and it would turn into one of the best bowl games ever.

It was a cloudy, damp, cool day at Raymond James Stadium, still almost 50,000 braved the elements...most of them wearing Orange and Blue. At the beginning it looked like it would be an Auburn romp. Kodi Burns scored on a one-yard touchdown run, and then Walt McFadden made it a 14–0 game in the blink of an eye on a 100-yard interception return for a touchdown.

The interception would be one of five on the day. Auburn led 21–7 at the half, but then the Wildcats came back with two scores to tie it up at 21. But Auburn answered with two fourth-quarter Ben Tate touchdown runs. Up 35–21, we all thought the Tigers had put this one away. But a long drive and a touchdown for Northwestern, followed by an Auburn fumble that led to another six points for the Wildcats tied the game again at 35 with only 75 seconds remaining. The game headed to overtime with Auburn getting the ball first. The Tigers had to settle for a field goal to take a 38–35 lead.

The Wildcats moved it to the Auburn 15-yard line in their overtime possession before linebacker Craig Stevens sacked Northwestern quarterback Mike Kafka for a 14-yard loss back to the 29. This led to a field goal attempt by the Wildcats kicker, Stefan Demos, who had already missed two field goals and a PAT on the day. A 37-yard attempt hit the right upright, and it appeared the Tigers had pulled it out, but flags were on the field as Demos had been roughed on the play. Demos was actually hurt on the play and was helped off.

Four plays later, Northwestern's head coach, Pat Fitzgerald, was faced with a decision. He was looking at fourth-and-goal from the 5. His regular placekicker had struggled all day long and was now hurt and unable to kick. He could go for the tie with an untested kicker in Steve Flaherty or go for the win. Fitzgerald decided to go for the tie...we thought.

STAN: They look like they're going for it.

Well let's see here...oh they are gonna do a little trick play..., they look for the goal line, to Markhasusen, he's hammered out of bounds at the THREE!

STAN: And Auburn wins it!

And Auburn FINALLY wins this football game! Neiko Thorpe was not fooled! They snapped it—did they snap it directly to Markhausen?—no they snapped it...

STAN: And he handed it underneath...

To Markhausen...and he ran it to the right, trying to get to the goal line and Auburn is the LAST...MAN...STANDING!

It was a wild finish to a wild game. Northwestern quarterback Mike Kafka had basically thrown the ball on the vast majority of plays. He set an Outback Bowl record with 78 attempts and had thrown for 523 yards. The Wildcats ran 115 plays to Auburn's 72 and outgained Auburn 625 yards to 425. But those five interceptions and rolling the dice on the last play cost them the win.

For Auburn, the win propelled them into the off-season. It would be an off-season that would lay the groundwork for quite possibly the most special football season in Auburn football history.

Chapter 8

2010—On Top of the College Football World

The 2010 season started taking shape with Auburn's spring football game on April 17. A record crowd of over 63,000 gathered to watch one person—Cameron Newton. What they saw was not much: Newton only threw seven passes and offensive coordinator Gus Malzahn showed very little of their offense. Gene Chizik said after the game that they were in no hurry to name a starting quarterback. Only 11 days later Newton was named the starter.

Most thought it surprising that Auburn wouldn't immediately name him the starter—after all that's why they signed him, right? In the end, they decided to waste no time. Newton was the man. However, at the time, most didn't realize there were some concerns as to whether or not Newton could handle the pressure of being a starting quarterback in the SEC. He had played very little while at Florida and the competition at Blinn Community College is not exactly the Southeastern Conference.

The fans didn't care, they were convinced Cam Newton would be the most electric quarterback Auburn had had in a very long time...maybe ever. The coaches, on the other hand, wanted to ease him in to the season. Arkansas State was the first test for Auburn and Cam Newton. We would almost immediately see the glimpses of greatness.

Arkansas State Game

We all remember the fairy tale about the Three Little Pigs…the trio head out on their own for the first time only to learn some valuable lessons about, among other things, the residential construction industry.

Last season the Auburn football team…on their own for the first time under a new head coach…had their share of good times but they had some tough times, too…learning that you need more than sticks and straw to withstand the huffing and puffing of the SEC…

While the Tigers built a solid foundation in '09, the coaching staff realized they still needed to upgrade their building standards, so they went out and added some new bricks and mortar to their construction plans.

Thirty new faces…many of which we will see tonight…will join the largest senior class in Auburn history in hopes of putting together a structure that can withstand the unpredictable elements of the Southeastern Conference.

The first test is tonight and it comes from Jonesboro, Arkansas, in an opponent that has nothing to lose.

But Auburn's version of the three little pigs have planned a housewarming party of epic proportion…as Chizik, Malzahn, and Roof have a few surprises waiting at the bottom of the chimney for this invading pack of Big Bad Red Wolves.

Arkansas State scored first, but Auburn scored the next 21 points including Cam Newton's first passing touchdown as a Tiger.

The game was unremarkable as you could see Auburn had the superior talent. The Red Wolves gave great effort and fought hard, but the Tigers clearly were the better team with the better quarterback. Newton's first touchdown run came from two yards out in the second quarter, but it was his second touchdown run later in the quarter that got everyone's attention. A 72-yard touchdown on the zone read. Newton out-ran everyone to the end zone.

The final score was 52–26. Although Auburn's new quarterback was the star, the coaching staff still didn't ask him to do much. You look at his passing numbers and he was 9-of-14 for 186 yards and two touchdowns. Those were pretty mundane statistics, but his rushing yardage of 177 yards and two scores were anything but mundane. Cam had established himself as a running threat—basically an extra running back that happened to line up in the shotgun. There were still questions about whether he could win a game through the air. Meanwhile, on defense, ends

Antoine Carter and Nick Fairley gave us a preview of the havoc they could create with four sacks between the two of them.

The Mississippi State Game

The first road test for Auburn came on a Thursday night. A short week of preparation had everyone a little nervous. The other storyline to this one featured Mississippi State head coach Dan Mullen, who had recruited Cam Newton hard to Starkville. He and his wife had also become good friends with Cam. The return of Cam to Starkville, even though he was never signed, drew the attention of the national media.

This game was a great example of thinking you know how a game is going to play out, but then the exact opposite occurs. This one was generally considered to be a game with a lot of points scored. That never happened. Neither team got out of the teens. It appeared to me that there was a conservative approach to the game by Auburn's offensive staff and head coach. Still not wanting to put too much on Newton, Auburn played this one close to the vest.

Auburn scored all their points in the first half, leading 17–7. Two Cam Newton touchdown passes and a Wes Byrum field goal gave the Tigers a 10-point advantage. Mississippi State scored another touchdown midway through the third quarter, and that was it. Neither offense could get anything going—nine straight possessions and nothing to show for it on either side. The Bulldogs drove it to the Auburn 41-yard line in the closing minutes, needing just a field goal to tie, but failed on fourth-and-10 with 22 seconds to go.

The Auburn defense preserved the victory with Nick Fairley leading the way with an interception, fumble recovery, and three sacks. Fairley was a junior from Mobile, Alabama, and his pick led to Auburn's second touchdown of the game and gave them the lead for good.

It was good to see Auburn's defense step up on a night where they had to. The offense was just okay, nothing spectacular, and at the time I believe most expectations we had for Cam Newton and the Auburn offense were tempered just a little. It would turn out to be the only time Auburn failed to reach 20 points during the regular season and only one of three times the Tigers failed to score 30.

The following week, Clemson was coming to town—Auburn's first real home test of the season.

145

Clemson Game

With a 1:14 remaining in the first half, you couldn't find too many Auburn folks thinking about a 3–0 start. Clemson jumped out quickly and Auburn couldn't get anything going on the offensive side of the football. The Tigers from South Carolina led 17–0 before Wes Byrum finally got Auburn on the board with a 35-yard field goal as time expired in the first half.

This was the first time we would get to see how good this staff was at making halftime adjustments, particularly Gus Malzahn. Auburn came out in the third quarter, forced three Clemson punts, and in turn scored 21 unanswered points—the last of the scores was a big-time pass play from Newton to Terrell Zachery for 78 yards and a touchdown.

Auburn led the game 24–17 as they headed to the fourth quarter. Clemson responded behind quarterback Kyle Parker. You'll remember Parker from the 2010 Clemson baseball team that came to Auburn for the NCAA Regionals. He could have easily played either sport professionally, and he chose the baseball route. Clemson marched 77 yards for the game-tying score.

The fourth quarter turned into a defensive struggle with both sides exchanging punts before heading to overtime. Byrum gave Auburn the overtime lead with a 39-yard field goal. On their first possession facing third-and-5 from the Auburn 8, Parker found a wide open receiver, Jaron Brown, but miraculously for Auburn, the ball just glanced off his fingertips. If that catch was made the game would have been over and Auburn's season would have taken a different turn.

Our stomachs sank in the booth. You could see the receiver flare out to the right wide open in the end zone, but it wasn't meant to be. Clemson had to settle for a game-tying 26-yard field goal. The first kick was good, but Clemson moved…the center moved the football prior to the snap. Freshman Chandler Catanzaro had to kick it again, and he hooked it left. Auburn survived, 27–24.

It was survival of the fittest with a little bit of luck mixed in. Auburn improved to 3–0. Head coach Gene Chizik wasn't happy about the physicality in which his offensive line played. The following week would be a turning point for them as they had a very difficult week of practice. It would pay off for the remainder of the season as the offensive line became dominant the rest of the way.

The South Carolina Game

Steve Spurrier's Gamecocks came to Auburn undefeated and ranked No. 12 in the country. On offense South Carolina featured two of the most dynamic offensive players in the country in tailback Marcus Lattimore and wide receiver Alshon Jeffery. Up to this point South Carolina's rush defense had been the best in the league, allowing only 60 yards on the ground—334 Auburn rushing yards later, that average went way up.

Quarterback Cam Newton had what I would consider his breakout game. The game that at the very least made the nation take notice. He accounted for 178 rushing yards, three touchdowns on the ground and two through the air. His first touchdown electrified the crowd…it occurred on Auburn's first possession of the game. Newton left the ground almost five yards out and he dove in the end zone—Superman *can* fly.

The old head ball coach responded with 20 unanswered before Cam ran another one in from three yards out to make it 20–14 Gamecocks going to half. Both teams swapped touchdowns in the third quarter, and South Carolina led 27–21 going to the fourth.

By this time you could see the renewed physicality of the offensive line starting to take effect. South Carolina's defense was starting to wither. With just over 13 minutes to go, Newton found one of his favorite targets, Philip Lutzenkirchen, from seven yards out to give Auburn the lead for good. Then Emory Blake made one of the best runs after the catch I've ever seen to make it 35–27 with just over six minutes remaining.

Meanwhile, Auburn's defense was just getting started and forced four turnovers on South Carolina's last four possessions. Two fumbles by starting quarterback Stephen Garcia and then two interceptions for backup Connor Shaw but the Gamecocks still had one more shot to send it to overtime. Alshon Jeffrey had two huge catches to get South Carolina inside the Auburn 20. With 39 seconds to go, the Tigers' defense rose to the occasion again when Shaw went for the end zone, where the ball was tipped in the air and Demond Washington once again came up with a big play…this time an interception.

The last of those four straight turnovers was a game winner. While the defense had a hard time shutting down Jeffrey, they completely neutralized Lattimore, who only rushed for 33 yards. Gene Chizik thought stopping their run attack was the key and set up everything else. He was right.

The win vaulted Auburn into the top 10, and two weeks later they were ranked No. 8 in the country as they prepared to play their second conference road game at Kentucky. Auburn was a big favorite against a Kentucky team that was winless in conference.

The Kentucky Game

Leading up to the night game in Lexington, the crew sat around the TVs in the main press box watching South Carolina host Alabama. A loss by Alabama would give Auburn a chance with a win to take the front-runner's role in the SEC West. The Gamecocks obliged with a 35–21 win over No. 1 Alabama. The first win over a top-ranked opponent in school history set up a very big game for the No. 8 Tigers against a Wildcats team that was more than ready to play.

> *If this were a horse race, the Auburn Tigers would be entering the backstretch of the 2010 season. The month of October typically determines who are at the front of the pack and who are the also-rans. Appropriate for the Tigers to start this all important portion of the SEC race...here in the land of thoroughbred champions...*
>
> *As we enter the backstretch...Auburn has consistently stayed out in front of the pack. With only a few stumbles along the way, the Tigers have consistently shown they are in it for the long haul.*
>
> *Their opponent tonight surged out of the gates...only to get caught up in the pack the last two weeks. Don't let them fool you...they have a stable full of talented stallions...that have proven in their careers...they can outrun anyone at any time.*
>
> *Just ask Auburn...they experienced in person on their own track a year ago as Cobb, Locke, and company pulled away, snapping a 15-game losing streak against the Tigers.*
>
> *That game signaled the start of Auburn's fade down the homestretch...but that was last year...this is a new race...the first of four here in the month of October that will determine who is good and who is great.*
>
> *This past week marked the 21st anniversary of the passing of possibly the greatest horse ever to race...Secretariat. When the Triple Crown winner died... doctors discovered his heart was two and a half times the size of a normal horse.*

To say he had the heart of a champion would be an understatement...it's that same kind of heart that Auburn will need to get through these next four weeks as we begin the backstretch and start heading for home.

It should have been an easy win. If you looked at the two teams, Auburn was clearly the better team, but it just goes to show you how one player can have a huge impact. In this game, for both sides, that was clear. Cam Newton for Auburn and running back/receiver/return man Randall Cobb for Kentucky.

The way the game started it looked like an easy win for the Tigers. Midway through the second quarter the score was 24–7, and at halftime it was 31–17. The way Auburn had been a second-half team through the first half of the season, this one appeared to be win number six just 30 minutes into the game. However, Kentucky's Cobb had something to say about that. He had already been responsible for both Wildcat touchdowns with a two-yard run and a six-yard toss to Jordan Aumiller. Before the third quarter was done, Cobb had caught a touchdown pass and run in another to tie the game at 31–31. All of a sudden we were headed to a fourth quarter that would define the rest of the season.

Wes Byrum gave Auburn a 34–31 lead early in the fourth on a short 19-yard field goal. Kentucky came back and simply wouldn't give the ball back to the defense. The Wildcats held on to the ball for the next 6:37 settling for a game-tying field goal with 7:31 to go in the game. There was still plenty of time remaining for both teams, but there seemed to be a sense of urgency for Auburn. The team had piddled around and not taken care of business. The nation had taken notice of this Auburn team. This game was for the outright lead in the Western Division, but Auburn hadn't played like it. They had not played like a champion. I'll never forget prior to what turned out to be the last possession for either team sending it down to Quentin Riggins on the sidelines. To this day, I point to his words as a harbinger of things to come—he nailed it on the importance of the Auburn drive coming up:

Quentin: Rod, with two teams in the West having lost today and you think about Auburn and you think about LSU undefeated...Auburn controls its own destiny... and you talk about championship drives, trying to get to Atlanta—it starts right here in Lexington...so let's see what No. 2 Cam Newton can do for this Auburn Tiger team...I think they shut it down too early, I think they got too conservative early in the second half...and they never could fire it back up...guys, with 7:31 to go in this ballgame, tied 34–34, ALL the momentum on Kentucky's side, championship drive starts right here, guys, on this kick return.

All night it had been the Cam Newton/Randall Cobb show. Newton had already run for four touchdowns. Cobb had been responsible for four as well for Kentucky. You had the feeling whichever guy had the ball in his hands last would win it for his team. Auburn and Cam Newton were determined not to let Cobb or Kentucky touch it again.

Auburn started at their own 7-yard line with 7:22 to go. Nineteen plays later, Wes Byrum kicked the game winner as time expired.

It is still one of the most amazing drives I've ever witnessed. Of the 14 plays in the drive, Cam Newton either ran or threw on 10 of them.

I'm not sure you will ever see many drives like that one. Quentin was right, a drive like that is what makes a champion. It wasn't the prettiest game Auburn played, they probably should have put it away in the third quarter, but they found a way to win and Cam Newton had solidly put himself in the Heisman Trophy conversation.

There was no rest however, up next were Arkansas and LSU. Both were western division foes, and both were top 12 teams coming to Jordan-Hare Stadium.

The Arkansas Game

When the westward expansion took place in the 1800s…a new code of behavior began. People no longer had to retreat when threatened…a code that dated back to our country's British roots…instead the code of the West dictated that a man did not have to back away from a fight.

He could also pursue an adversary even if it resulted in death…in the SEC West that same code of conduct holds true as we head to the second half of the season… the only question is who will be the last man standing.

In towns like Baton Rouge, Fayetteville, Tuscaloosa, and right here in Auburn, the townsfolk are preparing for a gunfight. A duel to see who emerges as the top cowboy in the Western Division.

In the old West…names like Earp, James, Wild Bill, and Masterson became legends.

By the end of this day it could be Newton, Fairley, Adams, or Byrum that will make their mark on history.

Sheriff Gene Chizik and his posse hope to turn back Bobby Petrino's gang...a task that has been difficult over the last four years.

In fact, you have to go back to when Auburn's sheriff was just a deputy, to find a time when the Tigers won a duel with the Hogs here at Jordan-Hare Stadium.

But today is a different day...Auburn has a gunslinger unlike any other...ready to go toe to toe with the Razorback sharpshooter from Texarkana.

Oh yes...the code of the West is in full effect today.

No retreat...no backing down...for either side.

So get ready...and you might want to take cover...the bullets are about to start flying...here in the Wild Wild West.

If it were not for the Iron Bowl later that season, this game might have been the most entertaining one of that magical year—108 total points were scored, breaking a Southeastern Conference record for points in a game that did not go to overtime.

Cam Newton was the offensive star and once again staked his claim to the frontrunner title as a Heisman Trophy candidate. Newton ran for 188 yards and threw for another 140. He was responsible, in some form or fashion, for four touchdowns. His signature touchdown on this day would come with about four minutes to go in the third quarter to give Auburn a 37–28 lead:

Shotgun and Byron Isom actually lines up in the backfield...and Cam LEAPS— HIGH into the air! Lights, Cameron, action! Touchdown Auburn!

As spectacular as that play was, Arkansas came back with 15 unanswered points to take a 43–37 lead early in the fourth quarter. Now there aren't many defenses that could bounce back after giving up 47 points through just over three quarters, but Auburn's did. In fact, they ultimately were the reason why the Tigers won on this day. After Cam found Emory Blake on a 15-yard touchdown pass, the defense rose to the occasion on the very next possession when Zac Etheridge picked up an Arkansas fumble and ran it in for the touchdown from 47 yards out.

It was a controversial play as the officials reviewed the call. It was the second of the day that could have gone either way. Earlier, Mario Fannin had the ball knocked loose as he crossed the goal line. The officials looked at that one for almost four minutes before ruling that he did score. This one was very similar. Although it appeared as if the runner was down, there was no clear-cut video evidence that he was, so the play stood. You sensed it took the wind out of Arkansas. In their next two possessions backup quarterback Tyler Wilson threw two interceptions. Auburn in turn scored 28 unanswered in the final quarter to win, 65–43.

The fourth quarter was the difference again as head coach Gene Chizik pointed out after the game. "We just believe in the fourth quarter. We emphasize it daily, weekly. Our team gets together at the end of every third quarter, and basically the mantra is that if we are not ahead, we are going to win it and come ahead and get ahead, and that if we are ahead, we are going to keep the lead. That is pretty much it in a nutshell. They get together and they sprint down the field right now and the message is that we are going to have energy in the fourth quarter, and we expect to win those games, and I think we've found different ways to do that all year."

There were still five games remaining to the regular season, and up next was Auburn's first game against a top 10 opponent, LSU. If the Arkansas game firmly established Cam Newton as the Heisman frontrunner, the LSU game basically won it for him.

The LSU Game

It's not the longest series nor is it the biggest rivalry in the SEC but what these two teams HAVE produced are some of college football's most amazing games.

However, today, the stakes have never been higher...never have two unbeaten/untied teams met in Jordan-Hare Stadium this late in the season...oh my goodness what will the next chapter hold in this classic tale...

Yep...this series has been a real page turner over the years.

In 1988...an earthquake rocked Auburn's national championship hopes.

1994—Auburn intercepted victory.

The next year...a little voodoo magic intervened on the bayou as Auburn fell to a phantom menace.

Not to be outdone by a little sorcery the following season, Auburn's chance at victory went up in smoke...as the old Auburn Sports Arena went up in flames.

And let's not forget two Auburn comebacks that led to a division and conference title in 1997 and 2004.

That brings us to the here and now...another chapter about to unfold...

On one hand...you have the Mad Hatter...whose decision making at times has at best been innovative...at worse, resembling that of Tweedledee and Tweedledum...

On the other…a young man with a grin as big and mischievous as the Cheshire Cat…who's now you see him, now you don't moves have left the opposition out on a limb.

Hope you enjoy your tea with a little spice, because it's sure to be a wild one… with the winner stepping through the looking glass into a wonderland of endless possibilities…

LSU's defense came in ranked third in the country, but it would be Auburn's defense that shined and the Cam Newton–led offense that would hold the spotlight. At the end of the first half the game was tied at 10. Both teams had trouble doing much of anything offensively, but like every game before, in the second half Auburn began to wear down the opponent.

The first score of the second half is still one of those plays you see replayed over and over. It was Cam being Cam. You can say what you want, but I still think this play won him the Hesiman Trophy that season.

First down and 10 from just inside of midfield, here's Cam on the fake, right up the middle, breaks a tackle at the 40, stays on his feet 35-30, 25-20, Peterson the one man to beat, at the 5, he…IS…IN! Touchdoooown Auburn!! Flash that smile, Cam! Tigers lead!

STAN: WOW! And he (dragged) the all-American Patrick Peterson from the 5-yard line into the end zone, right up the middle…Cam Newton takes the lead again for the Auburn Tigers…

What…an unbelievable run…that is…

STAN: That's an historical moment right there.

That kind of run makes you want to strike a pose, doesn't it, Stan?

The 49 yards were a large chunk of Cam's 217 that day, but LSU wasn't done. Early in the fourth quarter, LSU's Rueben Randle hit Spencer Ware on a halfback pass for 39 yards and a score to tie the game at 17–17. On LSU's next offensive possession they faced third-and-6 from their 44-yard line trying to drive for the go-ahead score with just under seven minutes to go. Nick Fairley ripped down backup quarterback Jordan Jefferson.

The sack ignited the sold-out stadium. LSU had to punt away. Auburn took over with 6:10 remaining at their 10-yard line. Cam ran for 16 yards, and Michael Dyer took it around right end for another four yards. On the next play, Gus Malzahn decided to stretch the defense to the other side of the field. Onterio

McCalebb turned the corner and ran 70 yards for what turned out to be the game-winning touchdown.

The extra point made it 24–17. Our sideline reporter, Quentin Riggins, was to our far left as we look at the field. He was positioned on the near sideline. One of my favorite pictures from that 2010 season came from that play. It's a shot of Quentin with microphone in hand pointing to the end zone indicating McCalebb was gone. It brings a smile to my face every time I see it.

Cam Newton continued his march through the Auburn record books, establishing a new Auburn single-season rushing mark for a quarterback by breaking Jimmy Sidle's record from 1963. He also surpassed Heisman Trophy winner Pat Sullivan by breaking Sullivan's record of 26 touchdowns in a single season.

The following week the Tigers climbed to No. 3 in the polls and No. 1 in the BCS standings as they prepared for their first road trip since the squeaker at Kentucky.

The Ole Miss Game

What is your biggest fear? Spiders, snakes? Maybe flying?

For the better part of the last month…college football's greatest phobia has been a fear of heights as the last three weeks No. 1 has fallen from its perch…into the depths of pigskin purgatory.

It is now Auburn's turn at the top…they are ready…are you?…

Fear is defined as a "feeling of anxiety that something bad is about to happen."

For three straight weeks…that feeling was justified…if you were Alabama, Ohio State, or Oklahoma.

So I ask the question…have you enjoyed the past week…or are you scared… fearful of what might happen now that Auburn is at the top of the BCS world.

Sure, some of the national talking heads still refuse to give your Tigers credit… no worries, I can't find a single example where they affect what happens on the field. Ignore them…you're No. 1.

Certainly anything can happen over the next month…but right now the view looks pretty good from up here…I'm not scared of heights…are you? I didn't think so.

You're not Ohio State or Oklahoma…and you're certainly not that other team. You are Auburn…you are unbeaten…you have a spirit that is unafraid.

So save the tricks and treats...the ghosts and goblins and all the truly scary things for tomorrow night...on this evening...it's all about the Ole Miss Rebels...it's all about focus, finish, and frontrunner...when you belong...there's nothing to fear.

Auburn was a heavy favorite as they headed into Vaught-Hemingway Stadium. That's what made the start of the game a little unsettling. Just 26 seconds into the contest Ole Miss led 7–0 thanks to an 83-yard touchdown run by Jeff Scott. However, after that it was all Auburn. On the Tigers' first possession Newton showed us he truly could deliver a little bit of everything.

Here's Kodi Burns, they're gonna run the wildcat here with Kodi...he takes the snap, he's gonna throw, Cameron Newton is the intended receiver in the end zone... did he catch it?? YES!!! Touchdown Auburn in the corner of the end zone! Burns to Newton...26 yards on a beautiful pass from Kodi!

The "wow" factor was at an all-time high. The touchdown basically told Ole Miss, "Congrats on the long run to start the game, but let's not forget who you're playing."

The game was tied at 14–14 late in the first quarter, but the second quarter belonged to Auburn. The Tigers outscored Ole Miss 20–3, highlighted by a huge special teams play from Demond Washington.

Washington from the 6...to the 10, 15, 20, 25, small hole to the 30, 35-40, 45-50 there goes Demond...he's at the 40, he's at the 30, footrace 20...15, 10, 5, Goooooooone!! Touchdown Auburn!

Auburn went on to win, 51–31. Michael Dyer rushed for a career-high 180 yards and a touchdown, and Newton rolled up another 274 yards of total offense with three scores. They were 9–0 overall and 6–0 in the SEC. The following week was Homecoming against Chattanooga. It was a chance to rest and get ready for the final gauntlet.

The Georgia Game

After dismissing Chattanooga 62–24, it was time to get ready for Georgia. The week was not without a distraction. News reports came out about the recruitment of Cam Newton and whether or not his father was "shopping" his services. I won't rehash them here because they have since been completely shot down. Needless to say the "drive-by" journalistic tactics were in full force as Auburn prepared to take on their oldest rival.

I've really never seen anything quite like it. It was as if the so-called "unbiased" media really wanted the allegations to be true. They, of course, were not. Gene Chizik called them "garbage." The team and coaches circled the wagons in their week of practice.

Looking back, I don't think Coach Chizik gets enough credit on how he handled the situation. How this did not become a major distraction is still amazing to me. He kept the team together and focused. Meanwhile, Cam was about to show the world what kind of leader he was...vocal in the huddle...his actions did the talking on the field.

It's about tradition...it's about honor...it's about the Deep South and its favorite pastime...it's Auburn...it's Georgia...it's time to play.

They come from all over for this one...

In section six...there's an elderly couple...they've been coming to games together for 50 years. They remember their first Auburn-Georgia game—1960—first time ever the Bulldogs came to the plains.

In section 44...top row...there are a group of guys...two Auburn...two Georgia...this is a ritual...a day of tailgating...a night of bragging...for two of them.

In section 20...there's a boy...there's a girl...two Auburn students on their first date...they will remember this day for a long time...

Then in section 99...way up in the upper deck...there's a father with his 7-year-old son...he promised him he would bring him to his first Auburn game this season...he works weekends so it was tough...turns out this was the only game he could attend...he paid an arm and a leg for the tix...worth every penny though... Anything to give his son a chance to see his Tigers and "No. 2" play...play for a trip to the SEC Championship Game...

So enough with the "garbage" that's been thrown around this week...enough with the talk...this team...these fans are ready for action...

It's time to lean on each other, Auburn family...it's time to pull back the curtain...and take out the trash...if you're not on board...you best get out of the way.

The atmosphere was electric with a good helping of angst and defiance. Auburn fans were anxiously waiting to see if Cam was playing. There was some doubt leading into the game whether or not he would be eligible. We found out before everyone else that he would indeed play. So we knew what to watch for when he finally came out on the field. When he did, the stadium erupted... almost as if Auburn had just scored a touchdown. Down in front of our radio booth there was a particular ESPN reporter (who will go unnamed) who had been releasing information throughout the week based on innuendo and rumor... facts be damned. When Newton appeared he began texting on his phone like a little school girl letting her friends know, "He's here, he's here...I can't believe he had the guts to show up with her!" The entire broadcast crew had had just about enough of all the misinformation that was being reported as fact. We were all rather fired up for the game. Probably more so than any I can remember.

It didn't take Cam long to show the crowd that the distractions hadn't affected him. He ran for 13 yards on the first play from scrimmage. Four plays later, he ran over two defenders and into the end zone for Auburn's first score.

After that score, things settled down a little bit for both sides. Georgia came back with 21 unanswered in the first quarter, but there was never a sense of panic. Time and again during the season, this team had shown a unique quality that enabled them to come back in games. Two touchdowns in the second evened the game at 21 going to the half. After swapping scores in the third quarter, Auburn took control in the fourth, basically icing the game with eight minutes to go on the second touchdown of the day for the late Philip Lutzenkirchen.

Auburn went on to a 49–31 win. Michael Dyer broke Bo Jackson's freshman rushing record (one that had stood for 28 years), leading to one of those images you will never forget. In the fourth quarter, Ric Smith, Jordan-Hare Stadium's public address announcer, told the crowd of the achievement. Bo, who was on the sidelines for that game, went to Michael Dyer and gave him a big bear hug. They showed it up on the big video board in the south end zone. Obviously, the crowd went nuts. Too bad Michael Dyer had some demons he was wrestling with that got him into a little trouble later on in his Auburn career. We all thought at that moment he could be one of the special running backs at Auburn. Unfortunately, it wasn't to be. However, he would have a great impact on the rest of the 2010 season.

Once the dust settled, Auburn had clinched a trip to Atlanta with another Western Division title. But there was no time to celebrate, the bigger prize was still out there. Two wins and Auburn was playing for their first national title since 1957. To get there, however, a trip to Tuscaloosa stood in the way. It was an Alabama team that had (by their standards) a disappointing season. Still, it was a very good Nick Saban–coached Alabama team that awaited the Tigers. The 2010 Iron Bowl was their national championship game. It would also turn out to be one of the greatest Iron Bowls ever played.

The Alabama Game

The last time Auburn went to Tuscaloosa it was Tommy Tuberville's last game as Auburn's head coach. It was also one of the most dominating victories in the series by Alabama—36–0 was the final. Going in to that contest, there was very little hope for Auburn, and the writing was on the wall for Tuberville. Still, we are there to bring some hope. I tried to do that with my tease…here's how it went in 2008:

> *In the dictionary, the word believe is defined: to have confidence in the truth or the reliability of something, without having absolute proof that one is right in doing so. I would say that's a pretty accurate definition as it applies to today's game. Now the question is…do you believe?*
>
> *We believed in 1972…against all odds…two blocked punts and a 17–16 victory. We believed in 1982…Bo over the top. We believed in 1989 when something Ray Perkins said would never happen…did.*
>
> *And in 2002, we believed in little Tre Smith and big old Robert Johnson. 17–7 and the streak began.*
>
> *Not since that game has Auburn been this much of an underdog to its archrival. As if it were their birthright, the opposition today has all but been given a victory by the state's media experts…Auburn…a mere speed bump on the road to a championship.*
>
> *There's no questioning their talent and success this season…it has been impressive…at the same time…none of that matters today…11–0, 5–6, and six in a row are all just numbers…insignificant for the next three-plus hours.*
>
> *So that brings us back to the original question…do you believe? By god, you better…if you don't, turn the other way, we don't need you…believe…believe like you've never believed before…believe in your Auburn Tigers.*

At halftime of that 2008 game it was respectable with Alabama holding a 10–0 lead, but by the time the third quarter ended it was 29–0 and the game was over. Throw out the tease…there seemed to be no reason to believe anymore.

Fast forward just two years into the future to the 75th Iron Bowl. Although Auburn was in the top two of the BCS Standings, the in-state media still didn't give Auburn an overwhelming vote of confidence in their picks—14 of the 22 did side with the Tigers, but all picked very tight games. With 2008 fresh in the minds of most, there was still that little seed of doubt among some…so I felt it necessary to open the 2010 Iron Bowl with a reference to what happened just 24 months earlier.

> *Two years ago we stood in this very radio booth and asked you to believe… believe on a day where you didn't have much reason to…my goodness what a difference two years make.*
>
> *Hello again everybody and War Eagle, I'm Rod Bramblett with Stan White, and Quentin Riggins at Bryant-Denny Stadium where over 100,000 have gathered…the largest crowd ever to watch Auburn and Alabama play football.*
>
> *Oh the reasons to believe are plenty…week in and week out we have seen them…*
>
> *It started with the debut of a quarterback…giving us a glimpse of what the future would hold.*
>
> *A challenge accepted by an offensive line.*
>
> *A fourth-quarter drive in the Bluegrass and a game-winning field goal. Oh yes…this could be something special.*
>
> *A Heisman-winning performance and a statement…a statement that because we are "All In"…Auburn is here to stay.*
>
> *The largest senior class in school history and a record season for a freshman tailback…sealed with a kiss from No. 34…a division champion crowned.*
>
> *And even with all this…there are those on the outside looking in that just don't seem to believe…there's no way this team is prepared to handle the hostile environment they are about to face…as if to say this team will somehow be intimidated by the proceedings today.*
>
> *But here's the thing…when you believe…there's no reason to fear…it has no place in the heart of a champion.*
>
> *So like two years ago we ask you to believe…my goodness what a difference two years make…when all you do is win.*

"Son of a Preacher Man" and "Take the Money and Run" were the songs of choice during pregame warm-ups inside Bryant-Denny Stadium that cool, cloudy November afternoon and the tone was set for one of the more hostile, tense Iron Bowls in recent memory. Of course, the intent was to "poke" at the troubles of Cam Newton. Not sure who made that decision, but I do believe they were relieved of their duties after that game was done.

I asked Auburn fans to believe again going into this game. After one quarter of play, that faith was certainly challenged. Alabama came out and scored on its first three possessions and looked to be headed for their 21st consecutive win at home. I still am amazed when I think about that game. Auburn was down 21–0 after just 15 minutes of play…on the road…at Alabama…with the weight of the college football world on their shoulders. How could they come back? Nick Saban seemed to have figured out a way to stop the running threat Newton presented. Without Cam's ability to run, how could Auburn come back in this one?

The second quarter rolled around and Auburn continued to struggle on offense, but the defense came up big on a play that could have just as easily ended all Auburn hope…but the effort of the defense and a little luck with the bounce of the ball kept the Tigers' hopes alive. Alabama's Heisman Trophy–winning tailback, Mark Ingram, was off to the races again, down the far sideline going from our right to left. He stumbled at the 20-yard line when Antonio Coleman knocked the ball out from behind. I'm not sure how the ball stayed in bounds, but it did, until it reached the end zone for the touchback. One slight kick to the right and Alabama would have kept the ball.

At the time, you didn't think too much about the play, but looking back it's almost as if the football gods were smiling on the Tigers that day. Still… Auburn couldn't do anything on offense, and at least the Tigers held Alabama to just a field goal, making it 24–0. Boy oh boy, this was still looking a lot like 2008…then something happened…a slight shift in the momentum. It was barely noticeable at the time but in the grand scheme it was an indication of the resiliency of this Auburn football team. Newton hit Emory Blake for 36 yards, and the Tigers were on the board.

There was still a lot of work to be done at 24–7, but at least we were on the board. Let's just get a stop, maybe score before the half. However, it didn't quite work out to plan. Alabama drove the ball down the field methodically and in eight plays they were on the Auburn 8-yard line at second-and-goal and looking at least at a chip-shot field goal or possibly a touchdown, Either would have been a backbreaker after Auburn had just scored for the first time. With just 62 seconds remaining in the half another sign of things to come in this game and Alabama deep in Auburn territory, Nick Fairley jarred the ball loose from quarterback Greg McElroy and then Fairley fell on it at the 13, keeping the Crimson Tide from putting more points on the board before intermission.

Halftime finally arrived with Auburn down by 17. The broadcast crew retreated to the main media area at Bryant-Denny Stadium. We all sat around a table just staring at one another. I don't remember who it was—heck, it could have been me, but I don't think so—said, "You know, if we come out and score on this first possession then it's an all new ball game." Actually, I know it wasn't me because I wasn't quite ready to buy that line of thinking. Alabama had moved the ball at will. Auburn was fortunate to force a couple of turnovers to keep the game respectable. However, by the time I strapped the headset on I had semi-convinced myself that could be the case.

Auburn started the third quarter at their own 31 and the first play from scrimmage was much like many in the first half...Cam Newton was dropped for a one-yard loss...then...

Newton directs traffic, waiting for the snap...fakes that handoff, steps back... wants to throw, goes downfield...Zachery...makes the catch 35-30, 25-20, 15, 10, 5...TOUCHDOWN AUBURN!!! 70 yards!

That's when I looked at Stan White during the break and said, "We are going to win this football game." You could feel it in the stadium. The crowd was silent. They could feel it. Auburn had already come from behind in seven games that season. As unlikely as it seemed when it was 24–0...it now seemed almost as likely that Auburn would find a way. Two possessions later Auburn scored again on a Cam Newton one-yard run. The Tigers had scored 21 unanswered points, and Bryant-Denny Stadium was in full-blown panic mode save for the several thousand Auburn fans in the northeast corner.

On their next possession, Alabama was forced to punt, but the normally sure-handed Quindarius Carr fumbled the return to give the Crimson Tide the ball on the Auburn 27-yard line with less than three minutes to go in the third. In my opinion this is the possession that tends to get lost in the shuffle when talking about Auburn's amazing comeback. Alabama had it deep in Auburn territory with a chance to take a double-digit lead again. The margin of error for Auburn was very small since they had already expended so much energy in getting the game back to where it was. A touchdown would have ignited the crowd again and then who knows what would have happened.

First play Greg McElroy hit Julio Jones, getting the ball down to the 12, then another pass the Jones put it at the seven. A five-yard false start penalty put it back at the 12 to set up a third-and-10. Eltoro Freeman sacked McElroy back at the 15-yard line.

It forced Alabama into kicking a field goal that they made, sending the score to 27–21, Crimson Tide. That sack by Freeman went just as far in ensuring Auburn's victory as any touchdown scored in the comeback.

Auburn went back to work as the third quarter ended. Two plays into the final period, Gene Chizik and Gus Malzahn were faced with a decision. Looking at fourth-and-3 from the Alabama 47, they could either punt it and pin Alabama deep or roll the dice and go for it. There was still almost 14 minutes left to play, so logic (we thought) would dictate letting your defense get the ball for you, but sometimes you have to go with your gut. Newton zipped one to the far boundary where Darvin Adams, with toes just in bounds, made a huge catch at the 39 to give the Tigers a first down.

I saw Cam throw a lot of tough passes…none were tougher than that one. And Darvin Adams? Best catch I ever saw him make. Five plays later Lutzenkirchen danced all over Bryant-Denny Stadium:

Ball just inside the 7, third down and about three…Tigers down by six…Fannin in the backfield with Newton…Cam takes the snap…looking for the receiver… HE'S GOT LUTZENKIRCHEN!! TOUCHDOWN AUBURN! TOUCHDOWN AUBURN!! Lutzenkirchen!! He threw it back across the field…seven-yard play… touchdown Tigers! We're tied at 27!

STAN: What a play call right there—a little half roll to the wide side, and Philip Lutzenkirchen sneaks out of the backfield, does a drag route across to the weak side, and a perfect throw and execution and a nice grab, and Auburn is poised to take the lead!

Josh Harris to snap it to Neil Caudle…there it is…Byrum kicks it…and it is GOOD! For the first time today, Auburn leads…28–27…that 24-point deficit a distant memory with 11:55 to go in the football game, the Tigers have the lead!

Alabama's next possession ended with Greg McElroy being slung to the ground by T'Sharvan Bell. The good, clean hit knocked McElroy out of the game. Backup quarterback A.J. McCarron would get one more chance…but it wasn't much of one.

The Auburn crowd, on their feet in the North end zone…here's your ball game… McCarron drops back, throws, and it is INCOMPLETE! Neiko Thorpe broke it up at the 25-yard line…intended for Julio Jones…Auburn's gonna win. Auburn is gonna win.

For the eighth time in 11 meetings, Auburn defeats Alabama…and today, inside the walls of Bryant's court, Newton's Law reigns supreme. Tigers 28, Alabama 27…a 24-point deficit erased, and Auburn finishes the regular season 12–0, and they go to Atlanta for the chance to play for a trip to Glendale, Arizona.

After the game, Cam Newton ran up and down the length of the Auburn sidelines with his hand over his mouth to show that he and Auburn had silenced the critics and the haters. Those that so desperately wanted the Cam Newton "scandal" to be true would ultimately discover it was not. Auburn had the last laugh. They had just made the biggest comeback in school history against their archrival in what very well could have been the greatest Iron Bowl ever played (at least up to that point). I wrote this the following week:

> *In my 25 years in the radio business, I have seen some amazing things. I have seen unbelievable comebacks. I have witnessed meltdowns of epic proportions. There have been games that I have broadcast where one team shows the character and poise it takes to win championships. Friday, November 26, in Tuscaloosa, Alabama, we got all of the above in one game…one game like no other that I've ever been a part of.*
>
> *Let's all admit it…we were all a little shell-shocked as we looked at the scoreboard in the second quarter and it was 24–0. "What in the world is going on?"…that's what I was thinking. "Can it get any worse?" The answer to that question seemed to be yes…on a couple different occasions.*
>
> *But things didn't get worse, instead Antoine Carter forces a Mark Ingram fumble…looking back I should have seen this as an omen. That fumble was just the second time in his Alabama career that the defending Heisman Trophy winner lost a fumble. The second "omen" occurred when the normally sure-handed Trent Richardson dropped a sure-fire touchdown pass from Greg McElroy. Couple that with Nick Fairley's forced fumble and recovery then we all immediately knew that at least there was a shot for the Tigers.*

Now I don't know about you, but at the moment Terrell Zachery crossed the goal line to pull Auburn within 10 points and almost an entire half remaining that's when I knew the Tigers were going to win. I've seen it too many times this season. Like a light switch, Auburn's offense started clicking and the defense again dominated the second half. All of a sudden the roles were reversed, Auburn became the team that was trying to win a game and Alabama was the team trying not to lose.

So as the clock wound down late Friday afternoon, I looked to the sky...a sky that had been a dingy gray all afternoon, but in the fourth quarter the sun finally broke through. As it hit the horizon, there was an orange and blue hue cast across the sky... now that's an omen. Auburn 28, Alabama 27. The comeback was complete.

Once again, a team whose motto this year has been "Good to Great" proved their mission was complete. It's now just "Great." No matter what happens the rest of the way, the 2010 Auburn Tigers will go down in the history books as one special team...a team that always found a way...the right way...to win.

Now it's on to Atlanta, this one will be tougher than any of the previous 12 games. But as long as the Tigers lock and load and keep doing what they do, there's no hurdle to high.

SEC Championship Game vs. South Carolina

We might not have vocalized it, but we all knew it. After what Auburn was able to do to Alabama there was very little chance South Carolina would end the Tigers' magical season. We were right as we headed to Atlanta for a rematch against the Gamecocks.

Six times before it has happened...six times before a championship won in the toughest and best football conference in the land...six times before an SEC title brought back to the loveliest village...a chance at number seven is in front of them today.

Hello again everybody and War Eagle, I'm Rod Bramblett with Stan White, Quentin Riggins, and Andy Burcham at the Georgia Dome in Atlanta as we get ready for the 19th annual SEC Championship Game.

In 1957 Auburn won its first SEC crown...and a national title...names like Nix, Lorino, Phillips, and Zeke would forever be remembered. Only 28 points allowed all season...untouchable.

*26 years later...Pat Dye returned the program to the top of the league...
Campbell, Carr, James, and a freshman by the name of Bo...long overdue.*

1987...Burger, Bruce, Rocker, and Tillman...the first of three straight.

*The next two years another Rocker, a Riggins and a Reeves were some of the
names that helped complete the three-year dominance.*

*The next championship wouldn't come for 15 years...but when it did...it came
with a bang...Campbell, Cadillac, and Ronnie...Rogers, Rosegreen, and T-Will...
undefeated and in all of our minds, undeniably the best team in the country.*

*All of these teams were unique...different in how they won championships...
and yet they were all the same...same in character...same in leadership...same in
heart and determination.*

*The 2010 version of the Auburn Tigers is unlike any of the previous champions...
yet they are the same...the same spirit...the same faith...the same family...*

Going for number seven today...and a date in the desert.

During the week, the NCAA officially cleared Cam Newton to play, all but erasing any concern over the story that blew up in the weeks preceding. Now the focus could solely be on the game.

Through the first quarter it appeared that the rematch would be very similar to the first meeting, a close game throughout as touchdowns were scored on four of the first five drives. The Tigers led 21–7 after the first quarter when both teams started to sputter on offense. After a couple of turnovers and missed field goals, the Gamecocks made it interesting on a one-yard touchdown pass from Stephen Garcia to Alshon Jeffery.

There were only 16 seconds remaining when Newton and the Tigers got the ball back. An eight-yard pass to Emory Blake got Auburn out to its own 41-yard line when the entire complexion of the game changed on that desperation heave.

Trips to the far side...Auburn may just launch it deep here...Newton runs to his right...looking, looking, throws it deep downfield, into the end zone, tipped up AND CAUGHT!! IT'S CAUGHT!! Darvin Adams off the deflection!! Touchdown Auburn!!

STAN: Worked to PERFECTION right there–first of all, the line has to give Cam Newton the time to roll out...he bought time, and he lofts it up and I can't tell who tipped it at first, but Darvin Adams grabs it off of the tip and Auburn takes a two touchdown lead again!

Unbelievable…unbelievable…

At the half the score was 28–14, and that's as close as South Carolina would get. Auburn went on to score 21 unanswered and it wasn't just the offense, the Tigers' defense had (as usual for the 2010 season) a spectacular second half. Midway through the third quarter it was the defense that really put the game away. Craig Stevens whacked South Carolina quarterback Stephen Garcia pretty good…just as he threw. The ball went right into the hands of T'Sharvan Bell. The Kissimmee, Florida, native took it in for a touchdown and a 42–14 lead.

The old saying goes "turn out the lights the party's over." Well, you could turn off the lights on this one, but the party was far from over. Auburn went on to win 56–17 as Cam Newton was responsible for six touchdowns. The Heisman Trophy was his, the SEC title belonged to Auburn, and now the wait and hype began. The Tigers were headed to Arizona to play Oregon for their first national championship in 53 years.

BCS Championship vs Oregon

The time between the SEC Championship Game and the BCS National Championship Game dragged on for what seemed like forever. During the 37 days between games we did have the pleasure of watching the postseason honors roll in. Of course, Cam won the Heisman, becoming Auburn's third Heisman Trophy winner. Nick Fairley brought home the Lombardi Award, given out to the nation's best lineman or linebacker. Newton, Fairley, and Lee Ziemba all were named All-Americans. Ryan Pugh joined those three as All-SEC team members. Michael Dyer and Corey Lemonier were named All-Freshmen in the league.

I spent the next month calling Auburn basketball. It was the first year of the Tony Barbee era. The month of December that year wasn't too bad with the Tigers winning more than they lost. The month was also spent making plans for how we (the radio network) were going to handle this historic trip to Arizona.

Personally, I wanted to take my entire family, but we just couldn't afford it. Plus, I knew I would be incredibly busy with interviews, special events, etc. We were allowed to bring one person (paid for) with us so my wife tagged along. I really didn't know when I would be required to go out to Phoenix until mid-December. Auburn athletics asked if I could come out to assist in their coverage of the week's festivities. Obviously, the answer was yes, but due to the fact we

My favorite picture of Cam Newton. That's my wife next to him. We took the picture at the senior banquet. We joked that she knocked over four co-eds to get to him.

waited a good week before making travel arrangements…how we were to get out there was a challenge.

After a couple of days of research and trial and error, I finally admitted to myself there was no way to get a direct flight to Phoenix for less than the price of my firstborn. So I had to get creative. Now you might ask why was it so hard to get out there? Here's why. Auburn fans started making their arrangements as early as the week before the SEC Championship Game. When Darvin Adams caught the Hail Mary at the end of the first half of that same game, even more Auburn folks started booking their reservations. I heard stories of fans sitting in the stands on their smartphones booking flights, buying tickets, and getting rooms. So by the time mid-December rolled around what few seats on direct flights to Phoenix remained were ridiculously priced. Being the good employee that I am, I still wanted to make sure the company didn't have to pay an arm and a leg, so the hunt began.

Finally, I pulled the trigger on the most unorthodox itinerary you'll ever see. My wife and I flew out of Atlanta on the Wednesday (January 5) before the game.

Our first leg was to Las Vegas where we rented a car and drove to the team hotel in Scottsdale, Arizona. It was mid-afternoon when we arrived. We then drove south, stopping at the Hoover Dam on the way. We got there just before dark so we couldn't go inside for the tour, but still, it was a pretty cool experience. Then it was off to Scottsdale. After a quick stop in Kingman, Arizona, for dinner at a Cracker Barrel we arrived in Scottsdale about five hours later. By the time we pulled into the team hotel (Scottsdale Plaza) it was close to midnight local time. Exhausted, we headed to the room.

As difficult as it was to get there...it would be even tougher getting back to Auburn. We couldn't get a flight out the day after the game...nor could we get a flight out of Phoenix. So we had to drive to Tuscon the day after the game then fly back to Auburn Wednesday (two days after the game). I actually missed the first two conference basketball games of that season. I didn't miss much as we lost to both LSU and Kentucky.

As you can imagine, the days leading up to the game were hectic but fun. Under Armour hosted an event at the team hotel that was a blast. All sorts of Auburn celebrities were in attendance. Charles Barkley held court for most of the

At our "Tiger Talk" BCS show. From L to R: Andy Burcham, Stan White, me, and Quentin Riggins on stage.

night. My wife, who doesn't care anything about sports, even wanted her picture taken with the "Round Mound of Rebound."

The university and athletic department hosted a huge event at the team hotel, as well. A mariachi band played as people mingled. It felt as if the entire Auburn fan base was in Arizona.

Our big event before the game was our special "Tiger Talk" at the Upper Deck Sports Bar & Grill in downtown Scottsdale. I'm not sure the place even exists any more, but I know this…they made a lot of money on the evening of Sunday, January 9. There was an open area outside the restaurant where they had hosted numerous Super Bowl shows similar to ours. The folks at the restaurant were quite confident they could handle the Auburn crowd that would attend the event…uh, yeah right.

The show started at 5:00 pm local time. The plan was for everyone to arrive around 4:00. We drove over in two or three different cars. On the way over we got word that it was "crazy" over there. The crowd had been slowly building for an hour or so. We were told the area in front of our stage was already "full." Still, we didn't grasp how many people were there because none of us had seen the setup or the area.

View of the thousands in attendance at our show in Scottsdale, Arizona.

We couldn't park anywhere close to the place. There was Orange and Blue everywhere you looked. We started walking. The closer we got the more we began to realize this was going to be much bigger than we could ever have anticipated. We all had brought our spouses. There was a special area set up for them in front of and around the stage. The only problem? We couldn't get there. The crowd had grown so big they were packed in shoulder to shoulder. By our unofficial count there were a couple thousand Auburn fans there to see the show in an area probably designed to hold half that number.

The broadcast crew had to literally fight our way through the crowd. Some fans recognized us, some did not, and we had to get a little physical with just to get them to move. There was no clear path to the stage. Our significant others were either not happy or a little nervous...so were we. We'd never experienced anything quite like this. Finally, we reached the stage. What followed was one of those moments you never ever forget.

You know when you go to a concert and your favorite artist finally appears on stage. The crowd goes bonkers. Well, that's what happened to the entire broadcast crew. It was surreal. When we walked up on stage (still a good 30 minutes before we were to go on the air) the crowd exploded with cheers. All of us still talk about

Picture of Oregon fan headquarters right across the street from our "Tiger Talk" location. To say Auburn had a few more fans would be an understatement.

Our show had numerous special guests, including AU alum and Hollywood star Michael O'Neill (L), along with Quentin Riggins and myself.

it today. We also like to remind our wives—which immediately draws the rolling of the eyes.

Prior to the show, we warmed up the crowd (not that they needed it). What was ironic, and funny, was the official sports bar for the Oregon Ducks was right across the street from our location. I couldn't resist when I asked the thousands of Auburn fans to wave to the 10 or 12 Oregon fans. One of those Oregon fans indicated that we were No. 1…which was actually an accurate assessment…she just used the wrong finger.

For the next two hours, we talked to former players, university representatives, and our own favorite Hollywood celebrity, Michael O'Neill. Michael is an Auburn grad (he graduated with Paul Ellen) and is a great friend to our broadcasts. But all of our guests played to the crowd that was frothing at the mouth. In just about 24 hours they were about to witness history. I'm sure many of them didn't have tickets to the game, but they didn't care. They were in Arizona with their team playing for all the marbles.

After "Tiger Talk," half of the crew went off to have dinner, the other half of us still had another event to attend. Stan, Quentin, and myself drove over 30 minutes across town to get to the Auburn "All In" party sponsored by the Auburn Alumni Association. The crowd was even bigger at this event that started at 8:00 pm. The Renaissance right next to the University of Phoenix Stadium was the site of the event. There had to be at least another 3,000-4,000 Auburn fans in attendance. Basically a big pep rally, we were joined by even more former Auburn players and celebrities. After spending a couple hours there, it was time to go back to the team hotel. The preliminaries were over. It was time for the reason we were all here.

Thankfully, we were able to sleep in just a little since the game was at night, although I'm not sure many of us were able to do that. Our pregame show was three hours long instead of the usual two. So we were at the stadium around 1:30 that afternoon. We went on the air at 3:30. It took us a while to get in as security was tight. While we waited in line to go in, Auburn fans came by to say "War Eagle" or just hello. When we got in it was up to the booth, and it was one of the worst locations I've ever broadcast from—but we didn't care. We were looking straight down at the goal line to the right. At pro stadiums this is common practice. So it was just something we had to get used to.

Our entire broadcast crew on the field prior to the BCS National Championship Game. From L to R: producer Brad Law, statistician Gene Dulaney, pre and postgame host Paul Ellen, then president (Auburn Network) Mike Hubbard, Stan White, general manager Jon Cole, me, locker room host Andy Burcham, spotter Beau Benton, and engineer Larry Wilkins.

After setting up the entire crew went down on the field to get a photo. After all, this could be a once in a lifetime moment we were experiencing. It had been 53 years since it last happened. If it takes that long again, it's doubtful any of us will be around.

We returned to the booth where the broadcast began. We were off and running. I was as nervous as I was on that first broadcast back in 2003. I knew I couldn't blow this one.

The wait began 37 days ago…as the confetti and streamers settled on the floor of the Georgia Dome…at the time it all seemed very surreal…tonight…it is very real… tonight…the wait ends…it is time to play for a national championship.

I guess you could say the wait actually began 53 years ago…1957…Auburn's first and only national title.

Tonight is for every Auburn player and coach since…that laid it on the line for this university.

Tonight is for those that came oh so close to the grandest prize of all only to come up short.

Tonight is for all of those great Auburn people who are no longer with us in body, but certainly are with us in spirit…for me…it's for my grandfather, for Sam, for Jim.

Tonight is about showing the entire college football world what Auburn is all about…a family built on names like Donahue, Heisman, Jordan, and Dye.

Picture of the field during the National Anthem at BCS National Championship Game. This was taken from our radio booth.

A family that has come from all over the globe, descending upon the desert like a perfect blue and orange sunset over Camelback Mountain.

In many ways, Auburn has already won…enduring a season that featured the highest of highs and the lowest of lows…emerging on the other side fearless and true.

Ah yes…the wait is over…the fourteenth and final chapter about to be written.

This is real…this is now…

On to victory…strike up the band…tonight is ours to make history.

Going in this was expected to be an offensive shootout, but it turned into anything but that. Both defensive coordinators, Ted Roof for Auburn and Oregon's Nick Aliotti obviously took advantage of the long layoff to come up with excellent defensive plans. I'm not sure what Oregon's plan was, but Auburn was determined to defend the edges, which they could do with their team speed on defense, forcing Oregon to the middle of the field and the waiting arms of Nick Fairley, Josh Bynes, and company.

A rather uneventful first quarter led to the opposite in the second. Oregon scored first on a field goal, but the lead didn't last long.

Single receiver Adams left, slot formation right with Burns and Zachery… McCalebb in the backfield…pump fake by Cam, finds Newton—or rather Burns— wide open 20, 15, 10, 5…DIVES!!—Touchdown Auburn!! Kodi Burns! Across the middle on the pump fake from Newton—35 yards and the Tigers score!

Oregon came back with a touchdown and two-point conversion to make it 11–7, and all of a sudden it looked like it might turn into the offensive shootout we expected. On the Ducks' next possession Auburn's Mike Blanc got two points back on a safety. Six plays later Auburn took the lead back…the team would never trail again.

From just inside the 30 of Oregon…trips to the near side, Adams the lone receiver to the far side…Dyer the tailback with Newton—Auburn a new play from the sideline…under two minutes to go, Blake in motion right to left…Cam to throw…Cam feeling pressure, eludes the man, wide open, he's got it—Blake—walks in! Touchdown Auburn! 30 yards! And Auburn regains the lead, 15–11, with a minute-47 to go in the first half.

The only scoring in the third quarter was a Wes Byrum field goal to make it 19–11. The teams traded the ball on several possessions until late in the fourth quarter. After Cam Newton fumbled, the Ducks tied it up on a touchdown and another two-point conversion. Only 2:33 remained. The game appeared headed to overtime, but as we all knew 2:33 was more than enough time for Gus Malzahn, Cam Newton, and the Auburn offense.

On the first play of the final drive, Cam Newton hit Emory Blake for 15 yards to get the ball out to the Auburn 40-yard line, then freshman tailback Michael Dyer made one of the most incredible runs you will ever see.

First down and 10 now from the Auburn 40...2:09 to go...inside handoff to Dyer...spun around at the 45...and he's still on his feet—he's still on his feet 40! 35, 30, 25—they never whistled it dead...he never went down...he just kept goin'! You've got to be kidding me!

Two plays later with 16 seconds to go I made one of my favorite calls of all-time...that will never be replayed.

Here's Cam Newton, gives it Dyer right up the middle, to the five, HE IS...IN!!! TOUCHDOWN AUBURN!!! TOUCHDOWN AUBURN!! TOUCHDOWN AUBURN! Ten seconds to go! Michael Dyer...from 18 yards out...may have just run Auburn right to the national title!

Are you kidding me? The officials got it right, he was down, but still a really good call was wasted. However, two plays later I would get a chance to make up for it.

Byrum waits for the snap and the place...there it is...the kick is up...the KICK... IS GOOD!!! AUBURN WINS!!! 22–19!!

STAN: Oh my goodness...oh my goodness!

And now...here in the desert...Auburn's journey is complete. 53 years of waiting...of hoping...of dreaming...of coming so close...it's all over. The Auburn Tigers are on top of the college football world, and the view from up here is sheer perfection! Auburn 22, Oregon 19—the Tigers are BCS national champions!

It was over. All the buildup all came down to nothing more than an extra point attempt, but it didn't diminish the importance. The final call is the only one where I've jotted down what I wanted to say. Leading up to that final play and ever since I've never scripted anything. But I knew on this night, if I was fortunate enough to get the opportunity it needed to be perfect. I don't know if it was, but the last thing I wanted to do was bungle a call that would be played forever.

As the crystal ball was being handed out, we immediately started our postgame coverage with interviews from the field. Andy Burcham, Quentin Riggins, and others were grabbing players and coaches randomly. The scene was

The morning after the Auburn win, my wife and I rolled a cactus (Toomer's Corner style) at the team hotel before making our journey back to Auburn.

incredible with the confetti falling from the sky we were truly broadcasting from the seat of our pants, and it was fantastic! It was great radio as you could hear the celebrating going on in the background during each interview. It was the best postgame show ever.

Once the dust settled and the broadcast ended we all left the radio booth to allow our engineer to break down our equipment. All of us sat around a table out in the main press box area. Every member of the crew sat there and said nothing. We didn't know what to say. This was all new to us. What do you say when you've just won the national championship? I'm not sure who it was…I think our statistician Gene Dulaney…who just laughed. The rest of us joined in and then for the next 30 minutes we talked nonstop about the game. Our favorite plays… the "what could have been" moments. At the time we all thought we'll never have this chance again as a crew…at least not the same people…to relive a night we'll never forget. I put my words (and feelings) into a column about a week after the victory.

A Moment To Reflect

I'm not sure I can add anything to what has already been said about Auburn's win over Oregon in the BCS National Championship Game. I thought about writing a new column the day after the win, but instead I chose to give it some time…give me some time…to come back down to earth and reflect.

There are so many moments I will remember from this season. I remember talking with Coach Chizik during the preseason and him telling me that he just wasn't sure about how this team would respond when their backs were against the wall. He was very concerned about their ability to handle adversity. Well…after several come-from-behind victories and major distractions I think we got our answer.

I'll always remember Cam Newton diving into the end zone against South Carolina…did he really do that? Yes he did! I'll never forget the emergence of Philip Lutzenkirchen and those great hands. Although he does need to work on those dance moves. And what about those seniors…Kodi Burns, Lee Ziemba, Terrell Zachery, Mario Fannin, and all the rest. As resilient a group as you will ever see. Thank you!

And speaking of thank yous…thanks to Nick Fairley…Mr. Lombardi Award–winner. He single-handedly knocked out about half of the SEC quarterbacks he faced. Nick and that baby-face grin will be missed but when you're going to be the No. 1 overall pick in the draft, you can't turn that down.

At the centerpiece of it all…Cameron Newton, listed 21st among the Tiger newcomers in the media guide. Page 62…check it out. He didn't stay in the shadows long. The young man endured more than any college player should have to…but his faith, his coaches, his family kept him focused…he kept himself focused en route to possibly the greatest season ever by an Auburn football player.

On a personal note, I want to thank our entire broadcast crew. Stan, Quentin, Andy, Paul, Brad, Beau, Gene, Larry, Mike, Jon, and everyone else behind the scenes…I couldn't have asked for a better group of folks to share this season with.

There were plenty of hugs, high fives and yes, even tears following the win. But that's okay. You have to understand one thing about our crew…every single one of us either graduated from Auburn or have been working with Auburn athletics for 20 years or more. We have a passion for Auburn. I doubt there is a single radio crew in the country at a major college that has the love for their school like we do. My thanks to them for an unbelievable season.

I was told on many occasions by folks, "Enjoy this, it could be a once-in-a-lifetime deal." Sure it could...but I don't think so. As long as we have the kind of leadership we have now, the sky's the limit, not only for football but all our athletic programs.

And I was right, it would be three years in the making and a new head football coach, but the once-in-a-lifetime experience would repeat itself in 2013. It would do so in remarkable fashion with two finishes that will go down in college football lore...one of them would change my career forever.

Chapter 9

The Scene Is Set
for an Amazing Finish

What Is Old Is New Again

Tuesday, December 4, 2012, less than a year after he left to take the head coaching job at Arkansas State, Gus Malzahn was back—this time as Auburn's 26th head coach. A packed Rane Room inside the Auburn Athletics Complex was the scene. If I remember correctly it was a relatively late press conference/ introduction. If you believed what you read Auburn had considered the likes of Florida State head coach Jimbo Fisher and Alabama defensive coordinator Kirby Smart, but in the end Jay Jacobs and his search committee that consisted of Auburn greats Bo Jackson and Pat Sullivan along with noted Auburn alum and successful businessman Mac Crawford went with a man they knew—the man who helped lead Auburn's first national championship since 1957 and the man whose offensive philosophy caused all defensive coaches to stay awake at night trying to figure out a way, not to stop it, but just to slow it down!

While the hire didn't receive the "underwhelming" tone from the national media like the Gene Chizik hire did, it wasn't necessarily considered a "big splash" hire, either. I believe most considered it a somewhat safe decision. On the surface it appeared to be Auburn athletic director Jay Jacobs going with someone (like Chizik) that he knew and was comfortable with...certainly that was true... but it wasn't the main reason. All the committee and Jacobs had to do was look at the resume. Everywhere Gus Malzahn had gone championships were won. His attention to detail was impeccable. Gus Malzahn was made to do one thing—coach football.

However, this being only his second college head coaching job (after only one year at Arkansas State) it was still important that he hire an experienced staff of outstanding coaches and equally important...recruiters. He did just that with a combination of new faces and old ones who were very familiar with Auburn.

Malzahn went out and hired three guys who were either the recruiting coordinators or considered to be their previous school's best recruiter. Dameyune Craig, who played quarterback at Auburn and was a legend at his school, was hired away from Florida State where he was outstanding for the Seminoles as a recruiter. Rodney Garner, another former Tiger, was hired away from Georgia where he was their recruiting coordinator. Tim Horton was snatched away from Arkansas where he coached running backs and was the recruiting coordinator for several years.

Add to the mix veteran defensive coordinator Ellis Johnson, Malzahn's protégé Rhett Lashlee (offensive coordinator), veteran offensive line coach J.B. Grimes, and defensive coaches Charlie Harbison and Melvin Smith (also considered to be among the best recruiters in the game), and you had a staff that was impressive from top to bottom. Malzahn also kept Scott Fountain from the previous staff. Fountain was one of the more well-liked coaches and was assigned special teams and tight ends responsibilities.

The staff was in place for the first year of the Gus Malzahn era. First on the docket was a spring football game for the ages. An audience of 83,401 showed up for the largest attended spring game in the country. Why was this one such a big deal you might ask? Well, three reasons I believe. First, by this time everyone was excited about Coach Malzahn and the prospect of a significantly better offense than in 2012. Second, Nick Marshall had signed in January, and although he wasn't enrolled yet, I believe fans knew better days were ahead. Third, and most likely the most important reason, the Toomer's Oaks had a send-off party like no other.

While I didn't feel the need to go into it in this book, the Toomer's Oaks had been poisoned by a misguided (to say the least) Alabama fan by the name of Harvey Updyke shortly after the Iron Bowl comeback in 2010. Over the course of the next two years attempts were made to save the trees; however, in the end there was just too much poison used and there was no hope for the trees that were the gathering spot of every significant event in Auburn athletics modern history. The university came up with a plan to completely remodel the corner in which the oaks resided. Included in that plan were two new Toomer's Oaks. That meant the old ones had to be removed.

A-Day was one last time for fans to roll the historic oaks. Several thousand gathered after the game at Toomer's Corner. I didn't go, knowing how crazy it would be in downtown. Instead, I took my family there the day after. There were still hundreds of people milling about on a beautiful Sunday morning. Many were with their young kids some of which would never remember the experience other than the photos being taken. There were many crying...the trees meant that much to the Auburn Family.

It was no different for me...admittedly it was emotional. It had been many years since I actually experienced a rolling of Toomer's Corner. The last football rolling I actually participated in was back in 1989 after the Alabama game—the first one ever at Jordan-Hare Stadium. My job responsibilities just didn't allow me to get up there after big wins. Looking around on this day at the ground completely covered in several layers of toilet paper and the trees full of the white stuff, I should have known this was a harbinger for many special moments to come in 2013.

With the A-Day game behind them the concern became how quickly could the coaching staff mold this team that had some obvious holes into one that could compete in the Southeastern Conference. It started with filling the most obvious hole on the team—quarterback. Like he did in 2010, Malzahn went out and found a junior-college kid looking for a second chance. Much like Cam Newton, Auburn found Nick Marshall. Other than having an amazing season in his first year, that's where the similarities end...they were two completely different kinds of players. Marshall, from little bitty Pineview, Georgia, didn't have the size of Newton, but he had speed and elusiveness. He also had the ability to run Malzahn's read option as good as if not better than Newton.

Marshall did not make it in for spring practice so he did not have the same advantage as Newton, but in the fall it didn't take him long to establish himself as the starter over freshman Jeremy Johnson and returning quarterback Jonathan Wallace. Marshall put up big numbers at Garden City Community College in Kansas. He threw for 3,142 yards, ran for another 1,095 yards, and accounted for 37 total touchdowns. However, the 20 interceptions he threw was a concern, and

Rhett Lashlee and Marshall worked on that during the first few weeks of preseason practice. On August 17, Marshall was named the starter. With that behind them, the team could focus solely on the season opener against Washington State.

The Washington State Game

All across this great land of ours…people awoke to a new day. For Auburn fans, that has more meaning than you can ever imagine. When they looked out their window… they saw the dawn of a new day…full of hope and excitement…the Auburn Family is energized and ready for the sun to shine brighter than ever before…

Everywhere there is an Auburn fan…today is a new day…

In Birmingham…a 1957 graduate awoke to a new day as the city's Vulcan monument was covered with an orange and blue sunrise.

In New York City a 2009 alum was War Eagled on an early morning jog through Central Park.

At the Grand Canyon…a 1988 graduate who works there as a park ranger saw what he could have sworn was a golden eagle flying overhead…really…on this day…hard to believe.

And in some dusty camp in Afghanistan…a group of young troops…some who graduated from Auburn…some who have adopted the Tigers as their team…have their AU flags proudly displayed on their dusty old jeep…they count the minutes to when they can huddle around their computers to listen as their team kicks off a new era.

From L.A. to D.C.…Seattle to Miami…and all points in between…no matter where you are…I'm not sure there's ever been a time when the start of a new football season was needed more…

Yes…it's the dawn of a new day…but in reality we all know that it is a return to an old day. A day where Auburn football was known for its mental and physical toughness, character, and championship pedigree.

That's really what this day is all about…step one will be taken tonight with an old face leading the way on a new day. And we're all in this thing…together.

So as the head coach would say…let's hurry up and get this thing started.

Considering what eventually happened in the 2013 season and where Auburn ended up, it's easy to forget the season opener was very dicey. Mike

Leach's Washington State team came in and played Auburn right to the finish. The Tigers won the game on big plays by both the offense and defense.

Washington State took a 14–8 lead midway through the second quarter. The first big play of the night occurred when Tre Mason ran a kickoff back for 100 yards.

The Cougars, however, scored on their very next possession to make it 21–15, then on the first play from scrimmage another big play from the Tigers gave Auburn the lead for good. This time it was Corey Grant for 75 yards and the touchdown.

It was Grant's first touchdown as a Tiger. He had originally signed with Alabama out high school in nearby Opelika. Corey then decided to come back closer to home. Considered to be the fastest player on the team with world-class sprinter speed, he was able to show off those abilities early in the 2013 season. He and Tre Mason gave us a glimpse of what kind of weapons they could be in the season opener.

In the end, it was Auburn's defense that came up big. With a chance to tie the score with less than five minutes to go in the game, Washington State drove it all the way down to the Auburn 8-yard line when Robenson Therezie intercepted a pass in the end zone to help preserve the win.

It was Therezie's second interception of the game. The Cougars got one more chance to send it to overtime, but with less than two minutes to go Auburn stopped them on a fourth-down attempt inside the Tigers' 30-yard line. The game ended with Gus Malzahn picking up his first win as head coach, 31–24 over Washington State.

It wasn't pretty, but it was a win. Coach Malzahn said after the game, "We talked about our goals, we're getting better after each practice and getting better each game, we've got a lot of work to do but we're committed to doing that." At that time there was no hint at all as to what this team would eventually become. We all simply thought, *"Well, let's move on to the next week when Coach Malzahn's old team would come to town."*

The Arkansas State Game

They say you can't go home again...that's kind of the feeling you get tonight...the only question is where is home...Gus Malzahn has returned to a place he called home to find him facing some familiar faces from another place he called home albeit for just a short time.

Gus Malzahn called Jonesboro, Arkansas, home for not quite one year... Jonesboro...the birthplace of noted novelist John Grisham and voice actor Rodger Bumpass...most noted for being the voice of Squidward Tentacles on SpongeBob SquarePants.

But enough fun facts about Jonesboro...the fifth largest city in Arkansas.

Instead let's focus on tonight...as the Auburn head coach will have to face the monster he created in less than a year's time. The Red Wolves have the second longest winning streak in the FBS division...having won nine in a row...only Ohio State is better.

In their season opener, they featured four 100-yard rushers, becoming only the seventh FBS school to ever do that.

All of this set in motion by the now Auburn head coach...and now...Malzahn along with 12 members of his coaching and support staff must figure out a way to avoid the upset against a team that also features 16 players from the state of Alabama.

There are plenty of storylines that are good enough for a cheesy soap opera.

It's kinda like going out and splitting up with your steady to sow some wild oats...only to realize that you were better off with your old flame...getting back together...but then you run into you-know-who when you are out at a party...now, that can be a little awkward.

Thankfully we're hosting this shindig tonight...and don't mind showing the door to any unwelcome visitors.

This one was never in any doubt. It was 21–3 at halftime and by the time the game was over Auburn's defense ran its streak of not giving up a touchdown to six quarters. Nick Marshall looked much more comfortable at quarterback than he did in game one. Cameron Artis-Payne showed he could have an impact by rushing for more than 100 yards, and Tre Mason just missed that mark with 99 yards on the ground. However, the postgame comments by the head coach stood out to me. You could tell he was starting to see something in this team as he said, "I think this team has potential." He was right.

The Mississippi State Game

Sitting at 2–0, I thought all in all there had been progress. You could see some playmakers stepping up. To that point, the defense had been a bit of a surprise. Like the 2010 national champions, the 2013 defense showed the ability to get stronger as the game went along. So going into the SEC opener you felt good… at least compared to the previous season. Like 2010, the first conference test was against Mississippi State, the only team that really slowed down Gus Malzahn's offense that season was coming to Jordan-Hare Stadium. Auburn was also trying to snap a 10-game conference losing streak.

> *We gather here tonight to what we hope is the end of a drought. A drought that has lasted way too long here in East Central Alabama…a drought that dates back to October 2011. A drought that most thought would never have a chance of happening.*
> *When you look at history there have been many droughts…*
> *9 million people perished in the 1870s when a terrible dry spell hit China.*
> *In the 1980s a drought hit Africa that experts say one million suffered the consequences.*
> *And then of course, in the 1930s here in our own very country…the infamous Dust Bowl occurred…devastating people in the Midwest and crippling the economy.*
> *There is no comparison of any of these natural disasters to what we've seen over the past…almost two years…we're not saying that…but in the college football world Auburn's 10-game conference losing streak is pretty remarkable. Particularly for a program that was so recently on top of the college football world.*
> *We all know what causes a drought…below normal precipitation caused by an unusually persistent ridge of high pressure. Well that pressure has been building around these parts since October 29, 2011. It's time to shift it west to Starkville where many are calling this game tonight the biggest of his tenure.*
> *I know the skies are clear right now…but for some reason I think rain is a-coming…and it could be a downpour…so get your ponchos and umbrellas ready…I have a pretty good feeling…this dry spell is about to end.*

Like Cam Newton in 2010, I thought Nick Marshall in 2013 got steadily better through the first three games. Against Mississippi State, he wasn't perfect, but he was definitely even more comfortable in the Auburn offense. The Bulldogs' defensive plan was pretty clear: they were going to do whatever it took to slow down Auburn's rushing attack, forcing Marshall to beat them through the air. After an early field goal by Cody Parkey, Auburn took a double-digit lead with Nick Marshall using his elusiveness to create a big play and a long touchdown catch and run on a completion to Quan Bray.

Auburn faked the extra point, going for two instead and made it giving them an 11–0 lead; however, the Tigers wouldn't score another touchdown until the fourth quarter…managing only two more field goals to make it 20–17 Mississippi State going into the fourth quarter. It was an ugly game for the Tigers in the second, third, and early fourth quarters. Three drives ended with turnovers and four more ended with punts.

This sounds like a broken record, but Auburn's defense stood up again late in the second half, holding Mississippi State scoreless for the final 27 minutes of the game. Because of that Auburn got one final chance. For the first time the weight of a potential game-winning drive rested on the shoulders of Nick Marshall.

With 1:56 to go, Auburn started the drive at its 12-yard line. True freshman wide receiver Marcus Davis became Marshall's favorite target. Four of the first five passes thrown were to Davis, moving the Tigers all the way down to the State 27. Marshall used his feet two plays later on a third-and-10 to pick up 11 on a run to the far sideline to give Auburn the first down at the Bulldogs' 14. That was followed up by a Tre Mason three-yard run up the middle. Malzahn used a timeout—amazing that this turned out to be the only timeout needed on the possession despite having 88 yards to go and under 1:56 on the clock. I brought it up to Stan almost immediately that I thought Gus would dial up tight end C.J. Uzomah, and that's exactly what happened.

Uzomah is over here to the near side, would they float one to C.J. here?

STAN: I think, I think that's correct.

Marshall, pump fake, into the end zone Uzomah–TOUCHDOWN AUBURN! TOUCHDOWN AUBURN! C.J.! In the corner of the end zone! C.J. Uzomah gives Auburn the lead!!

STAN: Nice call!

23–20 with 10 seconds to go!

STAN: Nice call, partner!

The extra point made it 24–20, and in the end Auburn had shown they could win a game on Nick Marshall's arm. When it was all said and done, Marshall had thrown for almost 300 yards. He did it using nine different receivers.

Auburn had cleared the first hurdle. The team proved it had what it takes to win a game when there's no margin of error. There are those who look back at the 2013 season and say this was the most important game because it showed the guys they could win a game like this. I'm not sure I agree with the "most important" argument. It certainly was very big. At the very least it allowed them to shake the ghosts of 2012—a season where they lost game after game in the second half or fourth quarter. On this September night, the 2013 Tigers showed they could finish. Their first home test of the year passed...up next was their first road test.

The LSU Game

In many regards, this game was bigger than the Mississippi State game. It was a chance to get a road win in front of the most hostile environment in the league. LSU was ranked No. 6 in the country and unbeaten. The weather was a huge factor. The bottom fell out shortly before the game began and continued into the first half. Auburn didn't handle the conditions well, LSU did.

Nick Marshall fumbled the ball on the first possession of the game and it was downhill from there in the first half. Just over a quarter into the game, LSU had a commanding 21–0 lead. What was unique...the environment wasn't hostile at all. The heavy downpour had actually sent a lot of LSU fans home or back to their tailgate site. So that part of the equation wasn't nearly as bad as it could have been.

Halftime rolled around and the head coach wasn't happy. In the locker room he challenged his team. It was one of those points in the season where it could have gone either way. Would Auburn roll over (as in 2012) or would they continue to fight despite the odds?

In the second half Auburn outplayed LSU. While they never got the game closer than two touchdowns, you left Baton Rouge with a feeling that like Mississippi State, Auburn had cleared another hurdle. They lost the game 35–21, but you got the impression they had exorcised another demon and did not quit in the second half. In fact, if the game was a five-quarter affair, Auburn probably would have found a way to win.

I truly believe this was the game Auburn came together as one unit. The Tigers showed their maturity. An ability to give great effort for four quarters was displayed in Red Stick. Auburn now had two weeks to prepare for Ole Miss. You could see the confidence building and the open week came at a perfect time.

The Ole Miss Game

October is here...a month filled with changing colors...county fairs...trick or treaters...and cooler temperatures...for the Auburn football team it is a month that could make or break their season...starting tonight as a bunch of black bears infiltrate the loveliest village.

October is a month of change...the question for Auburn is what they change after a week off to evaluate where they are after a third of the season. In reality, I'm not sure this team needs to change its colors. Despite losing to LSU, Auburn's offense was almost unstoppable in the second half.

And the week off allowed the defense to get healthy as we expect to see players tonight that we haven't seen in a while.

Ole Miss on the other hand was carved up nicer than a Halloween pumpkin last week against Alabama. Bryant-Denny Stadium was certainly no fun house for the Johnny Rebs as they were shut out for the first time since 1998.

For both teams...a win tonight could go a long way in insuring that it is not a long cold winter.

Ole Miss hopes it's an early freeze as they get back on track in the middle of the most grueling part of their schedule that still has them playing Texas A&M and LSU the next two weeks.

Meanwhile, Auburn simply wants to send the Rebel Black Bears back to their caves and into an early hibernation.

Ole Miss came into the game ranked 24th in the country. Auburn had lost 10 straight to ranked opponents dating back to October 1, 2011, when they defeated South Carolina in Columbia.

Auburn's defense played their best game of the season thus far, time and time again getting in the backfield and forcing Ole Miss quarterback Bo Wallace to make decisions under duress. Leading 6–3 late in the first quarter the Rebels appeared to be driving toward either a game-tying field goal or score for the lead.

Second-and-12 from the 21...shotgun snap to Wallace...shoots it to the left side and it's intercepted...intercepted down the far sideline...Therezie at midfield, to the 40, to the 30...TAIL LIGHTS! Touchdoooooown Auburn!!

Auburn eventually stretched the lead to 27–6 before Bo Wallace got it going with a couple of touchdown passes in the third and fourth quarters to make it 27–22. A Cody Parkey field goal made it an eight-point game. The Rebels had one more chance, and appropriately, the Tigers' defense sealed the deal. Gabe Wright and Carl Lawson sacked Bo Wallace on back-to-back plays to end all hope for the Rebels, and the final was 30–22.

Six sacks and two interceptions were the difference on a night where Ole Miss actually had more offensive yardage than Auburn and ran 24 more plays. After the game defensive tackle Gabe Wright talked about the pressure put on their defense and the need to take their game to another level, "I feel like the pressure has been put on us by our coaches that it was time we stepped up. In the LSU loss, we felt like the defensive line could have stepped up. I feel like we took a step forward tonight, and will keep improving through the course of the year."

After the LSU loss, you could really see in this game how far Malzahn and staff had developed this team. I could see something starting to change in the culture of the program. The following week it was an easy 62–3 Homecoming win over Western Carolina. Auburn moved into the top 25 for the first time since the end of the 2011 season as they prepared for a trip to College Station, Texas, for the first time...and a meeting with the seventh-ranked Aggies and Johnny Manziel. It was the game that, in my opinion, showed me this team had something special brewing.

The Texas A&M Game

I know today is the first time Auburn has ever played a football game at Kyle Field...but for some reason...I look down from high atop this beautiful stadium... and it resembles places we've all been before...places where the improbable was commonplace.

Yep...we most definitely have been down this road before...this road has taken us to Athens, Georgia...2005...where the fifth-ranked Bulldogs were sitting pretty... that was...before Brandon found Devin on fourth down...and John Vaughn found redemption.

This road has taken us to Tuscaloosa...in 2002...with a converted TE at fullback and only one running back to their name...little ol' unranked Auburn beat a top 10 Alabama team...the first of six in a row.

And twice...this road has taken us to Gainesville...in 2007 when Wes Byrum beat fourth-ranked Florida twice even though only one counted...and in 1994 when we learned even a No. 1-ranked Gator could get skinned in his own Swamp.

The visions are as vivid as if they occurred yesterday...going down a road that should end in disappointment...but somehow...someway...doesn't.

So forgive me...even though this is our first trip to Kyle Field...to me...it still has a familiar feel...like we've been here before...given little to no chance...only to prove that the improbable is more likely when you believe in yourself and when you are together.

The 2013 season will be remembered for many things...one of those is Tre Mason. What you might not remember is through the first six games of the season he had only two 100-yard rushing performances and had not really taken over the dominant back role on this offense. His season to that point was just...okay. That would change on a beautiful Saturday afternoon in south central Texas.

Both offenses were on full display. The Nick Marshall vs. Johnny Manziel angle had been played up all week. Both lived up to their billing, but it was Tre Mason who ended the day with 178 yards and made a name for himself. It was also, up to that point, the most entertaining game I had ever called.

At the end of the first quarter, it was 14–10 Texas A&M. Johnny Manziel did not hurt Auburn running the football...he just threw it up to his All-American wide receiver Mike Evans for a couple of scores. But after one, Auburn was in the game. The Tigers took the lead in the second quarter on a Nick Marshall touchdown pass to Quan Bray. However, a couple possessions later A&M retook the lead. For the third time in the first half Manziel found Evans on another big play...a 42-yard strike for a score. Auburn was down by only a touchdown at the half, 24–17.

The second half began in ho-hum fashion as both teams exchanged punts... the rest of the game would be far from ho-hum. The final combined 10 possessions would produce a total of 45 points beginning with Sammie Coates making a terrific catch and run for 43 yards to tie the game.

And the back and forth game was on when Mike Evans caught his fourth touchdown of the day to make it 31–24. A field goal on their next possession gave the Aggies their biggest lead of the day at 34–24...but also on that drive Manziel went out with an injured shoulder. Judging from the looks of it none of us in the booth thought he would come back out...he missed one possession but it would turn out to be a big one. The way this game was going, it was imperative Auburn score on their next possession. Seven plays later they did on a Marshall keeper over right end from 13 yards out.

There weren't many stops by either team, but with Auburn now down by only a field goal again they were able to stop a Texas A&M offense without Manziel and got the ball back at their own 31. Three plays later the Tigers faced a big third-and-1 to keep the drive alive. Tre Mason busted one for 58 yards and more than enough for the first down.

Two plays after that electrifying run, the fresh legs of Cameron Artis-Payne gave the Tigers their first lead since it was 17–14 as he spun off a defender to get into the end zone with just over nine minutes to play.

The frenetic pace continued. Manziel, miraculously, was back out there in obvious pain. The defending Heisman Trophy winner showed why he was one of the best players in the country as he led the Aggies on a 12-play drive to retake the lead, 41–38.

Five minutes remained. Auburn had been here before…with even less time. With their dramatic win over Mississippi State in our minds, we knew there was a chance. But this was different…this was on the road…in front of almost 90,000. The go-ahead score was 75 yards away. How many more bullets did they have left in the gun?

The drive was a thing of beauty. There was no panic. Auburn methodically moved down the field. Nick Marshall, Tre Mason, and Cameron Artis-Payne were the only ones to touch the ball on the drive…that is save for one play. It was third-and-9 from the Aggies' 39-yard line.

Four-down territory here for Auburn you would think…here's the snap… Marshall fires upfield…pass is…CAUGHT…IT'S CAUGHT, IT'S CAUGHT at the 15-yard line, down to the 12-yard line…the freshman Marcus Davis in traffic defended (but) well, 27 yards, and Marcus Davis has it down to the 12-yard line of Texas A&M!

It was the third of three third-down conversions on the drive. I have no idea how Davis caught the ball. The defender was draped all over him, and he was looking directly into the sun. It was also a perfect pass from Marshall, but the catch was simply amazing. Two plays later the Tigers had the lead for good on Tre Mason's only touchdown of the day.

The pressure turned back to the defense because Manziel still had 79 seconds to work with. Thankfully, with the score 45–41, Texas A&M had to score a touchdown. Manziel drove the Aggies to inside the Auburn 30. Just as it had two weeks earlier, Auburn's defense made the decisive final plays. Gus Malzahn had his first signature win as Auburn's head coach.

Manziel waiting for the snap from center…Auburn's gotta be prepared for anything here…here's the snap to Manziel, pressure off the edge, he's flushed out, he's runnin' around, he's in trouble…he's goin' down!!

STAN: YES!!

The Tigers are gonna win…the Tigers are gonna win! Johnny Manziel goes down in a heap back at the 44-yard line. And a flag late. It was Dee Ford comin' off the edge and with 11 seconds to go, the Auburn Tigers are gonna win against the No. 7 Texas A&M Aggies here at Kyle Field in College Station, Texas!!

STAN: There's another SEC West team that wants to have a say in who goes to Atlanta…

The game was over and Auburn was relevant again.

The greatest formation in college football…anywhere, particularly on the road, the victory formation…Marshall will take a knee, that will end it, and here in the home of the 12th Man…the Auburn Tigers have served notice to the college football world that THEY ARE BACK!

The offensive numbers in this one were staggering. Almost 170 plays were run by both teams combined. Each had over 600 yards of offense. We mentioned the day Tre Mason had, but Marshall also ran for 100 yards and was responsible for four touchdowns. In the end, it was the defense that stepped up big on a day where defensive plays were hard to come by on either side.

With this victory, we all knew this could be a championship team. The memory of 3–9 and 0–8 (SEC) in 2012 had faded away. Auburn made a statement in the first game of the second half of the season that they were a force to be reckoned with. This was the game where the turnaround was complete…no matter what happened the rest of the way.

The Arkansas Game

After an easy win over Florida Atlantic, Auburn vaulted into the top 10 at No. 8. The final month of the regular season began with back-to-back road trips. The first was to Gus Malzahn's home state and a stadium where he was 0–3 in his previous three visits—Reynolds Razorback Stadium to take on first-year head coach Bret Bielema.

It was an interesting buildup to the game with Bielema making comments suggesting he was trying to implement "normal American football" in Fayetteville. He was also one of the biggest opponents to Malzahn's up-tempo style of play. Bielema cited "safety" concerns that had already been proven false…but still it made for good fodder going into a game where Auburn was the heavy favorite.

The month of November is here…and for college football fans all across the country, it's the month that can make or break many a season. And after an undefeated October…the Auburn Tigers are hoping to make it a November to remember…but to do that they will have to navigate the twenty-first century version of Amen Corner.

Coach Pat Dye called it Amen Corner…in his time that consisted of the Tigers final three conference games…Florida, Georgia, and Auburn. If you were able to win those games…typically, an SEC title was well within your grasp.

With the creation of divisions and the addition of more teams…the original Amen Corner is no more…the new one, however, is just as challenging and carries just as much weight for the Tigers.

The first leg begins in the foothills of the Ozarks…in Northwest Arkansas… where they are learning what "normal American football" is all about under a first-year head coach.

So far, the learning curve has been steep…and there have been struggles to be sure…but a week of rest could be the cure to some of their ills.

Meanwhile, on the visitor's sideline…a prodigal son returns home again…to show the fine "Arkansans" he grew up with…his version of "normal."

So get your cameras ready…you might want to film this…and please make sure you get "all" of it…Amen Corner begins with two drastically different philosophies. And to be honest…I like our version of "normal" better than theirs…

Basically, Arkansas' philosophy was to play keep away from Auburn's offense. They did a pretty good job, running 74 plays to Auburn's 55. However, the problem…when Auburn had the ball for those 55 plays, the Hogs had a hard time stopping them. Auburn only threw the ball eight times during the game. There was no need to throw because Tre Mason and Nick Marshall were running through and around the Arkansas defense. Mason in particular was spectacular, racking up 163 yards and four touchdowns.

The Tigers led 14–3 at half, which was probably about as good as Arkansas could have hoped for, but Auburn opened the second half with a long 11-play touchdown drive and then on their next possession Marshall put it away with one of the few big plays of the game. A long touchdown pass to Sammie Coates made it 28–3, and that weird, new-fangled Auburn offense had gotten the better of Arkansas. The final was 35–17 in a game that wasn't all that close even though the stats didn't show it. The story was really Tre Mason who, in his last two conference games, had averaged 173 yards on the ground and scored five times. Next up was Tennessee on Rocky Top where the "Marshall and Mason Show" would be in full effect in a game full of big plays.

The Tennessee Game

For 35 consecutive seasons...you could mark it down...the last Saturday in September meant Auburn and Tennessee met on the gridiron...unfortunately the modern game of college football caught up and with expansion and divisions in the SEC the two teams could no longer play on an annual basis. It's doubtful that will ever change...but tonight on the second Saturday of November memories and the rivalry are rekindled with two first-year head coaches at the helm.

The modern day series began in Birmingham in 1956 despite objections from then Tennessee athletic director general Robert Neyland. Tennessee won the first meeting...Auburn won the second the next year on the way to a national title.

It has been a rather heated rivalry at times...after the game in 1973 Shug Jordan refused to shake the hand of Vol head man Bill Battle...saying Battle refused to shake his prior to the contest.

It has seen its amazing games, too...who can forget one of the few times a 26–26 tie felt like a win...in 1990 when my broadcast partner...in his first year as the starting quarterback...led a furious comeback from a 26–9 deficit in the fourth quarter.

Then of course, there was 2004...when Cadillac, Brown, Campbell, and Rosegreen roared out to a 31–3 halftime lead...and this stadium saw 100,000-plus Volunteers dwindle down to about 15,000 elated Auburn Tigers.

Today...Auburn makes another ascent up Rocky Top...looking for their sixth consecutive win in the series...and when they reach the pinnacle they can enjoy the *view…and on a crystal clear day like today…you should be able to see Athens and Tuscaloosa without any problem.*

This had the potential to be a "trap" game…Auburn cruising along with Georgia and Alabama on the horizon. It looked like it could be headed that way early in the second quarter when the Vols took a 13–6 lead after a first quarter in which Auburn sputtered out of the gate.

It was as if that touchdown was the wake-up call Auburn needed…the switch was flipped and the game was tied on a 13-yard Tre Mason touchdown run four plays later. The defense then forced a punt to set up the first really big play of the game…it wouldn't be the last…but it was the one that gave Auburn the lead for good.

Palardy back at his own 16 to punt it away…Chris Davis waits for it…high kick that will turn over…Davis takes it. No, he dropped it at the 15, but he picks it back up…20…running left 25, far sideline 30, 40, to the 50, down the far sideline 40, still on his feet got blockers in front…he's…gonna go…all the way!! Touchdown Auburn! 85 yards for No. 11, and the Tigers are on top, 19 to 13.

STAN: 41-yard return, oh, wait a minute, 85-yard return…two today! That is TWO for a hundred and 26 yards if my math is correct to put Auburn back on top. Chris Davis—senior—Birmingham, Alabama!

At half it was 34–20. The game wasn't over and Tennessee was battling hard, but it was clear they did not have the team speed needed to compete with Auburn. Still…a turnover here or there and they could really make it a game. However, that was not going to happen. On the first play of the second half, Corey Grant made sure the Volunteers never got a sniff of victory on this chilly November afternoon.

…angling toward that far sideline, taken by Grant at the 10, 15, 20, cuts it back across the field, 25, he's at the 30, speeds away 40, he's at the 50, near sideline to the 30, to the 20, 15–TAIL LIGHTS! Touchdown Auburn! 90 yards!

The return was the capper to a record-setting day as Auburn piled up a school record 312 combined return yards.

Auburn went on and won the game, 55–23. The Tigers ran for 444 yards… throwing the football only seven times for 35 yards. I'm not sure I will ever see that kind of stat again. Offensive coordinator Rhett Lashlee came out after the game as we were preparing to shoot Coach Malzahn's TV show and told me, "I promise Rod, we can throw the football." To which my response was, "I'm good with throwing it seven times if we're still scoring 55 points!" Up to that point it was the most dominating rushing performance I had ever seen.

Nick Marshall ended up with 214 rushing yards and two touchdowns. Tre Mason ran for a paltry (ha, ha) 117 yards and three scores. At the end of the day Auburn had scored the most points ever in the series. Georgia was next, and little did we know at the time the following weekend would be the first of two "incredible finishes."

Chapter 10

A Miracle and a Kick

The Georgia Game

Auburn and Georgia had met 117 times before—with the Tigers winning 55 times and the Bulldogs winning 54 times to go along with eight ties. Much more than the Iron Bowl, the Deep South's Oldest Rivalry produced its fair share of upsets. Typically, in the Iron Bowl the favorite always wins...if the underdog wins, it's usually Auburn. But in this series there have been some upsets. However, on this day, in a series that has been going on since 1892 and has seen just about everything, this game would become the stuff legends are made of as Nick Marshall (from Georgia) would lead his new team against his old team.

Everyone loves a good comeback story...we love it because we can relate to it...who hasn't been knocked off their feet...kicked to the curb...forced to find your way back...today is all about another story of rebirth.

Today we tell a story of rebirth...the rebirth of a program and a player...

Pineview, Georgia, population 532...on the northern edge of Wilcox County in South Central Georgia...nary a stop light in the entire county...hard to believe this is where the story begins...an athlete unlike any other to come out of the small Georgia county was headed to play for state university...a dream come true.

Things didn't work out...whatever it was...wrong place wrong time...doesn't matter...damage done. He had a choice...quit...or prove himself, to some degree reinvent himself. He chose the latter.

And now we stand here today…witness to a second chance seized…a young man…not as young…but more of a man…ready to put his mark on the Deep South's Oldest Rivalry.

We also stand here today…witness to the rebirth of a program…led by the man who gave someone a second chance…and that has translated into something amazing…not since Roy Hobbs has the world seen a comeback like this one.

With their own version of "Wonderboy" leading the way…the Auburn Tigers have been reborn in the image of their head coach…focused, confident…and today ready to take on the challenge of a new day.

As they say, the atmosphere was "electric" at Jordan-Hare Stadium. Georgia came to town just barely in the top 25 at 6–3 on the year. The momentum of the Tennessee win appeared to be carrying over as Auburn led by as much as 27–7 in the second quarter. A late Georgia field goal made it 27–10 at the half.

Both traded touchdowns in the third quarter, and we all thought this game was well in hand at 37–17 going into the fourth. After all, this Auburn team had become dominant in the fourth quarter. They had won the final 15 minutes in every game leading up to this one. However, Aaron Murray was not the quarterback in the previous contests. Couple that with the fact that Auburn went into "prevent" mode…probably too early…and things got interesting in a hurry.

A nine-play touchdown drive ended with a Murray touchdown pass to wide receiver Rantavious Wooten. Auburn went three-and-out on its next possession. Georgia and Murray proceeded to score on a five-play drive that ended on another touchdown pass…this time to tight end Arthur Lynch. With six minutes to play, the Bulldogs had cut the score to six at 37–31. For what could have been for the first time that season, Auburn went three-and-out a second consecutive time—giving Murray and Georgia just under five minutes to take it downfield for what would be the go-ahead score.

Georgia had to drive from the Auburn 45 after Steven Clark only managed a 31-yard punt. We could see it coming…for the first time since the LSU game Auburn seemed to be discombobulated. "Totally out of whack," as I described it on the radio. Georgia had the momentum, and Aaron Murray will go down as one of the greatest quarterbacks to ever come through Athens. This was it… the end of the magical run. Murray drove them down to the 5-yard line when he decided to keep it himself on fourth-and-goal.

Whatever your religion is, say a prayer, too…fourth-and-goal at the 5 for the Bulldogs with 1:56 to go…Auburn needs one more stop. Here's Murray, looking, in trouble, running, he is…I think he's stopped sh- NO they called a touchdown! They called it a touchdown! Murray running straight ahead, and they called it a touchdown!

The play was under review. We saw several different angles in the booth. Looking through Orange and Blue glasses it sure looked as if he never made it. In fact, to this day, I don't think he did. However, the replay official ruled there was not indisputable evidence he did not make it in, so with the extra point the Bulldogs had taken a 38–37 lead.

Not since the LSU first half had we seen this Auburn team. They appeared to be totally out of whack on both the offensive and defensive sides of the football. In what seemed like the blink of an eye, the chance at playing for a Western Division title seemed to have slipped away. After all, Auburn only had a 1:49 to drive down the field and score. The one solace…it didn't have to be a touchdown. A field goal would suffice.

Auburn got the ball at their own 22-yard line. The offense churned out one first down to get it out to the 35. Then things got really dire. A loss of two yards on a completion to Sammie Coates—54 seconds to go. An incomplete pass to Trovon Reed—48 seconds to go. Marshall sacked for a loss of six yards—36 seconds to go and it was fourth-and-18. Auburn used a timeout, then Georgia used one, as well.

Then it was time…Gus Malzahn said later that Nick Marshall had two options on the fourth-down play. The first option was to Sammie Coates on a "dig" route across the middle about 25-30 yards downfield. Remember, Auburn only needed to get into field goal range. The other option was Ricardo Louis on the post. Looking back at the film, Coates was wide open and Louis was not—Marshall chose option No. 2.

Alright here we go, fourth-and-18 for the Tigers…here's your ball game…Nick Marshall stands in, steps up…gonna throw downfield, just a home run ball and it is tipped up—and Louis caught it on the deflection, Louis is gonna score! Louis is gonna score! Louis is gonna score! Touchdown Auburn! Touchdown Auburn! A miracle at Jordan-Hare, a miracle at Jordan-Hare, 73 yards…and the Tigers, with 25 seconds to go, lead 43 to 38. Holy Cow!

STAN: my goodness…oh my goodness…wow…can you believe it?

To quote one of my idols in the business, Larry Munson…I think I just broke my chair.

The amazing catch by Ricardo Louis set up what would be an even more amazing finish two weeks later.

Offensive coordinator Rhett Lashlee tells the story that Gus Malzahn (who had his back to the play) turned to him during the play and said something along the lines of, "Please tell me he threw to Sammie." Lashlee's response, "No coach, he threw the post." This was as the ball was in the air. I've seen hundreds of games inside Jordan-Hare Stadium. I was there for the 1989 Alabama game… the first Iron Bowl ever played on campus at Auburn. That was the loudest I'd ever heard that stadium from start to finish. But in that one singular moment, as Louis pulled the ball in as if he was playing with a yo-yo, I believe Jordan-Hare Stadium was the loudest it had ever been. The ground shook.

In the booth, there was spontaneous combustion. However, the game was not over, Aaron Murray would get one more chance. Unlike Auburn on the drive before, Georgia had to find a way to get it into the end zone with only 25 seconds remaining. Two plays and two Georgia timeouts later, the Bulldogs and Aaron Murray had moved it 50 yards to within striking distance at the Auburn 25. *"Please God, no,"* is what I thought. We had just witnessed one of the most miraculous and spectacular catches in college football history. Auburn had snatched victory from the jaws of defeat—surely there was no way it could be snatched right back. The Bulldogs had one more shot with only eight seconds left.

And here's your ballgame…here's Murray…steps up, in trouble, he's on the run, hit as he throws, INCOMPLETE!! Tigers WIN! Tigers win! Dee Ford knocked the ball loose, and Auburn has done it in unbelievable, remarkable, unlikely, incredible fashion! 43–38…War Eagle, everybody!!

After the game Ricardo Louis told the media, "The only thing that was going through my mind was try to make a play. At first I was going to try and jump for it, but they took the angle, so I just kept my eyes on the ball over my shoulder and watched the ball all the way in. It was unbelievable, I thought I was going to drop it for real. Coach Craig always tells us to always look the ball all the way in. Coach Craig is the reason I caught that ball. He says stay focused on the ball all the time, and I did."

And what about Sammie Coates on that play, "I turned around when I came out of my cut, I saw that no one was around me and then I saw the ball in the air. I didn't know what to think. I just hoped someone came down with the ball, and Ricardo did."

Well one thing's for sure I thought there was no way the Iron Bowl two weeks later could top this! Ha...right!

The Alabama Game

It was probably a good thing Auburn had two weeks to prepare for Alabama. Not sure how you would come down off that emotional high in time to have a chance to defeat the No. 1 team in the country.

For me, I spent the better part of two weeks rehashing the Georgia finish. I must have done 20 different radio shows the week following the game. Even as we got closer to kickoff of the Iron Bowl, the finish to the Georgia game was a significant topic of conversation. The finish captured national attention. I was honored to be a part of a feature on *GameDay*...on "What is a miracle?" Again, how could anything top that game?

Finally, game week rolled around. Alabama was ranked No. 1, Auburn was No. 4. The last time both teams were ranked in the top five when they met was November 27, 1971. Auburn was fifth and Alabama was third. That game turned out to be no contest as the Crimson Tide easily won, 31–7. But that game didn't have the same aura to it. The winner of this game, 42 years later, won the Western Division title and earned a shot at an SEC Championship the following week. The winner of this game had a shot at a national title. In a state where college football is religion to some, this Iron Bowl was of biblical proportion.

I'm not sure I can stand here today and describe the meaning of this game...I can't say anything that hasn't already been said...never have the stakes been so high as they are on this bright sunny November afternoon.

You walk around this campus and you see if you feel it...the passion...a quiet confidence...the fever pitch among Auburn fans...we all know it...this one is big.

Rarely have these two teams played when both were at their peak...that's not the case today.

You have the obvious SEC and national ramifications...but there's more...like we've had to do so many times...written off for dead...given no chance...Auburn will rise once more.

Despite 10 wins and quite possibly a trip to New Orleans in hand...Auburn is still considered David against Goliath today as it steps onto the field of battle...I'm not sure why...after all, over the last three decades this is a team they have disposed of more than the other way around.

But we will do...what we've always done...sometimes with more success than others...never yield.

I think back to the image of Patrick Fain Dye in 1982...with tears in his eyes as the Tigers ended the streak...he looked out over Legion Field realizing a new day had dawned for this program.

Which brings us to the here and now...31 years later...a new day again.

The time for talk has passed...I can't do it justice...the time to play for a championship is now. It is time for the mother of all Iron Bowls.

The buildup was unprecedented. It was so massive that by Wednesday of game week, you were ready to crawl in a hole and tell someone to come get you when it was time for kickoff. Everyone was just ready for the game to start. The atmosphere at the stadium was more than electric. I'm not sure there were any words to describe excitement, tension, emotion...whatever you want to call it... that permeated Jordan-Hare.

Alabama won the toss and elected to receive. A little surprising but an early indication that Nick Saban thought he would have to score often in this one. The Crimson Tide came up empty as the usually sure-footed Cade Foster missed a 44-yard field goal. Two possessions later, Auburn scored first on the first big play of the game for Nick Marshall as he ran one in off the zone read from 45 yards out.

Alabama tied it up at seven two possessions later and proceeded to score a total of 21 unanswered points to take a 21–7 lead with 3:48 to go in the first half. On their next possession I thought Auburn really made a statement of what they planned to do the rest of the game. Starting from their own 19-yard line, Tre Mason ran the ball on five consecutive plays. Gains of eight, 40, 10, 6, and one yard moved the ball deep into Alabama territory at the 16-yard line. Alabama's vaunted defense was gasping for air and had no answer for Nick Marshall, who ran it down to the 1. Appropriately, Tre Mason finished off the drive with a one-yard touchdown score. Auburn was basically saying, "We know, you know what we are going to do…but we are going to do it anyway because we don't think you can stop us." And they didn't. It was 21–14 going to half with Auburn set to get the ball first coming out of the locker room.

On that first third-quarter possession it was Tre Mason and Nick Marshall carrying the load running the football. Nine plays into the first possession of the second half, Auburn was deep in Alabama territory again at the 13 when they went to an old standby play call that had worked against Mississippi State earlier in the season—a pass to C.J. Uzomah in the corner of the end zone.

Auburn had now scored 14 unanswered points to tie the game at 21–21, and we were off and running in the second half…this was about to get real good.

The remainder of the third quarter was scoreless with Alabama ending it by driving the football all the way down to the Auburn 11-yard line. A 14-play drive ended with yet another missed Cade Foster field goal…this one from just 33 yards out. However, Auburn couldn't do anything on its next possession that ended with one of the best punts you will ever see by Steven Clark. The tall drink of water from Kansas City, Missouri, pinned Alabama at their own 1-yard line.

All appeared well in Tiger land, until Nick Saban decided to go the non-conservative route with his back to his own end zone. A.J. McCarron took the shotgun snap and heaved it down the near sideline where one of the best receivers ever to play the game, Amari Cooper, hauled it in and took it the distance…99 yards.

Boom! Just like that the stadium was silenced. The longest pass play in Iron Bowl history had given Alabama the momentum and the lead 28–21 with 10:28 to go in the game. On the next possession, Auburn was the one that gambled as Gus Malzahn decided to go for it on fourth-and-1 from his own 35-yard line. To be honest, we were a little surprised in the booth. Adrian Hubbard dropped Nick Marshall for no gain. The ball went to Alabama on downs, and the Crimson Tide had a short field to work with. Up by a touchdown, another here at this stage of the game could have been deadly for Auburn.

Like Auburn had done in the second quarter, Alabama tried the same approach on this possession, turning to their star running back, T.J. Yeldon, who got the ball four consecutive times. His first carry went for 13 yards and a first down, but the next three left Alabama one-yard short of a first down. Knowing a touchdown could seal the deal, Saban went for it.

5:52, 5:51, clock continues to run...Auburn...trying to hold on fourth-and-inches...McCarron under center...he may just sneak it...down to two, down to one, he's gonna turn and hand it to Yeldon...AND THEY STOPPED HIM! Auburn stopped him!! On fourth down they stopped 'em!! 5:34 to go! And Auburn has stopped Alabama on fourth-and-inches!!

In what was quite possibly the biggest play of the season, the Auburn defense reignited the crowd, but unfortunately it didn't bleed over to the offense, which went three-and-out and had to punt it away. It marked four consecutive drives where Auburn came up empty. It appeared the Alabama defense had figured some things out with the Auburn offense by focusing on the running attack and basically daring the Tigers to throw.

Only 4:26 seconds remained when Alabama started their next drive on the Auburn 25-yard line. Clark had to punt from his own end zone and could only get it out to the 44, and Christion Jones took it back 19 yards. Now it was a situation where a field goal would basically end Auburn's hopes. The Tigers' defense, at the very least, actually held Alabama in check and forcing a field goal attempt of 44 yards. Cade Foster, who had missed two already, was given the opportunity to be the guy who closed out Auburn in their own stadium and send his team on to the SEC Championship Game as the No. 1 team in the country.

Well, here's Cade Foster...he could redeem himself big-time right here...this could all but seal it for Alabama...a 44-yard field goal attempt for Foster...let's see if Auburn goes after the kick...here they come...and it's BLOCKED! Auburn's blocked it! Picked out of the air by Ryan Smith!

There was still a breath of life left for the Tigers, but they would have to move the ball 80 yards in just 2:30 minutes against an Alabama defense that had stopped them on four straight possessions.

An unsportsmanlike penalty on Alabama helped on the first play, moving the ball out to the 35-yard line. Remember that drive we talked about in the second quarter? The one where Auburn dared Alabama to stop Tre Mason and they couldn't? Well, Gus Malzahn used the same blueprint with the game on the line. Mason for seven yards up the middle. Mason for one yard up the middle. Timeout called by Alabama with 1:43 to go. Mason up the middle for five yards. Mason over left guard for five yards. Mason three yards up the middle. Mason five yards up the middle.

The no-huddle fast pace had taken its toll on Alabama. There wasn't one single "big" run, but they kept hammering at the heart of the Crimson Tide defense. But now, time was definitely a factor. With just under one minute to go, Auburn was at the Alabama 39-yard line. Looking back, I truly think because Auburn had hammered the middle time and time again, the Crimson Tide defense became solely focused on stopping Tre Mason…that's why this play worked to perfection.

47 seconds to go in the football game…clock starts again, Auburn on the move again…first-and-10…this time it'll be Marshall on the keeper, and then he throws. Oh he's got Coates at the 20! To the 10, to the 5. Touchdown Auburn! Touchdown Auburn! Razzle dazzle from Gus Malzahn! 32 seconds to go…Cyrus Jones bit on the Marshall run and then Nick dumped it over the top! Holy cow, Sammie Coates scores!

At that point with so little time remaining, my thoughts went directly to overtime. I really didn't think Alabama would have time to get into field goal range. I also thought, *"Wow, this might be the greatest Iron Bowl ever played."* It was…and it was about to get even better.

Alabama got the ball at their 29-yard line with 25 seconds remaining. An 11-yard pass, followed by two T.J. Yeldon draw play runs totaling 33 yards and the clock said 0:00. I thought the game was headed to overtime. Stan White thought the game was heading to overtime. Alabama head coach Nick Saban did not. So the officials reviewed the last play. We watched the replay over and over and finally had to admit…yes…there should be one second put back on the clock.

What would Saban do? With all the struggles his kicker had already been through, surely he would lob one up for his All-American wide receiver Amari Cooper and take a chance at the hail mary—but no. Out comes Adam Griffith, who had attempted only a few field goals all year. He had the stronger leg of the two kickers. My mind had visions of Van Tiffin. In 1985, Auburn was ranked seventh in the country and faced an unranked Alabama team at Legion Field in Birmingham. Tiffin nailed a 52-yard field goal as time expired to break Auburn's heart, 25–23. Surely, history wouldn't repeat itself here.

Chris Davis is gonna drop back into the end zone in single safety...well I guess if this thing comes up short he can field it, and run it out...alright, here we go...56 yarder...it's got, no, does not have the leg...and Chris Davis takes it in the back of the end zone...he'll run it out to the 10, 15, 20, 25-30, 35-40, 45-50, 45—THERE GOES DAVIS!

STAN: *Oh my gosh!*

Davis is gonna run it all the way back! Auburn's gonna win the football game! Auburn's gonna win the football game! He ran the missed field goal back—he ran it back 109 yards! They're not gonna keep 'em off the field tonight! Holy cow! Oh my god! Auburn wins! Auburn has won the Iron Bowl! Auburn has won the Iron Bowl in the most unbelievable fashion you will ever see! I cannot believe it! 34–28! And we thought a miracle at Jordan-Hare was amazing! Oh my Lord in heaven! Chris Davis just ran it 109 yards and Auburn is goin' to the Championship Game!

STAN: *You got plans next week, my friend? 'Cause I'll be in Atlanta! I will be in Atlanta!*

Never...in all my days...have I seen anything like THAT!

STAN: *Do you say this is the most epic Iron Bowl in history? Oh my goodness— they're storming the field. They can't get 'em off, they can't be denied!*

Hats off to the replay booth, because without that overturn Chris Davis would never have had that opportunity, and as hard as they're gonna try, they're not keeping this bunch of Auburn fans off this field tonight.

STAN: *I can't believe it...a hundred yards...one hundred yards...can YOU believe it? I still can't believe it! Oh my goodness! My friend, do you have plans for next weekend?*

I'll tell ya what...(laughs) last one out, turn the lights off, lock the gates, and we'll see you in Atlanta!

STAN: *Hey...I know some folks I'd like to join at Toomer's Corner! What do you think? You think there'll be anybody over there tonight? 'Cause we're gonna celebrate, my friend!*

Into the wee hours of the mornin'! War Eagle, everybody! 34–28...the Tigers are SEC Western Division champions!

The radio booth was total bedlam. I had Stan White, my spotter Beau Benton, statistician Gene Dulaney, producer Jessi Duval hanging all over me. It's amazing I was able to say anything or get my headset ripped from my head. I remember high-fiving Stan and Paul Ellen (who is on the row behind us). It's fuzzy, but Stan and I might have kissed (ha, ha). All professional decorum went out the window. It was a moment that will never be topped. There I said it… as long as I live…I don't think I will ever experience a moment like that. What made it so special (outside of the play itself) were the people I got to share it with. All of us call Auburn our alma mater…all of us have great passion for Auburn athletics. To be with that group of guys (and Jessi) when Chris Davis crossed that goal line is something I wouldn't trade for anything in the world.

Normally, once we are done it takes me about five minutes to pack up my stuff and head on down to the field to get ready to tape our TV show ("Auburn Football Review"). We shoot the show on the field. On that night, there was no way I was getting to the field for a very long time. The waves of fans continued to pour onto the field 10-15 minutes after the game ended. It was truly a "sea of Orange and Blue." I heard stories the following weeks of fans injuring themselves

An image which will go down in Auburn history. From the end zone, the moment we all knew Chris Davis was going to score. But my favorite is the picture of the celebration in the radio booth which took place moments later. From L to R: statistician Gene Dulaney, me, spotter Beau Benton, and Stan White.

trying to leap the hedges that line both sides of the stadium. But every story also included a quote along the lines of, "It was well worth it."

For me, all I could do at that point was sit and watch. Most everyone else in the booth left in search of spouses, family members, and friends. Jessi, Paul, Ben Leard (former Auburn quarterback who at that time assisted on our postgame show), and our engineer Patrick Tisdale couldn't leave as we had another hour or so of coverage left on the radio. By the way, Patrick is another unsung hero in all of this. When Stan screamed, "Oh my god!" Patrick immediately turned off his headset mic. Otherwise, you wouldn't have been able to hear a thing I said. But Stan's "Oh my god!" is still my favorite part of the call. If you listen, you can still hear my good friend saying it over and over (to go along with some giddy laughter).

Since I couldn't go anywhere, I just sat there. I guess the adrenaline at one point just rushed out of my body and the realization of what I had just witnessed and been a part of hit me. All I could do was put my face in the palms of my hands. The emotion ran over me like a freight train, and for about a minute I literally cried like a baby. No one knew it at the time. Everyone around me was doing their job, while I was gathering myself.

It was about this time the play appeared up on the big video board in the South end zone. It was part of the highlight montage the video crew put together and play after every win. Now remember, like the Ricardo Louis catch two weeks earlier, I had no idea what I had said during the runback. They got to the play and the crowd (thousands) on the field and the thousands in the stands came to almost complete silence. The call echoed through Jordan-Hare Stadium…with every five-yard increment covered by Davis, the noise rose higher and higher. Until you couldn't hear the call after Stan screamed. I heard about half of the call, but I still didn't know what I had said from start to finish. The reaction of the fans was good enough for me—dang it, here come the tears again. It was at that moment that I realized what this play meant, not only to Auburn, but to college football. It was a "the band is on the field" moment, but bigger. There were no national ramifications to the crazy play in the Cal-Stanford game back in 1982. It was only the fourth time a college game had ended in that fashion. It was later dubbed "the greatest finish in college football history" by many media outlets.

Once I got myself together it was time to head down to the field (or in this case the locker room) to get ready for the TV show. As you would expect, it took longer than usual to get the show done. Instead of filming on the field (where there were still thousands of fans) we had to shoot the show in the locker room. So we had to wait until it cleared out, which can take a while. By this time the adrenaline had kicked back in and was like that little cartoon dog that hops around his much bigger dog friend/boss with so much energy while his bigger partner is the calm and collected one. I couldn't wait to talk with Coach Malzahn. Normally very focused and reserved, surely Malzahn would be different after this game. This was going to be the best "Auburn Football Review" ever! So here he comes around the corner. Takes his visor off and sits down next to me. I was giddy, "Coach, wow! What a finish! Congratulations! What was it like to be on the field?!" He responded in typical Gus Malzahn fashion with measured emotion, "Yep, that was something else. Unbelievable. We ready to knock this (TV Show) out?" That was it. The same as he was after the Washington State game to start the season. It baffled me at first, but I realized later, he had already moved onto the SEC Championship Game. He was already thinking about Missouri and the challenges of getting his team up and ready for one of the nation's best defenses. That's what makes him great. The singular focus on the next game, not the last one or the one two weeks down the road...just the next game.

The Aftermath of the Alabama Game

I finally got to hear my call of the Chris Davis run on my way home after the game. I was listening to ESPN Radio (I believe) and they played it not once but multiple times. I flipped around to Fox Sports...same thing. Everywhere you turned the radio that call was being played. In the process, my head was getting bigger and bigger. I had convinced myself that when I got home, my family, who usually didn't have the same passion for collegiate athletics and in particular what I did for a living, would finally see the light and appreciate how important my job was (I'm being facetious) to the entire world!

By the time I arrived home, it was after nine o'clock. I walked in through our garage where I was greeted with two garbage bags that needed to be taken out, and everyone was in their respective rooms getting ready for bed. I guess I expected a greeting of, "Oh father we are so proud of you! You are the greatest announcer in the world!" Instead I got nothing, which is why my wife and children are the best in the world. Keeping me grounded and in check at all times. I don't recall what time I actually got to bed that night, but it was late. Not surprising...I saw and heard the play call several times on ESPN. I guess maybe this is a big deal, but for me, it was time to move to the next broadcast. A trip to Ames, Iowa, with men's basketball awaited me the next day.

The next 48 hours would be the most whirlwind of my career. The morning after the Iron Bowl, was not too terribly unusual. I took the family out to breakfast as we always try to do on Sunday mornings. The only difference was that I tried to find every newspaper I could just so I could save them. I didn't watch much TV on this day, as I had to pack and get ready for my first ever trip to Ames. We (the basketball traveling party) departed from the Auburn airport late in the afternoon Sunday. I had received a few interview requests via email or text, but nothing out of the ordinary. By the time I landed in Ames, my email box had blown up with requests. I really didn't know how I would fulfill all the requests, so I had to pick and choose who I talked to. I did a couple Sunday night from the hotel room in Ames, but the bulk of the requests were for Monday. I do have one favorite request because of how I received it.

While I was sound asleep in Ames, Iowa, back in Auburn the phone rang about 2:00 in the morning. My wife was sound asleep. My then 10-year-old son had a stomach bug so he had climbed into bed with mom so she could keep an eye on him if he got sicker during the middle of the night. My wife is a heavy sleeper. She finally answered the phone. On the other end of the line chirped a perky voice, "Hello, I'm [don't remember the name] and I'm a producer with the *Fox and Friends* television show. Is Rod Bramblett available? We'd love to have him on to talk about his Iron Bowl call." My wife was still half asleep, and failed to remember I wasn't there so she said, "Yes, just a minute" and she proceeds to hand the phone to my son, "It's for you." To which he responds, "Who is it?" It was at this point, my wife realized her mistake and told the very happy young lady, "Oh, he's not here." I can only imagine what the Fox producer thought. Here was Mr. Bramblett's wife and the person in bed with her was not her husband. We get a huge chuckle out of this story. I love to tell it when I'm speaking to various groups.

Oh by the way, Fox finally got in touch with me, and I was on with them early Monday morning. That was just the first. Before the day was done I was interviewed by Tim Brando, Dan Patrick, the *New York Times*, ABC News, the *Wall Street Journal*, not to mention numerous radio stations (both local and national). It was nonstop from 6:30 am until 3:30 pm when I finally got a chance to shower and get ready for Auburn's game against Iowa State that Monday night. The following week the interviews continued. I had at least two a day for a couple weeks following the game. It was an honor to do every single one of them. I was representing my alma mater and the entire broadcast team. This was good for Auburn. The Tigers had become the national darlings of the 2013 football season.

And then you had the fans' reactions. My favorite was from a young lady who lived in Denver. I believe she was originally from North Carolina. She wasn't even an Auburn fan, but YouTube video of her lip syncing the call went viral. We connected on Twitter and have stayed in contact since. She said it took her about 10 times to get it right, but when she did, she nailed it. Then there were all the fan reaction videos that popped up online. You saw fans in their homes, at the game itself, with huge groups going nuts at the end of the game. I received emails from fans telling me where they were and when they heard the final call. The video with the call on the official Auburn Tigers athletic YouTube page (as of this writing) has almost 3.5 million views. When you factor in all of the videos with the call that are out there it probably tops 10 million. Amazing!

Over the course of the next month, there were a couple professional moments I will never forget…great indications of how that play and I guess that call impacted everyone, even those in our business. The following week we had longtime CBS announcer Verne Lundquist on our pregame show in Atlanta at the SEC Championship Game. Verne has been a great friend to our broadcasts. He also presented to me my first National Sportscasters and Sportswriters Alabama Broadcaster of the Year Award.

The previous week, when asked where that Iron Bowl ranked all-time in his career in terms of events he had called, he said second behind the Jack Nicklaus winning his final green jacket at the Masters in 1986. Of course, that's one of Verne's most famous calls as he screamed "Yes sir!" when Nicklaus' putt dropped on 16.

He was on with us for about five minutes. We talked about the game that day and, of course, the previous week. We were about to let him go when he stopped and said he had one more thing to say. It was then when he put his arm around me and brought up the fact he had said that Iron Bowl ranked second in his career. But he followed that by saying after listening to our call of the play over and over, coupled with the fan reaction, he thought that Iron Bowl was No. 1. He then looked at me and something along the lines of, "Rod, we will forever be linked to that moment." I told him after we went off the air how much that meant to me. I've always loved the way he called the big events. Never the center of attention...the game, the player, the moment always takes center stage when Verne is calling it.

The other professional moment I will never forget occurred at the Rose Bowl in Pasadena at the BCS National Championship game against Florida State. We were already on the air, but I was no longer needed in the booth so I had gone down in the stands to check on my family. As I returned to the press box (by the way, that press box is one of the worst I've ever seen for such a major event) I walked down the narrow hallway and headed back to our booth. There in the hallway was our own Quentin Riggins talking to Kirk Herbstreit, who, of course, was doing the color on the national television broadcast. I nodded as I walked past, but Quentin grabbed me by the arm and said Kirk wanted to talk to me... that he had been waiting on me to return. Kirk shook my hand and said he just wanted to tell me how much that call meant to him personally. That it was one of the best he'd ever heard and it was what made college athletics so special. He didn't have to say word one to me, but he did. I was greatly appreciative. Again, another example of how that play and call resonated across the country.

In one second my career was changed forever. All I was doing was my job. The ripple effect of that call will be felt for years. While Auburn ultimately had two more very big games to play, the ending of the Iron Bowl would be a topic of discussion everywhere I went, including the Georgia Dome in Atlanta where the Tigers had to somehow put behind them the emotion of the Alabama win.

The SEC Championship Game

It's hard to describe...it's hard to capture...it's hard to define...faith...that's why we are here today...because a team and its fans simply had faith.

Faith is defined as a confident belief in the truth, value, or trustworthiness of a person, idea, or thing.

If you didn't have or believe in faith before...you certainly have it now after witnessing Auburn's last two games.

Faith...in a throw...a deflection...a catch...a score.

Faith...in a kick...a return...a touchdown...

Limitless faith all wrapped up into just one second.

The one second one side wanted so badly…the faith that one second could make all the difference in the world…and it did…only not like anyone could have ever imagined.

Faith is also defined as belief that does not rest on logical proof.

What we have seen recently certainly defies any sort of proof that is founded in logic. But we all saw it…we all lived it…we screamed…we hugged…we cried… tears of joy and disbelief…but at the end of the day we all somehow…someway had faith.

So dig down deep…I know you have it…60 more minutes of faith is all we need…here in Atlanta and later in Indianapolis…man oh man can you imagine…I hear Pasadena is beautiful in January.

Going into this game, I had the same feeling that I had in 2010. Although the game against Alabama was emotionally draining beyond belief, I still had the feeling there wasn't much Missouri could do to stop Auburn for four quarters. However, we quickly found out that might not be the case. Missouri had been underappreciated throughout the season, but here they were at 11–1 overall and ranked fifth in the nation with one of the league's best defenses and one of the best defensive players in Michael Sam. The Black and Gold Tigers led the league in sacks. They were also outstanding on offense where they were second in the league in scoring and third in total offense.

The game was back and forth with seven lead changes. The final lead change came with 3:21 to go in the third quarter when Corey Grant ran it in from two yards out. The extra point gave Auburn a 38–34 advantage. You could start to see Missouri's defense faltering. The pace and physicality with which Auburn was playing was starting to wear on them. The fresh legs of Cameron Artis-Payne got them next on a 15-yard touchdown run to make it 45–34. I will give Missouri credit—they would not go down as James Franklin scored from five yards on their next possession to make it 45–42 Auburn. All of this happened in the last three minutes of the third quarter!

But the fourth quarter belonged to Auburn. Tre Mason continued to pound Missouri over and over again. At the end of the day, Mason had set an SEC Championship Game record with 304 rushing yards and four touchdowns. His final score from 13 yards out put it away with 4:22 to go in the game.

On top of Mason, Auburn's defense had more sacks (three) than Missouri's and the SEC's Defensive Player of the Year Michael Sam only had three tackles in the entire game. Auburn won the game 59–42. Now all we could do was sit back and wait. We knew at the very least a Sugar Bowl trip awaited us, but we needed Michigan State to beat Ohio State that night in the Big 10 Championship to get the big prize of going to the Rose Bowl.

My wife and daughter were on the trip and attended the game. After my duties were done, we walked down to the field to get some pictures. We stayed at the football team hotel at the airport the night before the game. It just so happened that basketball was playing the next day at Philips Arena (next to the Georgia Dome) so we packed our things and moved over to the basketball team hotel in downtown. On our way to the hotel, we stopped and got some fast food. The Michigan State–Ohio State game was already underway at Lucas Oil Stadium in Indianapolis.

Before we got to our new hotel, Michigan State was up 17–0 early in the second quarter. However, by the time we got to the new hotel, Ohio State had tied it up early in the third quarter. Then by the time we got to our room Braxton Miller had engineered another scoring drive. The Buckeyes had scored 24 unanswered points to take a touchdown lead with 5:56 to go in the third.

My daughter and I watched intently, while my wife read the magazines she had brought with her. My daughter wanted Michigan State to win so she could go to Hollywood. I wanted them to win for more obvious reasons. My wife didn't care either way. A Sparty field goal made it 24–20 Buckeyes going to the fourth quarter. With just under 12 minutes to play Michigan State scored again to make it 27–24. Now the Spartans had scored 10 unanswered to retake the lead. The next 10 minutes of that game was excruciating. Finally, Jeremy Langford ripped off a 26-yard touchdown run that gave a final score of Michigan State 34, Ohio State 24. It was done...as the clock hit zero I was jumping up and down like a kid. I took a flying leap and tackled my daughter, screaming, "We're going to California, we're going to California!" Meanwhile, my lovely bride was wondering how in the world we were going to pay for it all. But she was excited too, in her own way.

It had happened again...something I never expected to happen again... and yet it did...just three years removed from a trip to Arizona, Auburn was in another BCS National Championship Game. The magic carpet ride was going to continue on to LaLa land.

The BCS National Championship Game, Again

The preparations for this trip were different than the one to Glendale in 2010 (technically 2011). For one, for me personally, my entire family was going. In 2010, it was just my wife. So I had to put out a second and third mortgage to get four of us out to Los Angeles. They were all very excited to be going to California. My 14-year-old daughter was all about the Hollywood lifestyle…my 9-year-old son…well, he was just thrilled to be getting on a plane. Although I will say this, he does want to be a movie director someday. We arrived a few days before the actual game. I had responsibilities to shoot some video features for Auburn about the team's time in California.

One of the biggest differences in this trip as compared to the first one… was how much time we spent on the road. Unlike Arizona, things were much more spread out for this game in Pasadena. The team actually stayed in Newport Beach, which is (on a good day) an hour drive south of the Rose Bowl. Newport was the headquarters for both teams and the media. We stayed with the team. I think I spent more time in our rental going to and from locations than I did at the various venues we visited or worked.

Although it cost an arm and a leg to get the family out there, I was so happy they were able to go. I would have regretted it greatly if they did not get to experience that week. We were able to take the kids to Disneyland on a couple of days, but it was our ventures into Los Angeles where they had the most fun. We spent one day hitting the typical tourist spots like Sunset Boulevard, the Santa Monica Pier, and riding around trying to find various filming locations of my daughter's favorite TV show, *Bones*. My son's favorite stop was a car museum where they had the Batmobile from one of the movies along with other superhero-related vehicles. Hopefully, the kids will appreciate the trip and memories we created. I'm not saying it was a once-in-a-lifetime thing, but certainly not all kids get to visit L.A.

We did have a star sighting one night while out to eat. My friend and fellow broadcaster Mike Kelly (who is the play-by-play voice for the University of Missouri) recommended a spot to us in Newport Beach called Javier's. It was a rather upscale Mexican restaurant…very unlike the mom-and-pop-style places we are accustomed to in Auburn. The food was excellent. We were enjoying our dinner when my daughter spotted someone that looked like the actor David Spade. Sure enough, just a few tables over there he was with a large group of friends. To show you the generational differences, my daughter asked, "Isn't that the guy that was in the *Grown Ups* movie?" I had no idea who she was talking about until I turned around and saw him. My wife and I were thinking, *"Hey that's the guy who used to be on* Saturday Night Live *and starred in* Tommy Boy*!"* I tried to get the kids to go over and ask for an autograph and they wouldn't do it…ha, they asked me to do the same thing and I wouldn't, either. I tried to explain to them that celebrities like David (we are on a first name basis) and I wanted our privacy when going out. Of course, the eyes rolled from both of the kids…and deservedly so.

One of my favorite memories was (like the 2010 BCS trip) Tiger Talk the night before the game. In Glendale, we truly didn't have enough room for the fans. Thousands crammed into a very tight area, creating a rock star atmosphere for the radio crew. In Los Angeles, we felt like movie stars. Chris Davis, who was one of our account executives at the Auburn IMG Sports Network, and Debbie Shaw with the Auburn Alumni Association put together a setup that I'm not sure will ever be topped. Our special BCS "Tiger Talk" was at L.A. Live, which is a place adjacent to the Nokia Theater and across the street from the Staples Center.

It was a red carpet type event with again thousands of Auburn fans in attendance. From the stage the Nokia was to our right and straight out was Staples. Behind us was a huge video board…the event had all the glitz of Hollywood. Our guest lineup included Tiger…Auburn's golden eagle that flies at all the football games. Auburn alum and actor Michael O'Neill was with us in Arizona, but here we were in his backyard making it easy for him to join us. Former Auburn greats Reggie Slack, Steve Wallace, Ed Graham, Lee Ziemba, and Ryan Pugh were also

This was taken from behind our stage at the special BCS National Championship Game "Tiger Talk" at L.A. Live across the street from the Staples Center. Like the one in 2010, thousands of fans turned out to celebrate the season.

One of my all-time favorite pictures from my broadcasting career. This was taken after our show at L.A. Live and features our broadcasting family at the time. On the air and behind the scenes, these are the folks who make it work. From L to R: Andy Burcham, Patrick Tisdale (engineer), Steve Witten (sales), Chris Davis (sales), Jon Cole (GM), me, Ben Leard, Jessi Duval (producer), Stan White, Quentin Riggins, and Beau Benton. (Not pictured: Gene Dulaney)

on the show. All of these guys were terrific, each providing a different perspective. Ziemba and Pugh were on the 2010 national championship team and here only a few years later they were watching their school back in the biggest game of them all. We visited with athletic director Jay Jacobs and Mack Crawford, two of the men instrumental in bringing Gus Malzahn back to Auburn. It was a two-hour Auburn love-fest more than 2,000 miles from home. The event didn't have the same frenetic atmosphere as our Arizona "Tiger Talk," but it did have more of a "big event" feel to it. By the time the show ended darkness had fallen on L.A., and we were bathed in the neon lights of an area that had hosted countless movie premieres and award ceremonies. It was an amazing night I will never forget.

After the show, it was time for dinner. Most of us made the drive over to Santa Monica, where we had a terrific dinner at a place called One Pico. While the food was fine, the atmosphere was even better. It was directly on the beach. You could walk out with the Pacific Ocean as the backdrop and view the Santa Monica Pier lit up in the distance. It was a great finish to what had been a memorable week with my primary family and my secondary family…the broadcast crew. It was time now to head back to the hotel and get ready for game day inside the Rose Bowl.

Game Day in Pasadena

The game kicked off at 5:30 local time so our airtime was 2:30, which meant we needed to be at the stadium around 12:30. Taking into consideration the typical L.A. traffic, we left the team hotel at 11:00 am. My traveling partner was Andy

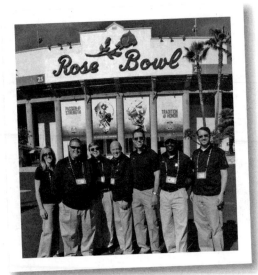

Outside the Rose Bowl before Auburn's title game versus Florida State. From L to R: Jessi Duval, Andy Burcham, me, Stan White, Quentin Riggins, and Patrick Tisdale.

Burcham. My family came with the team caravan a little later. The weather was beautiful…sunny and low 70s for a high during the day. Our route took us back to the Anaheim Angels baseball stadium then along the northern edge of Los Angeles and into Pasadena. The Rose Bowl resides in one of the most unique settings I've ever seen. It's in a natural valley right in the middle of a residential area. You are driving through neighborhoods as you wind your way down to the stadium. When we arrived the place was already crawling with fans. Unlike Glendale, Arizona, where there were many more Auburn fans in attendance than Oregon faithful, this time the numbers were a little more even, although Auburn still had a slight edge.

We stood in a long line to go through security. When we finally got in it was up to the booth. I had already received warning from our engineer, Patrick Tisdale, that the booth was small…that was an understatement. It was ridiculously small. Normally, there is room for at least four of us, if not five, across the front row. Normally, we can stand or sit comfortably, but at the Rose Bowl there was really only room for three…and that was a stretch. Stan, Jessi (our producer), and I had to stand behind our spotter Beau Benton and statistician Gene Dulaney. What was even worse…this was a renovated booth! Just an absolutely terrible setup, but on the plus side the view of the San Gabriel mountain range was spectacular!

After dropping off our bags in the radio booth, we headed down to the field and outside the Rose Bowl for some pictures of the crew. These are the moments

I try to soak in and cherish. The crew walking around and absorbing the history of this stadium was something I will always remember. On the field, walking up the ramp out of the stadium and getting photos with the famed Rose Bowl sign as the backdrop will always be one of the highlights of my career. It's one of the bucket list venues as a broadcaster you just dream of.

We headed back to the booth where it was show time. After a pregame show that included Mike Tirico, legendary Florida State announcer Gene Deckerhoff, and others, it was time to kick off the final BCS National Championship Game. There was pressure on both sides. Florida State had been criticized about having a weaker schedule than most because they played in the ACC. Auburn had the pressure of the SEC on their shoulders as the conference had won seven consecutive national titles.

> *Thirty days have passed since last we spoke...as we bid you farewell from the Georgia Dome we had no idea from where we would talk again...remember?... remember as we all went our separate ways to find a TV...Go Sparty, please win... and they did...remember what that moment was like...I know I will never forget it.*
>
> *Remember when...we all celebrated in Arizona...in Auburn...and all across the globe...go ahead and admit it...you had to wonder if it would ever happen again.*
>
> *It's okay...after all...it had been 53 years since Auburn had won it all. It was okay to think that was a once in a lifetime moment.*
>
> *But then something happened...a new day dawned...and with it...a program reborn...in the image of its leader...proving the doubters wrong at every turn...a team pushed itself to the edge of greatness.*
>
> *The final step will be taken tonight in the shadows of the San Gabriel Mountains...in a stadium that's the granddaddy of them all.*
>
> *So let's lock arms...it's what we do...it's how we got here...and we will leave the same way...together...with a crystal ball in hand...national champions again.*

I was unusually nervous before this game. I'm not sure why. Maybe it was the attention from the Georgia and Alabama calls. Maybe it was just because of the magnitude of the game, the venue, etc. But I didn't think I was particularly sharp in the first half of the game.

Florida State scored first on a field goal, and then Auburn scored 21 unanswered and really was dominating the Seminoles. The biggest play made it

My family at the Rose Bowl and BCS National Championship game. For a group that doesn't particularly get into sports, this was a special moment. Getting them to a game is a big deal.

21–3 early in the second quarter and it was to an unlikely candidate. Melvin Ray caught one down the middle for 50 yards and a touchdown. The momentum was fully in Auburn's court.

Auburn was clearly on the verge of blowing out the No. 1 team in the nation when Jimbo Fisher rolled the dice on their next possession. Facing a three-and-out he faked a punt on fourth down and converted. Our spotter, Beau Benton, immediately saw the fake coming because of the personnel on the field, but for some reason Auburn was caught off guard. Credit Florida State—they executed the play and went on to make it 21–10. That play was the first of a couple of critical breakdowns or simply tough breaks that allowed Florida State to eventually win the game.

Florida State scored the only points in the third quarter on a 41-yard field goal, but it was just part of what turned into a 24–3 run for the Seminoles. The last of which was an unlikely play as FSU's Kermit Whitfield ran a kickoff back 100 yards for a score. Unlikely because Auburn placekicker Cody Parkey all season had been kicking touchback after touchback, for whatever reason on this night, Parkey had trouble getting the ball to the end zone. Whitfield took advantage of a block on Jonathon Mincy, and he was gone. The play made it 27–24 with only 4:31 to go.

How would Auburn now respond to a play much like the ones they had used to beat Georgia and Alabama—a big play out of the blue when Florida State needed it most. Eight plays later we found out Auburn was far from done.

Ninety seconds remaining in the football game...Marshall waits for the snap, takes it, hands it off to Mason...bounces it out right side, he's at the 30, he's at the 20, he's at the 15...to the 10, to the 5, TOUCHDOWWWWN AUBURN!! A minute-19 to go, 37 yards! He broke a tackle at the 20, and he never stopped after that!

Auburn had left the Seminoles and their Heisman Trophy winner 1:11 to work with. Florida State started on its own 20-yard line, and on the second play of the drive Jameis Winston dumped off a pass for Rashad Greene, who then proceeded to run another 49 yards all the way to the Auburn 23-yard line. A weakness for this Auburn team had been its pass defense...once again that reared its ugly head. Now Winston was in striking distance with 56 seconds to play. With 17 seconds to go looking at first-and-goal from the 2-yard line, it was Florida State with the heartbreaking play for Auburn. Jameis Winston found his All-American receiver, Kelvin Benjamin, in the back of the end zone with only 13 seconds to go, and the Seminoles had a 34–31 lead.

After the kickoff, Auburn's final play was a trick play that was actually one or two blocks away from working, but the football gods didn't answer Auburn's prayers that night. The remarkable season came to an end. Any end of the season is emotional for me in most cases, particularly if it had been a special season like this one.

I don't remember much about the postgame show. After a loss you are just ready to get it done and get off the air. I do remember riding back to the team hotel in Newport Beach. It was just Andy Burcham and me. For one thing, it took forever to get out of the neighborhood surrounding the Rose Bowl. It must have taken us 90 minutes to get back to the team hotel. On the way back we begrudgingly listened to some of the national talking heads. Already they were talking about next year and the 2014 football season. It was different than 2010. After Auburn's win over Oregon, we all knew the Tigers would take a step back... probably a significant one. After all, you don't lose Cam Newton, Nick Fairley, and a senior class 30 strong and not go back a little bit. But the aftermath of this game was different. Auburn would return a core group on both sides of the football and they were being mentioned as one of the teams that could be a part of the first ever College Football Playoff.

Following the 2013 season, I was honored to be named Alabama Sportscaster of the Year and Sports Illustrated *named me National Broadcaster of the Year. Here I receive my state award from Marv Albert at the NSSA (National Sportscasters and Sportswriters Association) Awards banquet in Salisbury, North Carolina.*

Andy and I found comfort in the prospect of being right back in the thick of things the following year. As we know, that didn't happen. The 2014 season was not as spectacular as 2013…but then again how could it be? That team did not mature or develop like 2013. That's the nature of the game, particularly when you are in the SEC. Auburn still brought a formidable offense to the table…one of the best in the country. But it wasn't enough to withstand a finish that included road games in Athens and Tuscaloosa.

However, we'll always have 2013, and we still have the future that is very bright. Chris Davis, Ricardo Louis, Nick Marshall, and C.J. Uzomah are the names that we will never forget. As a broadcaster you hope to get that one big call in that one big game. Thanks to the 2013 Auburn football Tigers, this broadcaster got two career-making calls and another chance to describe a national championship game. As a broadcaster, so much of what defines your career is simple luck of the draw. There are plenty of us who will never come close to calling a championship of any sort. There are thousands of play-by-play guys who are better than me. I realize how lucky I am to have one of the top jobs in college athletics. I also realize I might never come close to getting moments like the ones during the 2013 Auburn football season, and I'm okay with that. I have been fortunate enough to climb the mountain on multiple occasions—the right person at the right time describing the moments that will be replayed for generations to come. And for that I am grateful beyond words.

Chapter 11

Random Items from the Junk Drawer

There are so many things I haven't covered and I don't know quite where to fit them, so I close out with a chapter contining a little bit of everything. Just interesting stuff…and a little bit of rambling, I'm sure.

Auburn Basketball

I wish I had more material to dedicate an entire chapter to Auburn basketball. But to be honest, the Tigers have struggled in my time as the Voice of the Tigers. When I started, Cliff Ellis was going into what would turn out to be his final year as head coach. Coach Ellis had raised Auburn's level of competition to an all-time high for a couple of years. In 1998–99, the Tigers went 29–4 and made it to the Sweet Sixteen before losing to Ohio State. The next year Auburn made it to the second round of the NCAA Tournament. In the year (2002–03) before I took over for Jim Fyffe, Marquis Daniels lead an Auburn team—that some didn't feel deserved to be in the tournament—to the Sweet Sixteen, losing to eventual national champion Syracuse. I was in Athens, Georgia, that night calling a thrilling 13-inning baseball win over the Bulldogs. Little did we know that it would be Jim Fyffe's final broadcast and that it would be Auburn's last NCAA Tournament appearance…at least through the 2014–15 season.

Jeff Lebo was hired after Coach Ellis was let go two years later. Coach Lebo was, and still is, an outstanding X's and O's coach. He was terrific to work with.

A halftime interview at an Auburn basketball game in Las Vegas in 2003. From L to R: Paul Ellen, Charles Barkley, and me.

His first couple of recruiting classes were very good, but he never could sustain the momentum. The highlight of his tenure and up until Auburn's SEC Tournament run (which I will talk about shortly) in 2015 the highlight of my Auburn basketball career came in 2008–09. Facing another disappointing season, the Tigers went 11–3 down the stretch. They won seven of their last eight conference games to finish second in the West. Unfortunately, it wasn't quite enough to earn an NCAA bid, but they did get a No. 1 seed in the NIT. After easily taking care of UT Martin and Tulsa, Auburn lost a heartbreaker at home to Baylor, coming up one game shy of the semifinals and a trip to Madison Square Garden.

The old Beard-Eaves Memorial Coliseum was electric for those three games. Every game sold out. Basketball was fun again. That season was also the year Auburn decided to build a new arena. The coliseum held a lot of history and tradition, but it was outdated. Auburn needed something new and…yes… smaller. I really thought that season would be the stepping stone to great things. After taking a big step back the following season (15–17 record), Jeff Lebo was let go as Auburn's head coach, giving way to Tony Barbee, who came to the Plains from Texas-El Paso.

Barbee was a John Calipari protégé. He played for him at UMass, and he coached with him at Memphis before going to UTEP as the head coach. When he was hired there was a great deal of buzz—Barbee was one of the up-and-comers. A young coach hired to revitalize the program; however, one thing got in his way...player attrition. In his four years at Auburn, multiple players his staff signed transferred out. Whether it was trouble they got themselves into or just not seeing eye-to-eye with the head coach's plan or style, Barbee never did hold onto an entire recruiting class. Anyone who knows will tell you...you can't build a program that way.

For both Barbee and Lebo, something else never worked out in their favor and that was generating the excitement in the fan base. Auburn needs a great promoter as well as a great head coach. Auburn is a small town that loves its football, but it has also shown that it will support its basketball program with similar passion. Unlike football, you need to draw the bulk of your basketball crowds from local people within a 40-45 mile radius. To do that you need to get out and promote the program if you are the head coach. Couple that with not enough wins and it's not a very good recipe. There wasn't much equity earned when things continued down a rough road.

In March 2014, Auburn finished the regular season 14–15 and 6–12 in the SEC. The future did not appear very bright. The SEC Tournament was held at the Georgia Dome that season. Auburn opened as the No. 12 seed against No. 13 seed South Carolina, a team they had already beaten twice that year. The game was never close. Auburn lost, 74–56. It appeared to be just a matter of time before Auburn made the call to dismiss Coach Barbee.

It took me about 30–45 minutes to get packed up after the game and head back to the team hotel. As I walked in the lobby, I saw many of the assistant coaches, players, and their families all huddled up talking. I made sure to remain positive, shaking hands and patting backs and saying something along the lines of, "We'll get 'em next year." I headed up to the room to get my wife (who had made the trip with me). We walked down the block to get a late night appetizer. I left my phone in the room by accident, but that was okay. It was nice to get away and just enjoy each other's company. We weren't gone but maybe 30 minutes when we returned to the hotel. Now the lobby was empty, and we went up to the room. My phone might as well have been on fire...I had numerous text message and emails saying Barbee had already been let go.

It didn't take athletics director Jay Jacobs long to pull the trigger. In the span of about 60 minutes after the game, Jacobs had dismissed Barbee. Turns out when I walked through the lobby earlier the news had already been delivered. I felt terrible because I was talking about next season, thanking everyone for their hard work, how much I enjoyed being around the coaches and players, blah, blah, blah. I had no idea what had taken place. I'm sure I've not forgotten my phone since!

That was on March 12, 2014. Six days later, after making a quick move on the previous head coach, Jay Jacobs and Auburn hired a man that is destined to turn the Auburn basketball program around and bring it to new heights. On March 18, 2014, Bruce Pearl was introduced as Auburn's 20th head basketball coach.

Bruce Pearl

On that same day, I had a chance to interview Coach Pearl for the first time. Immediately, I knew it was going to be fun working with this guy. He is genuine… what you see on the basketball court is exactly how he is all the time. Energetic, competitive, compassionate, and he understands what I do. He understands the big picture unlike any head coach I've ever been around.

He inherited a very difficult situation. Only seven scholarship players were coming back and that included freshman Jack Purchase, who had been recruited by the previous staff. So Coach Pearl and mainly his staff (Pearl could not actively recruit until his show-cause ended in August) had to somehow piece together their first class. They did it with a couple of one-and-done guys who had one year of eligibility left. Antoine Mason (the nation's leading returning scorer) came over from Niagara, and K.C. Ross-Miller transferred from New Mexico State. They then added Junior College Player of the Year Cinmeon Bowers, who had originally signed with Florida State. T.J. Lang was another freshman they signed. Lang's father is Duke legend Antonio Lang. Later in the season they got 7'2" Trayvon Reed, who had originally signed with Maryland. Marshall transfer point guard Kareem Canty was another arrival, but he had to sit out a year. Many considered him the best player on the team…at least of all the new guys.

But Bruce Pearl's first team at Auburn centered around KT Harrell. A senior from Montgomery, Alabama, Harrell had come to Auburn after signing with Virginia. He was a Barbee signee who didn't need much convincing to stay around for his last year. All involved were glad he did. He went on to lead the conference in scoring and quickly became one of my all-time favorite players to cover. He is an outstanding young man with a big heart and a deadly three-point shot.

226

It was remarkable what Coach Pearl and his staff did with his first team. They were undersized in every game they played. On top of the challenges on the court, there was adversity off the court. Antoine Mason missed a good chunk of the non-conference schedule with an ankle injury—so one of Auburn's main scoring threats (on a team that didn't have many) was gone. Then later in the conference season, Antoine's dad, Anthony, had a massive heart attack, which he never fully recovered from. He passed away on February 25, 2015. The former New York Knick great was the heart and soul of Antoine. During his battle after the heart attack, Antoine did everything he could to be with his father in New York and yet still be with his team at Auburn. It was tough on Antoine, but he somehow battled through it. He did miss the last three games of the regular season.

The Tigers were 12–19 overall and just 4–14 entering the SEC Tournament. Auburn was the 13th seed and taking on No. 12 Mississippi State. Expectations were not high going in, but I should have known not to undersell Coach Pearl and this team. To tell you how rough times had been for Auburn basketball since I started doing the play-by-play, in 11 previous SEC Tournaments my record calling Auburn basketball games was just 2–11. I was hoping just to get a win and stay an extra day in Nashville where the tournament was being held.

Auburn trailed by two at half against the Bulldogs but outscored them by eight in the second. An unlikely hero emerged as Alex Thompson scored a career-high 16 points off the bench. The Tigers had won their first SEC Tournament game since 2009, 74–68 over Mississippi State. It felt like an NCAA Tournament win to be honest...at least what I would imagine an NCAA Tournament win would feel like. I was so happy for the kids...no matter what they did the rest of the week they had already made a statement.

Up next for Auburn was Texas A&M...a team fighting for their NCAA Tournament lives. Oh, things did not look good for the Tigers. A sluggish first half led to a 33–23 deficit. However, Auburn roared out in the second half. By the time we hit the first media timeout with 15:41 to play, the Tigers had gone on a 16–1 run and led by five. They would never trail again. It was as good a half of basketball as we had seen all year. After scoring 19 against Mississippi State, KT Harrell poured in 25 against the Aggies. Auburn had ended Texas A&M's hopes for the NCAA Tournament and for the first time since 2000 they had won two games in the SEC Tournament. It was on to the quarterfinals to take on an

LSU team that was a lock for the NCAA Tournament and was sitting there fully rested, having received a double bye as the fourth seed.

By this time, Auburn and Bruce Pearl were the darlings of the tournament. The Pearl magic was in full effect. Everyone across the country was talking about Auburn's unlikely, incredible run. Like the first two games, Auburn trailed at the half to LSU and like the first two games, Auburn saved their best for last. Trailing by eight with just 2:45 to go it seemed to be slipping away. I'll admit I thought that the run was on its way to ending, but KT Harrell wasn't ready to call it a day. He hit a three-pointer to cut it to five. His next five points came from the free-throw line. It was 62–61 LSU with 57 seconds remaining. A couple of free throws by LSU made it 64–61 with just 8 seconds left. Auburn needed someone to step up and hit the big shot. With every person inside Bridgestone Arena knowing that someone was Harrell, including LSU, he still made the shot of a lifetime:

LSU's gonna make it tough, but Auburn's gonna try and get something here… in bounds to Canada, to Bowers, now to KT…catch, shoot, three—GOT IT! HE GOT IT! Auburn ties the ballgame! KT Harrell buries three! Oh, the senior from Montgomery, Alabama, sends this one to overtime, 64-all!

The game went to overtime where LSU never really recovered. Auburn took the lead and never let go winning, 73–70. The postgame was almost as if Auburn had won the title. Sure, they were getting Kentucky the next day in the semifinals. Sure, they had little-to-no chance to win that game, but it didn't matter. Auburn and Bruce Pearl had served notice to everyone in attendance, watching, and listening that this was just a glimpse of the future.

With former head coach Sonny Smith by my side, we interviewed assistant coach Chuck Person after every game. For those who don't know, Sonny recruited and coached Chuck back in Auburn basketball's heyday in the 1980s. To watch the two of them interact during that unbelievable run will be one of those broadcasting memories I will always cherish. The love for each other was open and unabashed. Coach Smith even told him on the air, "I don't mind telling you, I love you Chuck!" This from the same 78-year-old man who also said when we were joking about not having brought enough clothes for the week, "The heck with not enough clothes, I'm not sure I brought enough pills!"

The last time Auburn had won three games in the SEC Tournament, Chuck Person was an All-American playing for Coach Smith in 1985. That's when

Auburn became the first team to win four games in four days to win the SEC Tournament. It all had come full circle that week in Nashville.

I have seen some amazing things in my time as a broadcaster—things that you live for if you are a play-by-play man. I've watched a backup catcher hit a walk-off home run in his hometown to set up his team for a trip to the College World Series. I've seen a football team win its first national championship in over 50 years. I've witnessed a man run a missed field goal 109 yards for a touchdown to beat his archrival in the most unlikely fashion. All of those things are amazing to be sure, but the four days spent in Nashville, Tennessee, with a basketball team that finished 15–20 will rank right up there with all of those above mentioned moments.

Oh, the future is bright! I've never called an NCAA Tournament game. I have a sneaky suspicion that's about to change.

Top 10 Favorite Games

This is not a list of favorite moments…but my all-time favorite games. Games from start to finish that still stand out in my mind.

1. 2013 Alabama "Kick Six" Game—This is an obvious choice as No. 1. It is quite possibly the greatest college football game ever played, and it changed my career forever.
2. 2010 BCS National Championship Game—This one could easily (and maybe should) be No. 1. It was a great game on college football's biggest stage. It ended over a half-century drought as the Tigers claimed the national title.
3. 1997 David Ross Home Run vs. Florida State in the Tallahassee Regional— You're probably surprised at how high I have this one. Certainly the moment is what is most important but it was an incredible game, as well. Auburn trailed 7–1 going to the seventh and somehow found a way, capped off by the Tallahassee native's improbable walk-off winner.
4. 2010 Iron Bowl—The "Camback" wasn't necessarily the best game for four quarters, but Auburn had to win the game, showing the perseverance of a champion. Erasing a 24-point deficit in Tuscaloosa with everything on the line was simply remarkable.

5. 2013 Georgia Game—This one would have been higher, but because of the fact it probably shouldn't have come down to a Ricardo Louis catch off the deflection pushes it down the list just a little bit. Credit Georgia for erasing the big fourth quarter deficit, but credit Auburn more for again finding a way to win and setting up for more dramatics two weeks later.

6. 2015 SEC Basketball Tournament—LSU Game—For a team that finished 15–20 on the season, I bet you never expected to see a game from that year on my top 10 list. Auburn did something only one other Auburn team had done…win three games at the SEC Tournament. It all was capped off by the incredible game vs LSU. It wasn't a buzzer beater, but darn close to it as KT Harrell hit a three to send the game to overtime. Auburn went on to win it. Notice had been served.

7. 2010 Auburn Baseball Regional vs. Clemson—I've never seen Plainsman Park frothing at the mouth like it was on that night when Creede Simpson kept the Tigers alive in their own Regional. The moment was great, but the atmosphere for nine innings was unlike anything I had seen at that ballpark up to that point.

8. 2007 Auburn at Florida—After starting the year at just 2–2, the Tigers went to Gainesville and went toe-to-toe against Urban Myers' squad. Wes Byrum's *two* field goals (only one counted) beat Florida. The image of Byrum's, a Florida native, Gator chomp is one of those images Auburn fans will never forget.

9. 2010 Georgia Game—With all the so-called controversy surrounding Cam Newton that week, how Auburn came out and played that game was inspiring. Falling behind early but roaring back to pull away late. They clinched the SEC West and kept themselves on track for the national title.

10. 2004 LSU Game—It was without a doubt one of the most physical games I've ever seen. It was also the only game that was really all that close for what would turn into one of Auburn's best teams ever to walk on the field. Courtney Taylor's touchdown catch late and John Vaughn's second chance PAT to give Auburn the win catapulted that team to an undefeated season.

There are plenty more to choose from and it's probably not fair to narrow the list to just 10, but that's my best effort at picking my favorite games.

Best Places to Eat in the SEC

Out of respect to my longtime baseball broadcast partner Andy Burcham, I won't go into a lot of detail on this list. He and I have long wanted to do a book on the best places to eat on the road in the SEC and beyond, so here's a quick list of our favorite haunts in the league.

Tuscaloosa, Alabama—Dreamland Bar-B-Que (Original Location)
Known for its ribs, this is a must stop on our way into Tuscaloosa each year for basketball.

Fayetteville, Arkansas—Herman's Ribhouse
Without a doubt my favorite place in all of the SEC. It looks like a rundown house from the outside, but on the inside you can find some of the best ribs around. My favorite is the filet and the hashbrowns with the special Herman's sauce. Saltine crackers and salsa start you off. To finish things the waitress brings you a huge bowl of Tootsie Pops and Blow Pops.

Gainesville, Florida—Ballyhoo Grill
Great seafood place with a little bit of everything. Good wings, too. We've been known to hit it twice over the course of a baseball weekend.

Athens, Georgia—DePalma's Italian Cafe
To be honest, we don't have a go-to restaurant in Athens. I picked DePalma's mainly because my wife enjoys it. Located on the main drag (Broad Street), it's an Italian spot with a great menu and even better cozy atmosphere.

Lexington, Kentucky—Billy's Bar-B-Q
This could fall under the category of obituary: we never went to Billy's for the barbeque, although I'm sure it was delicious. Instead, it's where Andy Burcham introduced me to the breaded pork tenderloin sandwich. A delicacy in the Midwest, this simple sandwich is hard to find in the SEC. Unfortunately, Billy's closed in early 2016; Andy is still in a deep depression. Maybe he can find a good place in Columbia to get his all-time favorite sandwich.

Baton Rouge, Louisiana—Multiple spots.
As you can imagine, Baton Rouge is a good eating town. For football we'll either hit Walk On's Bistreaux and Bar (basically a sports bar) or Mike Anderson's Seafood. When traveling for basketball more times than not we go to Brusilla

Seafood Restaurant, another seafood place. In baseball, it's all of the above, plus a new place we discovered on our 2015 trip and that's Sammy's Grill. Seafood, cajun, po-boys, and crawfish are the specialties. A really good place that I can't believe took us so long to discover.

Starkville, Mississippi (or more specifically Columbus, Mississippi)—Old Hickory Steakhouse

There are some very good places to eat in Starkville proper, but 25 minutes away in Columbus is Old Hickory, one of the best hole-in-the-wall steakhouses you'll find. The prices are incredibly affordable and the ribeye with unlimited supply of garlic bread is amazing. It's my third favorite place to go in the league.

Columbia, Missouri—Booches Billiard Hall

Yep that's right…a billiard hall. It really is a fully operational billiard hall with some of the best burgers you will ever eat. In downtown Columbia, seating is limited, but worth the wait. The burgers are small, so I typically order two or three. They come to you on wax paper, and if you're going…it's cash only. Really, really neat place.

Oxford, Mississippi—Oxford Grillehouse

As anyone who has known me for any length of time can tell you, I love mozzarella sticks. I've become an aficionado of them, and while the Oxford Grillehouse has terrific steaks, their friend cheese is the best in the league and a must-get when we are in Oxford. They are located right on the historic square in downtown. The square in Oxford has many good eating options, but the Grillehouse is a go-to place whenever we are in town.

Columbia, South Carolina—Blue Marlin

Blue Marlin is borderline upscale (which is a bit unusual for our crew), but you can still dress casual. The main menu is great (with the filet being my favorite). I don't care for shrimp and grits, but theirs is supposed to be among the best. Dessert is why I go, it's one of the few places you can find a Crème Brûlée cheesecake—best dessert in the SEC.

Knoxville, Tennessee—Ye Olde Steakhouse

If it weren't for Herman's in Fayetteville, this would be No. 1 on the list. Located just south of Knoxville, Ye Olde has been the go-to place from the first time I went there with baseball. They have the best prime rib around. Also, if you go there and you are an Auburn fan, look around on the walls and find the letter written to Ye Olde Steakhouse by former Auburn football coaching legend Ralph "Shug" Jordan. Most don't know to look for it, but it's on the back wall of the main dining room. The letter simply compliments the restaurant on its food and service.

College Station, Texas—Hullabaloo Diner / Koppe Bridge Bar & Grill

One of the new additions to the SEC brings not only great tradition, but also great dining. For breakfast, it's Hullabaloo Diner. It's an actual diner brought in from New York City. They have the biggest pancakes I've ever seen. I would highly recommend going later in the morning because you won't need lunch after stopping at this place that is located on the outskirts south of College Station. For lunch or dinner, we always hit Koppe Bridge Bar & Grill. I've had the burger and the steak sandwich…both of which are among the best I've ever put in my mouth. The menu is large, and I'm looking forward to trying other items as we continue our visits to Texas A&M.

Nashville, Tennessee—Too many to name

Nashville is one of my if not *the* favorite city we visit. It's impossible to pick one place in a city that has every kind of food imaginable. Some of the best places are located in the West End area of Nashville where Vanderbilt University is located. Downtown Nashville is a little touristy, but you can find a spot or two if you look closely.

I left many off the list, but I encourage you to try any of these if you happen to be in one of these towns. It's a large part of what I enjoy most about the job. The towns and their restaurants are definitely one of the larger perks…and typically I can expense it!

A Saturday to Remember

The date was Saturday, January 30, 2010. We were in the middle of the conference basketball schedule and preparing for the start of what would turn out to be a baseball season that would end with a Western Division title. The day started with a 25th anniversary recognition of the 1985 SEC Basketball Tournament champions and ended with the preseason Auburn baseball banquet.

There they were…some of my college heroes of the hardwood…all lined up on the floor of Beard Eaves Memorial Coliseum. Players from the 1980s had returned to be honored…in particular the 1985 team. It was just one part of a Saturday that I'll never forget.

The day started with a lunch for the '80s players. It was beyond amazing to meet some of the same players that I cheered for while a student at Auburn from 1984–89. Watching Frank Ford, Gerald White, Chris Morris, and Chuck Person tell old stories, most of them true, was great fun.

Looking around at all these former players, it really made me realize how good Auburn basketball was in the '80s. Never before and never since has Auburn basketball had such a sustained high level of success. Five straight NCAA Tournament appearances, three seasons finishing in the top 25, an Elite Eight, and a Sweet Sixteen finish all marked a time when the Tigers were one of the powers in the SEC.

The man leading that group, of course, was Sonny Smith. He came to Auburn in 1979 and almost left in 1985. Frustrated with the lack of wins and lack of other areas of support, Coach Smith announced his resignation before the season ended. He decided to stay after his 1985 team became the first to win four games in four days at the SEC Tournament. That same team then made a run to the Sweet Sixteen and the rest, shall we say, is history. Coach Smith went on to take Auburn to three more NCAA Tournaments. His teams were exciting to watch and tough to beat at home. I should know, since I was in the stands for almost every home basketball game.

One of my more prized possessions: a picture of me with Dale Murphy at the 2010 Auburn baseball banquet. I grew up a huge Atlanta Braves fan and "Murph" was my all-time favorite.

Needless to say, just getting to be around those players and Coach Smith at the lunch and then watch them get honored at halftime of the Auburn-Alabama game was very special to me personally…by the way, Auburn also beat its archrival for the fourth straight time.

But wait, the day wasn't over! That night I would get to meet Dale Murphy, another of my childhood idols. The former Atlanta Braves All-Star and National League MVP was the speaker at the Auburn Diamond Club's banquet for the upcoming baseball season. The event itself was outstanding, but the true highlight for yours truly was hearing and meeting old No. 3.

My grandfather and I would spend countless hours from March through September listening and watching as our favorite team, the Atlanta Braves, slopped their way through the baseball season. Dale Murphy was always one of our favorites. He certainly was not an overnight sensation. Experiments at catcher and first base were miserable failures, but as he alluded to Saturday night, Bobby Cox never gave up on him. He put "Murph" in the outfield. Two consecutive National League MVP's, five consecutive Gold Gloves, and seven All-Star games later, Murphy was an Atlanta legend. He was my all-time favorite Brave.

Saturday, he talked about doing things the right way. He lambasted those guys who used steroids. He talked to the kids about how hard work and effort were all you needed…not artificial enhancements. My one regret from the evening was that my grandfather wasn't still alive to meet him, too.

After the banquet, I introduced myself. I did the whole fan thing. I got the picture. I got the autograph. But the topper was this…Dale (we're on a first name basis) told me he listened to the basketball broadcast earlier that day and enjoyed it. After I picked myself off the floor, I thanked him.

What a day! There's no way to put a price on getting to meet the guys you cheered for when you were just a fan. It's something I rarely get to do.

Memories of the World's Most Famous Beach

I have found that this business…my job…can bring back childhood memories. Many times those memories are stirred by the travel that comes with the job. Most places you travel in this business are just places…some more intriguing than others, but in the end they are just another city or venue that you can add to your list of "places I've been." In this case, it was the off week between the

Georgia and Alabama football games in November 2009, and I had to travel with Auburn basketball to Daytona Beach, Florida.

It was a three-game round-robin event as part of the Glenn Wilkes Classic. It didn't really occur to me until I was sitting under the gazebo of the team hotel enjoying some doughnuts and watching the waves of the Atlantic Ocean crash on shore that Daytona Beach was a large part of my summers as a youth.

When I think of the beach now it's typically the Alabama or Florida gulf coast…that's where we go as a family now. However, when I was young Daytona was the main destination for summertime fun. This is where my mother came when she was a little girl growing up in North Carolina and Georgia. This is where her parents, my grandparents, would bring us in the summer. This is where I went on my senior trip in high school. This is where a large group of my friends came when we were in college. This is where a lot of memories were made.

I haven't been back since 1988, and on the final day of the basketball tournament the sights and sounds of the past all of a sudden came rushing over me. I remembered my grandparents talking about making what would be my first trip to Daytona. They talked of how you could actually take your car on the beach, drive it and even park it right there. We did just that. I'll never forget popping the back of the Buick Grand Estate Station Wagon, spreading out the beach towels, and playing all day in the sand.

I remembered walking the Boardwalk, playing the arcade games, and most important buying a box of saltwater taffy. "You know, you can watch them make it right there looking through the window," my grandmother said. That was a big deal to a 10-year-old. A few years later, I remembered my grandparents allowing me to buy a certain T-shirt with a certain blonde television star on the front. That was also a very big deal. I could go back home with my head held high knowing I had Farrah Fawcett in a bathing suit plastered on my chest.

After high school graduation, five of us drove my old, faded yellow Pontiac Gran Torino (you know, the one like Starsky and Hutch drove—theirs was red, though) eight hours to the World's Most Famous Beach where we stayed a week at the Mainsail Beach Inn (amazingly it's still there—I checked). Five more nerdy guys you would never find…we certainly would not have made for a very interesting reality show. Nevertheless, we had a great time.

We pulled something similar in college when a bunch of us (guys and girls) decided to camp out at a local state park for a long weekend. It was just that…a long weekend considering we had to fight off raccoons stealing our food and mosquitoes just about carried us away. Still we had fun even though we all chalked it up in the "never will we do that again" category.

So there I sat, looking out my hotel window at what once was the old Boardwalk. They built this fancy new resort right on top of a historic location that was the heart of Daytona Beach. Much has changed about this place in 21 years. The only thing left is the old band shell at one end of the hotel, the old clock tower that now serves as a landmark directly behind the resort, and a few of the old shops and arcades that I remembered as a child.

I was left a little bit sad as I'm left missing many things about the past. I missed the old boardwalk. I missed my friends (both high school and college) with whom I've fallen out of touch. But most of all I missed my family, who didn't get to come on the trip because of work and school. I would love for my daughter and son to have experienced a little bit of the World's Most Famous Beach. I would love to bore them with my stories of what Daddy did when he was a kid.

Last But Not Least…Thanks For Listening

It's easy as a broadcaster to get wrapped up in the preparation each week. Working on spotting boards and score sheets, studying game notes, talking to coaches and players, and doing various talk shows can certainly take your focus away from what's most important…and that's the listening audience. I've been reminded of this on several occasions throughout the 25 years I've been doing this.

My first year as the lead announcer, we traveled to Nashville for a basketball game against Vanderbilt. About an hour before tip, I was walking back to press row when a gentleman tapped me on the shoulder and asked if he could introduce me to someone. I could tell this was an Auburn fan since he was decked out in his Orange and Blue. I walked back to the first row where they had set up some special spots for those fans in wheelchairs. There sat a young man who was about 9 or 10 years old. It was the man's son, and he was blind.

I kneeled down as he reached out for my hand. His dad said he always listened to the games on the Internet. I said hello, and his voice quivered with excitement. You could tell he immediately recognized the voice. With a grin from ear to ear he explained how he someday wanted to be an announcer, too. I gotta tell you…I was a little choked up. It was the first time in my career that I had an encounter like this. It was also the first time that I realized how we (as a broadcast crew) have the ability to touch others who've taken some tough shots in life.

Since that time, I've heard from several fans who are vision impaired. It reminds me that we are the eyes for many fans throughout the Auburn family. Our job is to paint a picture for those who can't be there. Hopefully, we accomplish that.

Another example from several years back…I received a letter from a fan that was living life in the Easterling Correctional Facility in Clio, Alabama. The letter was two-fold—to request an autographed picture and to just let me know how much he appreciated what all of us did at the network. It got me to thinking: here's someone who's obviously made some mistakes in life, telling me how much our radio broadcasts mean to him.

Judging from the letter, he made peace with himself for what he did (which was not mentioned) and he was just trying to serve his time and make the most of his remaining sentence. Again, without cable television, just a radio, we were his only way to follow his favorite team. The two-page letter gave me a new appreciation of the wide array of Auburn fans out there. Some listen by choice… some listen by necessity…either way, they love their Tigers.

Hopefully, I'm able to do this job for the rest of my professional life. There have been times where I've taken for granted what I do. Thank you to those who "jerked a knot in my neck" to make me realize this could all go away very quickly. I can't imagine doing anything else. I'm not sure I *could* do anything else.

Are there 25 more years of this in front of me? There's no way to know. At some point in time I need to think about my family and the things they've had to sacrifice because Rod/Daddy had to work all those weekends. But in the meantime, thanks to all who listen and who care so deeply about their Auburn Tigers. Most important, thanks to those who have helped shape my career and my life.

Until next time, War Eagle…and so long everybody!

Epilogue

t was December 10, 2014. Outside, a light snow was falling on Times Square in New York City. Inside, there I was, on stage in one of the main event rooms of the Marriott Marquis Times Square. I was sitting between Bill Roth, who is now the Voice of the UCLA Bruins, but at that time was the Voice of the Virginia Tech Hokies. A job he had held for 27 years…a man who is in the Virginia Sports Hall of Fame. He's a Syracuse grad and generally considered one of the top active broadcasting legends. He was to my right. Off to my left was Don Criqui… that's right…*that* Don Criqui. The man who called so many classic Orange Bowl games back in the 1980s. The same man who called what is still considered to be the greatest NFL game ever played—the 1982 playoff game between San Diego and Miami in the Orange Bowl was an overtime classic. And then there was me. I had been asked to join a panel at the IMG Intercollegiate Athletics Forum. The name of the panel, "College Radio Legends." Okay…I can buy that for the two guys on either side of me, but I didn't belong up there, did I? Of course I didn't, but there I was nonetheless.

We spent 30 minutes talking about our careers…or should I say Don and Bill talked about their careers. I had one play…that's all…one play that everyone wanted to talk about. The other two guys had many great moments to mention. Even though I've shared many memories and moments here in this book…I was there because of one play. But that one play was something else. I don't think in my entire broadcast career I will see another moment like that one play. I hope I never get tired of talking about that one play.

It was an honor to be there with two of the great broadcasters of our time. To think someone felt I fit into their category is quite humbling. But for someone who grew up in a small town in Alabama listening to the likes of Larry Munson, Pete Van Wieren, Ernie Johnson, and Skip Caray, I still couldn't believe I was sitting among these legends.

After the event was over, Bill Roth sent me a text telling me "good job" and he "enjoyed being a part of the panel" with me. I responded with a thank you and this: "I have to pinch myself every morning to make sure this isn't a dream." So far it hasn't been a dream…I don't think so at least…other than the fact this is a dream job many want but only a few get the opportunity to have.

It's all about being a part of the moment…describing that moment when Chris Davis gives you the greatest finish in college football history, when David Ross hits a storybook home run in the NCAA Regionals, or even when hearts are broken on a touchdown pass by Jameis Winston. That's what a play-by-play person lives for. I'm thankful I've had all of the moments in this book and hopefully, many more to come.

I am blessed, fortunate, and honored to be the "Voice of the Auburn Tigers." War Eagle!